INSTITUTE OF CLASSICAL ARCHITECTURE & CLASSICAL AMERICA
20 West 44th Street, Suite 310, New York, NY 10036-6603
telephone (212) 730-9646 facsimile (212) 730-9649 institute@classicist.org

WWW.CLASSICIST.ORG

EDITOR
Richard John

DESIGNER
Tom Maciag
Dyad Communications *design office*
Philadelphia, Pennsylvania

PRODUCTION MANAGER
Henrika Dyck Taylor

PRINTER
Pimlico Book Company
Manufactured in China

ISBN 978-0-9642601-2-2
ISSN 1076-2922

FRONT COVER: Carl Laubin, *Architecture Parlante*, 2006, Oil on Canvas, 117 x 204 cm. Private Collection. BACK COVER: Carl Laubin, *Verismo*, 2007, Oil on Canvas, 58 x 121cm. Collection of the Artist. END PAPERS: Details from Michel Etienne Turgot, *Plan de Paris*, (Paris 1739). PAGES 8–9: J. M. Gandy, *A Composition of Various Designs* (by courtesy of the Trustees of Sir John Soane's Museum). PAGES 44–45: Duncan Stroik, Detail of Thomas Aquinas College, Santa Paula, California. PAGES 92–93: Tim Kelly, YMCA for Manila Naval Base, Georgia Tech MS in Classical Design 2008. PAGES 116–17: Leonard Porter, *Tai-Yu Burying the Flower Petals*, 2002. ©Leonard Porter MMII. PAGES 134–35: Schauspielhaus, Berlin. Photograph by Wolfgang Staudt. PAGES 166–67: Temple of Artemis, Jerash, Jordan. Photograph by Askii.

The generous contributions of individuals and institutions who provided images for publication and the invaluable assistance of the anonymous peer reviewers of the academic articles in the Essays section are very gratefully acknowledged.

THE CLASSICIST NO. 8 IS MADE POSSIBLE IN PART WITH SUPPORT FROM
MARSHALL G. ALLAN AND KAREN LAGATTA.

THE CLASSICIST

№ 8: 2009

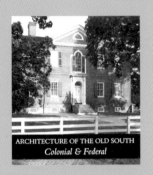

ARCHITECTURE OF THE OLD SOUTH
Colonial & Federal

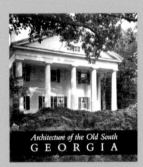

Architecture of the Old South
GEORGIA

ARCHITECTURE OF THE OLD SOUTH
Greek Revival & Romantic

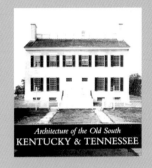

Architecture of the Old South
KENTUCKY & TENNESSEE

Architecture of the Old South
LOUISIANA

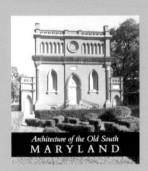

Architecture of the Old South
MARYLAND

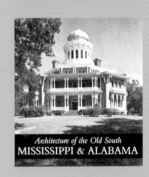

Architecture of the Old South
MISSISSIPPI & ALABAMA

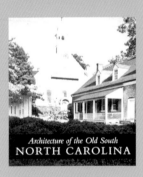

Architecture of the Old South
NORTH CAROLINA

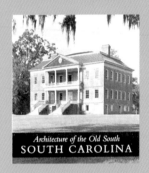

Architecture of the Old South
SOUTH CAROLINA

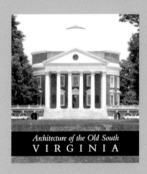

Architecture of the Old South
VIRGINIA

The INSTITUTE OF CLASSICAL ARCHITECTURE & CLASSICAL AMERICA
gratefully acknowledges the support of The Beehive Foundation, making possible the publication of
this eighth issue of *The Classicist.* Beehive is publisher of *Architecture of the Old South*, the pioneering
ten-volume series by Mills Bee Lane IV—scholar, historian, preservationist. It surveys, state by state and
then in summary volumes, historic buildings throughout the region. In an age of homogenized culture
created by cults of technology and bigness, speed and greed, it is a small triumph for one person, working
more or less single-handedly from the basement of an old house in Savannah, to have plodded along
for years to document, record and, in a sense, preserve an important aspect of the American South's
fast-disappearing culture. "Buildings," said Lane, "are three-dimensional history books that reflect the
comings and goings, successes and failures, aspirations and follies of real people."

www.beehivefoundation.org

The Classicist at Large
TOWARDS A RENEWED ARCHITECTURE

O ne often hears attempts to sway public opinion against a proposed classical building with the claim that such buildings are not of "our time." The suggestion, somehow, is that if this library / courthouse / town hall is built according to classical principles, derived from a millennial tradition, then the activities within should only be conducted while wearing togas, sporting periwigs, or writing with quill pens. Yet no one ever seems to impute a similar anachronism to the practice of democracy, the study of philosophy, or the use of rhetoric —not to mention the writing of history, acting of tragedies, or the application of mathematics —though these are all equally historic fields of human endeavour that owe their first flowering to Classical Greece. Like all other traditions of learning and scholarship, classical architecture has been repeatedly buoyed by periods of resurgence and constantly reinvigorated by innovation and new knowledge.

Human beings, when they have thought about it, have generally envisaged the path of history as following one or other of two forms: cyclical or linear. The rhythmic alternation of Golden Ages with periods of darkness is a standard trope in the mythistory of ancient cultures. Evidence for a cosmic clockwork was found by the pre-modern mind in the diurnal rhythm of night and day, in the waxing and waning of the moon, and in the irresistible sequence of the seasons. Each cycle had, of course, its mythological justification, generally associated with the deities of life, death, and rebirth. The onset of winter, for instance, was explained for the Greeks by Persephone's periodic return to Hades—drawn back to the underworld by the pomegranate seeds she had consumed during her first visit. These deities were central to mystery cults that led their initiates through cyclic rituals of death and rebirth. The concept of *renovatio* (renewal)—perhaps internalized through the popularity of mystery religions like Mithraism—fuelled a belief that political rejuvenation could be symbolized through architectural and urbanistic revivals such as

Constantine's emulation of Rome in his new imperial capital at Byzantium. This core concept of the classical tradition, that there is a limitless capacity for reinvention and rediscovery by returning *ad fontes*, to the sources, is also illustrated by the numerous later attempts to lay claim to the glory of Rome: from Charlemagne's coronation in 800 AD through the medieval notion of *Translatio Imperii* to the evocation of an Augustan Age in Georgian Britain and beyond.

In the sixteenth century a circular historiographical framework was applied by Giorgio Vasari to his account of the progress of painting, sculpture, and architecture, so that the development of a style or artistic movement traced a trajectory like that of the lifecycle of an organism—birth, youth, maturity, and, finally, decay. This interpretative structure, founded on a cyclical vision of history, endured in popular thought through the first decades of the twentieth century as witnessed by the success of books such as Oswald Spengler's *Der Untergang des Abendlandes* (1918) and Arnold J. Toynbee's *A Study of History* (1934). By then, however, a linear vision of progress was already being increasingly embraced, powered by the indefatigable twin engines of scientific positivism and historical determinism. As the twentieth century unfolded and the unimaginable cataclysms of two World Wars came to pass, this approach, replete with such fallacies as the *Zeitgeist*, became so commonplace that by 1989 Francis Fukuyama could ponder if we had reached "The End of History?"

The contrast between these two opposed interpretations of history is crucially important. With a linear world view coming to predominate in the twentieth century, it is not surprising that historians of architecture increasingly explained the succession of styles and theories of the eighteenth and nineteenth centuries as simply so many steps up to the temple mount of Modernism.

But the history of Western architecture, which has been suffused by the *koiné* of the classical tradition, is unquestionably cyclical. Not just

the major Renaissance revival of the *all'antica* style—but also smaller cycles and eddies within the larger tradition. In 121 AD, on Rome's birthday, 21 April, Hadrian renamed its celebratory games the *Romaia*, ceremoniously renewed the boundary (*pomerium*) of the city in conscious imitation of Romulus, and vowed his new Temple of Venus and Roma. This ambitious building, on a vast platform overlooking the Colosseum, deliberately recalled in its form the peripteral temples of ancient Greece and particularly the sanctuary of Olympian Zeus in Athens. For Hadrian, his *Pax Romana* was the Age of Pericles reborn.

Similar acts of conscious revival can be observed echoing down the corridors of history. In the service of Charlemagne's explicit quest for a *Renovatio Romani Imperii* (Renewal of the Roman Empire) his architect, Odo of Metz, referred to the sixth-century masterbuilders of Ravenna in designing the palatine chapel at Aachen. Six centuries later, Filippo Brunelleschi turned to the proto-Renaissance forms of San Miniato and the Baptistery as models for his Ospedale degli Innocenti to celebrate quattrocento Florence as the New Rome. Andrea Palladio (1508-1580) looked back not just to antiquity but also to the work of his immediate predecessor Donato Bramante (1444–1514), crowning him

an ancient Roman reborn. In turn, Palladio provided inspiration for Inigo Jones (1573-1652), then Lord Burlington (1694-1753), and later, John Soane (1753-1837), C. R. Cockerell (1788-1863) and Raymond Erith (1904-1973). Each of these, though sharing a wide range of common sources, made the tradition notably their own.

Classicism is not eternally young or eternally old, but rather constantly renewed. As the contributions to this eighth volume of *The Classicist* demonstrate—from Schinkel's nuanced details at the Schauspielhaus and Blomfield's advocacy of the "Grand Manner" to Leonard Porter's *Christ in Majesty* (2007) and Robert A. M. Stern's Jacksonville Public Library (2005)—this is a living tradition, coruscating with creative energy and universally understood. What better way to embark on the architectural challenges of the twenty-first century? —RTJ

(*opposite*): C. R. Cockerell, Taylorian Institute, Oxford. Photo by Br Lawrence Lew, O.P.

(*above*): Temple of Olympian Zeus, Athens with a view of the Acropolis in the background.

Essays

Whitmore's Palace

GEORGE WHITMORE AND THE PALACE OF ST. MICHAEL AND ST. GEORGE IN CORFU

By Richard M. Economakis

I

N A LITTLE-KNOWN episode in the history of Late Georgian architecture, the Greek island of Corfu, capital of the erstwhile Septinsular Republic (known also as the Ionian Island Republic) was graced with a number of impressive civic buildings designed by a British military engineer, Lieutenant Colonel George Whitmore [FIGURES 1 and 2].[1] While representing the first essays in Greek Revival architecture on Greek soil and displaying a number of remarkable features, the fickleness of history has ensured that these dignified Regency edifices should remain relatively unknown to architectural historians, and largely unappreciated in Greece for the cultural patrimony that they represent [FIGURES 3 and 4]. History books instead concentrate on the later neoclassical works of German, Danish, and French architects who followed the young King Otto of Greece, second son of King Louis I of Bavaria, from the temporary capital of liberated Greece in Nauplion to the official capital of Athens in 1834.[2]

Most of King Otto's appointed architects were accomplished professionals who worked with enthusiasm to transform Athens into a new center of art and culture, and who were assisted by scores of well-trained artists and artisans.[3] By contrast, George Whitmore could count on no formal education as an architect, lacked the advantage of precedent that his Athenian successors could rely on, and was required to supervise a polyglot team of Greek, Maltese, Albanian, and other builders and tradesmen with little experience in the execution of classical designs.[4] Furthermore, his principal client, Thomas Maitland, first Lord High Commissioner of the British Protectorate of the Septinsular Republic,[5] did not grant him the same kind of professional deference and financial assurance that would allow Whitmore's future rivals to more fully express their sensibilities. Whitmore's oeuvre[6] on Corfu is nevertheless remarkable for its skillful synthesis of a broad range of Georgian themes, from Palladian plan layouts and proportioning systems, to Adamesque decorative schemes on the interiors, to Greek Revival detail

and trim typical of the Regency period. Most extraordinary, however, is Whitmore's encryption in his buildings through devices like formal architectural progressions, symbolic numerical associations, and carefully considered sculptural programs with hopeful references to the nascent Ionian island state's political ambitions and Greek cultural self-awareness.

This essay, which builds on the research of Mr. Stelio Hourmouzios and especially the scholarship of Dr. J. Dimacopoulos, focuses on Whitmore's most important Corfuote commission, the Palace of St. Michael and St. George.[7] Aspects are here revealed of the Palace's original appearance and ordering that have gone unnoticed or that have yet to receive scholarly attention; for instance, the recurrence of the number seven in reference to the Septinsular Republic, the use of Palladian ideal proportions in the principal rooms, and the incorporation, originally, of a broad awning across the front of the Palace at the level of the piano nobile. Also considered are possible precedents for Whitmore's choice of forms beyond the work of Robert Adam and other eighteenth-century sources. Finally, this article will attempt to interpret the significance of the sculptural elements that formerly crowned the building, which appear to have comprised an allegorical reflection on the changing political situation in the region.

The picture that here emerges of Whitmore is of a highly sensitive and inventive designer who drew on a wide variety of sources in order to satisfy the often conflicting requirements of a grandiloquent British client and an ardent Greek audience at a time of hastening national expectations. While in many ways typifying early-nineteenth-century eclectic attitudes, the formal nuances, complex organizational strategies, and subtle cultural and political references that pervade Whitmore's work may be offered in *riposte* to the argument that Late Georgian architecture was compromised by rote copying, capricious application of antique and Renaissance precedent, and a disinclination toward

analytical and metaphorical thinking. As this essay attempts to show, the social and political intricacies of this age of expansion and enlightenment often prompted architects—consciously or otherwise—to fuse rich layers of meaning into their designs, many of which still await decipherment and interpretation. In that sense, the Palace of St. Michael and St. George is an open book—at once a testament to George Whitmore's creative talent and the cultural sophistication of his day.

Figure 1 (opposite): Portrait of General Sir George Whitmore in his retirement (Alan Sutton Publishing).

Figure 2 (above): View of the Palace of St. Michael and St. George from the southwest, with the statue of Sir Frederick Adam, the second Lord High Commissioner of the Ionian Island Republic, by the Corfuote sculptor Pavlos Prosalendis.

Figure 3 (next page): View of the Palace of St. Michael and St. George from the southwest; oil painting by Joseph Schrantz, c. 1830 (©Crown copyright: UK Government Art Collection).

The Palace of St. Michael and St. George is situated at the edge of a public park between Corfu's eponymous capital city and the Old Fort (Fortezza Vecchia), which was used by the Venetians from the thirteenth century until the brief French occupation of 1797 [FIGURE 5].[8] Built of imported Maltese limestone in 1819,[9] just four years after the Ionian Islands passed into British hands, the building was designed to serve as a combined seat of local government, ceremonial venue, and residence for the Lord High Commissioner, who acted as Governor when the Septinsular Republic became a Crown Protectorate.[10]

In plan, the Palace is a symmetrical, neo-Palladian assemblage of structures centered on a three-story, U-shaped principal building, with smaller pedimented wings that are connected by a long Doric colonnade [FIGURES 6 and 36]. This distinguishing stoa-like feature—which is at once portico and passage—resolves on either end into curved quadrants that attach to the building's wings [FIGURE 35]. It was conceived by Whitmore as a device to incorporate an older, existing pawnbroker's establishment to the west (the *Monte di Pietà*), which he then mirrored with a smaller guest wing.[11] Two massive archways are embedded in the colonnade on either side of the Palace's central volume,[12] which let into yards that are loosely enclosed by the outlying structures.

Originally the transition from the single-story stoa to the soaring Palace façade was mediated at the level of the piano nobile by a balustrade [FIGURE 3]—perhaps removed because of the incongruity of its Italianate pot-bellied members in connection with the Greek Doric order of the columns—and a massive awning, which contrivance, though mentioned by Whitmore in his memoirs,[13] has not been noted as yet in the existing scholarship [FIGURE 7]. According to Colonel Whitmore, this enormous, 2,250-square-feet rigging was destroyed in a violent downpour and windstorm, after which no effort was made to restore it by the British authorities. Judging from the colonnade's depth of about 15 feet—which was likely matched on the upper level by the awning—the structure would have been about 150 feet (50 meters) long and therefore spanned the length of the building's elevation from archway to archway. This conspicuous shading device—a kind of feature that was increasingly fashionable in the Regency period[14]—would have dramatically altered the Palace's now familiar elevation by reinforcing its already pronounced horizontal lines on the one hand, and, on the other, softening the effect of the plain ashlar walls.

The Palace's central mass is treated as a simple rectangular block with sheer, undifferentiated elevations on its three landward sides that are afforded some distinction by an Ionic cornice. The north-facing

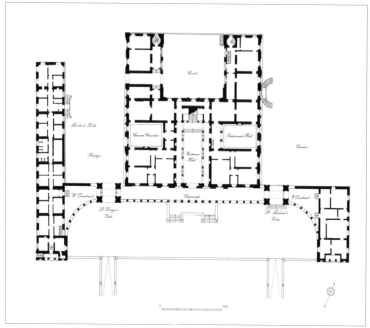

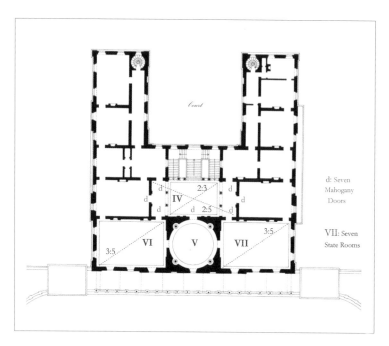

courtyard serves as the principal source of light for the Entrance Hall [FIGURES 6 and 8], which is accessed directly from the Doric colonnade. The Hall is divided by two rows of freestanding, unfluted Ionic columns into a central "nave" and raised passages or aisles. From the aisles one may enter the Corfuote Council Chamber on the west, and the Parliament Hall on the east.[15] Adding to the austerity of the Hall, the alternating niches and doors into these civic rooms are surmounted by chiaroscuro panels with scenes from the Iliad and Odyssey, copied from Flaxman's illustrations of Pope's Homer.[16] At the end of the Entrance Hall, two Ionic columns frame the Great Stair [FIGURES 8 and 9] which leads up to a spacious Gallery on the piano nobile [FIGURE 10] by way of returning, symmetrical flights of steps. This barrel-vaulted hall sits perpendicularly to the Great Stair, and is graced by pairs of free-standing Corinthian columns on three sides.

From the Gallery one proceeds into the most architecturally distinguished room in the Palace, the Rotunda (Ball Room). With its elaborate coffered dome, gilded plasterwork, blue Wedgwood motifs, and statuary niches with copies of Canova's figure of Vesta, this impressive Pantheon-like space [FIGURES 11 and 12] is situated at the center of the building's façade above the Entrance Hall[17] and overlooks the Spianada, the public park that stretches to the south of the Palace.[18] The Rotunda serves as a vestibule into the two most important ceremonial rooms in the Palace, the Halls of St. Michael (State Dining Room) on the west, and St. George (Throne Room) on the east [FIGURE 13]. Carefully fitted with satin wall fabrics and delicate Adamesque motifs, these grand spaces were normally reserved for state occasions, including the induction of native islanders and others who served the Crown into the new Most Distinguished Order of St. Michael and St. George.[19] On the same level and occupying the east and west sides of the Palace are the residential quarters where the Lord High Commissioner and high-ranking members of his retinue dwelled.

Work on the Palace commenced on St. George's Day, 1819, on the orders of Maitland. Whitmore had been appointed to design

Figure 4 (opposite): View of the Park of the Spianada with the Old Fort on the left, the Maitland Monument in the center, and a residential arcade on the right; oil painting by Joseph Schrantz, c. 1830 (©Crown copyright: UK Government Art Collection).

Figure 5 (top left): The Palace as seen from the Old Fort.

Figure 6 (above): Plans of the Palace of St. Michael and St. George.

"a future residence for the Lord High Commissioner, for so bad was his present one that the dining room windows looked into a house of ill fame and the ground floor was the public jail!"[20] The building was also intended to house the Treasury of the new Order of St. Michael and St. George and the Septinsular Republic's Council Chamber.[21] The "official" purpose of the edifice as seat of a Royal institution justified its designation as a Palace, which appellation would have suited Maitland's notoriously autocratic personality.[22] In cultivating the allegiance of the prominent local families, this new chivalrous Order performed a similar function to the earlier Venetian practice of bestowing titles and inscribing the recipients in the vaunted *Libro d'Oro*.[23]

What first strikes the visitor to the Palace is its strongly residential character. Its picturesque setting in a landscaped park—complete with romantic monuments and freestanding pavilions[24]—reinforces the impression of an aristocratic estate [FIGURES 3, 4, and 5]. Contributing to this effect would have been the great awning that stretched across the façade on top of the Doric colonnade [FIGURE 7]. In his memoirs, Whitmore acknowledged the incongruity of the Palace's domestic-looking exterior and ceremonial purpose, contrasting Sir Thomas's sober assessment of the state's available funds with the Corfuote Council's fervent calls for an "imposing structure."[25] Though Maitland gradually relaxed his "parsimony" in funding work on the Palace, Whitmore nevertheless expressed his dissatisfaction with the procedure, complaining that it would have "materially influenced the whole design had I from the first foreseen the subsequent latitude."[26] Whether or not Maitland, who appears to have favored a grand residential look, felt inconvenienced by Whitmore's ambitious civic vision and desire for greater monumentality, and therefore intervened to temper the building's effect, is hard to say with certainty. He did nevertheless extract from his architect a design that could pass for his own stately home, a grand sprawling edifice that was in the same league with any one of the great mansions that graced the British countryside.

The Palace's marriage of Greek and Palladian themes make it something of a throwback to the late-eighteenth-century eclecticism of Adam and Wyatt before Hellenic purism—or what J. Mordaunt Crook calls Greekomania[27]—gripped Britain in the first decades of the nineteenth century. This might seem all the more curious considering

---

Figure 7 (top left): Sketch view by the author of the Palace from the southwest, showing the balustrade and awning atop the façade colonnade as originally realized by Whitmore.

Figure 8 (center left): View of the Palace's Entrance Hall looking toward the Grand Stair.

Figure 9 (left): Detail of the Grand Stair.

Figure 10 (opposite left): The second-floor Gallery viewed from the Grand Stair.

Figure 11 (opposite right): The Rotunda with one of four reproductions of Canova's statue of Vesta.

the location of the building on Greek soil; however, as Mordaunt Crook reminds us, "the Greek Revival was never wholly Greek,"[28] and "there was at no time a complete embargo on the use of Renaissance precedents."[29] At the Palace, for instance, Whitmore incorporates Italianate features like balusters, engaged columns, broad cantons at the exterior corners, Palladian window surrounds, and bracketed cornices alongside typically Hellenic details. Where columns are needed, he is careful to employ Greek orders, but arranges them in canonical succession as specified in the Renaissance treatises,[30] beginning with the Doric entrance colonnade, continuing into the Ionic Entrance Hall, and concluding with the Corinthian Gallery on the piano nobile.[31]

Despite their Renaissance sequencing, Whitmore ensured that the Palace's orders were adapted from the most venerable ancient Greek monuments—Parthenon for the Doric, Temple of Athena Polias at Priene for the Ionic, and Monument of Lysicrates for the Corinthian order[32] [FIGURES 1, 8, and 10]. The progression also works chronologically beginning with the Periclean fifth century, continuing into the Hellenistic fourth, and, if one counts the astylar Rotunda as part of the sequence, ending in a space evocative of that first Greek revival of the second century AD, Hadrianic Rome. The precedents were no doubt selected for embodying the most admirable qualities associated with each columnar type and intended to invest the building with predominantly Hellenic qualities.[33] The exception in this regard is the base detail of the Athena Polias Ionic order [FIGURES 14 and 8], which, despite the elegance of its capital, comprises two diminutive scotiae set back awkwardly beneath an exaggerated torus.[34] This strikingly uncanonical model is likely to have been chosen for adaptation by Whitmore over the more graceful examples of the Erechtheion or Temple of Athena Nike in Athens because of Priene's location in Ionia, a fact which underlines the toponymic association—relished by the

locals though entirely coincidental—between the Ionian Island Republic and this ancient Greek region in Asia Minor.[35] The desire to bestow a predominantly Ionian character to the Palace is probably also what led Whitmore to crown the exterior of its main volume with a denticulated Ionic cornice [FIGURE 1]—dentils being particular to Ionia, and, with the singular exception of the Caryatid porch, atypical of the Ionic buildings of Periclean Athens.

A subtle device employed by Whitmore, likely to commemorate the creation of the Ionian Republic, was the symbolic numerical referencing of the seven Greek islands comprising this small Mediterranean state.[36] The Republic's emblem was a seven-pointed star;[37] which integer is a key to deciphering Whitmore's approach to the layout of the Palace [FIGURE 15]. Seven is the number of intercolumniations along the aisles on either side of the Entrance Hall—and two times seven are the freestanding Ionic columns in this space, including the couple that flank the approach to the Grand Stair. Seven are the intercolumniations in each curved quadrant of the Doric colonnade on the building's south elevation. Between the archways, there are twenty-one additional intercolumniations in the central part of the colonnade. Of

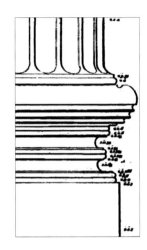

these, the seven central ones lead to the stepped landing of the approach from the Park of the Spianada, leaving seven on either side of the landing, respectively. Furthermore, there are seven public rooms in the Palace: The Entrance Hall, Council Chamber, and Parliament Hall on the ground floor, and the Gallery, Rotunda, Hall of St. Michael (Dining Room), and Hall of St. George (Throne Room) on the piano nobile. Finally, seven mahogany doors open from the Gallery, which acts as a spatial distributor on this floor level.

Dr. Dimacopoulos has discussed the Palladian aspects of the Palace, which are associated chiefly with the building's plan, especially its dominant central volume, symmetrically disposed pedimented wings, and colonnaded quadrant corners.[38] These features are characteristic of a number of well-known country residences by Palladio—for instance, the Villa Mocenigo on the river Brenta, and the Villa Badoer at La Frata [FIGURE 16]—buildings which exerted a strong influence on the eighteenth-century neo-Palladian movement in Britain. Although it is tempting to think that Whitmore's Palladian references were meant as a deliberate nod to Corfu's Venetian history and cultural connections, a number of objections come to mind. First, the Venetian buildings on Corfu have more in common with the work of Sanmicheli[39] and later Baroque expressions than they do with Palladio, something that the Colonel is certain to have realized [FIGURES 17 and 18]. Secondly, there is nothing in the Palace's layout and architectural themes that could not have been derived directly from eighteenth-century British neo-Palladian examples [FIGURE 19].

We know from his memoirs that Whitmore did not visit the Veneto before 1830, which was eleven years after beginning work on the Corfuote Palace.[40] When he finally had opportunity to inspect buildings by the Italian master, his commentary is brief, and surprisingly critical. Pointing to Palladio's use of balconies, for instance, he notes that "when they advance before the columns or pilasters they

Figure 12 (top left): Coffered ceiling of the Rotunda.

Figure 13 (left): View of the Hall of St. George (Throne Room).

Figure 14 (above right): Detail of a column from the temple of Athena Polias at Priene in Ionia, as erroneously reconstructed by the Society of Dilettanti in the first edition of *Ionian Antiquities*, 1769 (vol. I, ch. II, pl. II), and adapted in the Palace's Entrance Hall.

Figure 15 (opposite left and center): Plans of the Palace showing Whitmore's use of the number seven in reference to the Septinsular Republic.

Figure 16 (opposite top right): Palladio's Villa Badoer at La Frata, as shown in the *Quattro Libri* (Ware, pl. XXXI).

Figure 17 (opposite bottom): View of the sixteenth-century Venetian Loggia dei Nobili in Corfu (the second floor is a later addition).

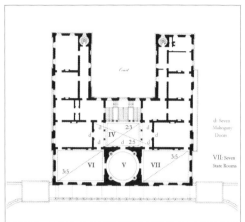

d: Seven
Mahogany
Doors

VII: Seven
State Rooms

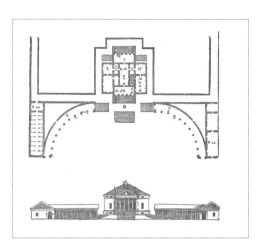

sadly injure the general effect."[41] In the Colonel's estimation, even the famous Teatro Olimpico "is but a model of a better thing—the proscenium is too broken, and the fixed scene representing the streets of the city is a childish invention to produce a trifling effect at great cost, which effect is destroyed in proportion to the advance of the actor towards the distance."[42]

Clearly, Whitmore felt no particular obligation to Palladio's legacy—and his disinterest is further borne out by the fact that he makes no reference at all in his memoirs to Palladio's treatise, the *Quattro Libri*. Nor is there anything that would suggest the influence of someone in Whitmore's circle who might have cultivated a particular interest in Palladio. On Corfu the Colonel consorted with a number of cultured members of the British establishment and the Lord High Commissioner's own entourage, all non-architects[43] who would have been more interested in the most contemporary trends—especially the Greek Revival—than in sifting for inspiration through the pages of a sixteenth-century Italian architectural dissertation that had seen its day in Britain, and whose influence in Corfu is nowhere apparent, save remotely perhaps in the seventeenth-century Church of San Giacomo [FIGURE 20]. We may therefore confidently attribute Whitmore's Palladianism to older, lingering Georgian attitudes, gleaned by himself from available eighteenth-century publications like Campbell's *Vitruvius Britannicus* and Adam's *Works*, and his familiarity with the recent classical traditions of his own homeland.

The neo-Palladian inspiration of the building—which is to say its British references to Palladio's work, i.e. oblique rather than direct—is borne out by closer analysis of the building's plan [FIGURE 6], which is organized around a linear colonnaded hall of the sort associated with well-known Georgian residences like Holkham and Kedleston Halls. The formal affinities of the Corfuote Palace with Kedleston, especially as delineated in the earlier version by Paine before Adam's alterations [FIGURES 21 and 22] have been noted by Stelio Hourmouzios[44] and one is indeed struck by its similarly proportioned Hall and axially situated Rotunda—a spatial pairing that is replicated at Corfu, albeit on separate floors and linked by a Grand Stair. Furthermore, unlike Palladio's villas the Palace's central volume does not include a pedimented portico, nor does it distinguish in any way the central fenestrated bay on the upper floors, despite the presence there of the building's grandest room, the Rotunda. In Palladio's country residences at least one of these two conditions is invariably met, whereas in British neo-Palladianism this is by no means requisite. Even the Palace's colonnade with curved quadrants is distinct from Palladio's examples in that it stretches entirely across the building's façade. This motif was instead increasingly common on the garden fronts of grand Georgian residences,[45] and seems especially to owe something to Wyatt's earlier colonnade at Frogmore House at Windsor [FIGURE 23].[46]

Another Palladian reverberation is found in the dimensions of the Palace's principal spaces and elevations, the most important of which Whitmore records in his memoirs.[47] These closely conform to the proportions recommended in Palladio's *Quattro Libri* for ideal room types—the circle, the square, and five rectangles derived from the square, the sides of which form the ratios 2:3, 3:4, 1:2, 3:5, and 1:2

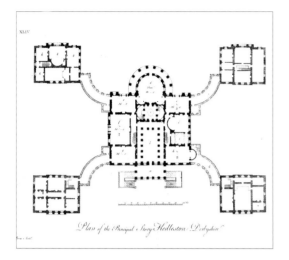
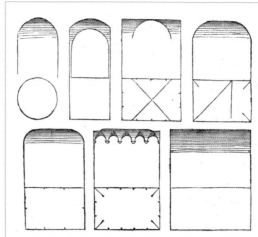
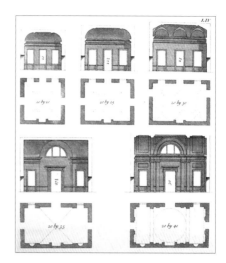

[FIGURE 24]. Thus, on the Palace's ground floor [FIGURE 15] the plan of the Council Chamber produces a 2:3 proportion; the Parliament Hall, 1:2; whereas the plan of the colonnaded Entrance Hall with the staircase yields a 1:2½ (2:5) proportion, which is a two-and-a-half square or square-plus-2:3 ratio that was sometimes employed by Palladio (though not specified in his treatise). On the piano nobile, the same 1:2½ proportion is found in the Gallery, the short elevations of which are perfect squares; the symmetrically disposed Halls of St. George and St. Michael each form a 3:5 rectangle in plan, while their long elevations describe precise 1:2 rectangles; the private Drawing and Dining Rooms define 2:3 rectangles, respectively, with square short elevations. Finally, the domed Rotunda has a height exactly equal to its diameter (35 feet)—a geometric relationship most famously associated with the Pantheon in Rome and recorded in Palladio's treatise.[48] With regard to the exterior elevations, and on the basis of a first superficial examination by the present author, the central part of the Palace that is comprised by the middle five windows articulates what appears to be a 2:3 rectangle from the ground to the top of the Ionic cornice, which proportion seems to repeat in the flanking areas.

Here again we must caution against assuming a deliberate Palladian reference in Whitmore's work, as Whitmore could more easily have derived his proportions from available British treatises and architectural manuals. For instance, in his *Rules for Drawing the Several Parts of Architecture* (1732), James Gibbs lists four of Palladio's seven ideal room proportions, adding one (4:7), and proposing to "standardize" the dimensions so that they are always divisible by five [FIGURE 26].[49] Gibbs' recommendations were echoed in numerous other manuals and pattern-books by authors like Chambers, Langley, Paine, Hoppus, and Salmon.

Dr. Dimacopoulos proposes that for the most characteristic external feature of the Palace, the Doric colonnade, Whitmore adapted Robert Adam's Admiralty Screen (1760) in Whitehall [FIGURE 27], increasing it in length to fit the greater span of the Corfuote building's façade.[50] There is much to recommend this idea, especially considering the association with Maitland's military "home base" and it must certainly be regarded as a real possibility. However, as Dimacopoulos

Figure 20 (opposite top): View of the seventeeth-century Catholic Cathedral of San Giacomo, Corfu.

Figure 21 (above left): Plan of Kedleston Hall, 1757-59, as designed by James Paine, before Adam's alterations, from his book *Plans, Elevations and Sections of Noblemen and Gentlemen's Houses,* pl. XLIV, 1767 (courtesy of the Trustees of Sir John Soane's Museum).

Figure 22 (opposite bottom): Section of Paine's original design for Kedleston Hall from his book *Plans, Elevations and Sections of Noblemen and Gentlemen's Houses,* pl. L, 1767 (courtesy of the Trustees of Sir John Soane's Museum).

Figure 23 (above): James Wyatt, garden elevation of Frogmore House, Windsor, 1798.

Figure 24 (top center): Diagram from Palladio's *Quattro Libri* illustrating the seven ideal room proportions (Ware, ch. XXIV).

Figure 26 (top right): Proportional rooms as proposed by Gibbs in his *Rules for Drawing the Several Parts of Architecture,* 1732 (pl. LIV).

Figure 27 (opposite middle): The Admiralty Screen at Whitehall, London, by Robert Adam, as illustrated in *The Works in Architecture of Robert and James Adam, Esquires,* 1761 (vol. I, IV, pl. I).

Elevation of the Gateway to Sion House and Porters Lodges, Fronting the great West Road, Eight Miles from London.

Elevation du Portail du Château de Sion, en face le grand chemin à l'ouest et à huit miles de Londres.

Plan of the Gateway and Porters Lodges.
Plan du Portail.

himself admits, the theme of an archway intercepting a colonnade or arcade with pedimented or otherwise formalized end-pavilions was common by the early nineteenth century [FIGURES 28 and 29].[51] Whitmore's innovation at Corfu consisted in doubling the type to include two archways disposed symmetrically on either side of the Palace's central volume. Nevertheless, and notwithstanding the curiously unstressed entrance that results from such an arrangement, which is more typically associated with garden façades where emphasis on a central doorway is not essential, the similarity of the Palace colonnade to Adam's design is true only in the most general sense.

For instance, whereas the Admiralty Screen makes use of a Renaissance Doric order, the Palace employs fluted Greek Doric columns, surmounted (originally) by a balustrade. Also, the embedded Corfuote archways are significantly more massive in appearance than their highly modulated and ornate Whitehall counterpart, and do not suppress their openings beneath the level of the entablature as in Adam's design. Furthermore, in their obvious evocation of Greek *distyle in antis* temples, the façades of the Palace's pedimented flanking pavilions differ appreciably from the bare walls and embedded niches of the

Whitehall end-pieces. Finally, the awning that originally stretched across the Palace's piano nobile would have effectively annulled any immediate resemblance of the Corfuote colonnade with the Admiralty Screen [FIGURE 7].

The ponderous Hellenic qualities and massing of the Palace's archways and end pavilions appear instead to have much more in common with contemporary Regency period designs like John Soane's gate and entrance lodges at Wimpole Hall, Cambridgeshire (1791-1794).[52] Indeed, Wimpole's almost identical *in antis* wings and stepped archway profile lead one naturally to suppose that, at least in this particular instance, Whitmore took direct inspiration from Soane [FIGURES 30 and 31].[53]

Dr. Dimacopoulos is however probably right in ascribing the Corfuote colonnade's affinity with the Admiralty Screen to more than coincidence. Whitmore's approach to design was clearly eclectic; at the Palace he appears to have liberally adapted and synthesized a variety of sources from the broader Georgian repertoire, including works by Paine (Kedleston Hall), Wyatt (Frogmore House), Soane (Wimpole Hall), and others in addition to Adam. Architectural design in eighteenth- and

Elévation perspective du Projet de l'Hôtel de Condé.

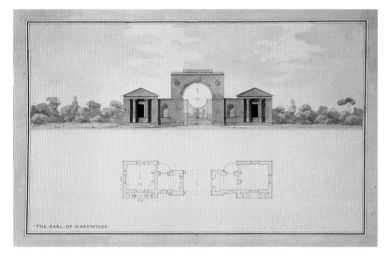

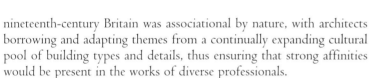

· THE EARL OF HARDWICKE ·

nineteenth-century Britain was associational by nature, with architects borrowing and adapting themes from a continually expanding cultural pool of building types and details, thus ensuring that strong affinities would be present in the works of diverse professionals.

As we have seen in his design for the Palace, Whitmore did not seek to make explicit references to Corfu's Venetian architectural legacy. It is, however, tempting to interpret an aspect of the building's sculptural program as a purposeful allusion to the Serene Republic's long history in the region. As Whitmore himself mentions in his memoirs, the Palace façade was originally crowned by a figure of Britannia seated above Corfu's traditional emblem, an antique rudderless ship, and a matching reclining lion [FIGURE 32].[54] Britannia and the lion were removed (no doubt for political reasons) after the secession of the Ionian Islands to Greece in 1864,[55] which resulted in the current eccentric appearance of the central block's cornice from the Park of the Spianada. In his memoirs, Whitmore informs us that the lion was "copied from one of those in Canova's tomb of Rezzonico."[56] By this he means the tomb executed at St. Peter's Basilica in Rome in 1783-92 by the sculptor Antonio Canova for Pope Clement XIII, a member of

Figure 28 (above left): Perspective of the Hôtel de Condé, Paris, as proposed by Marie-Joseph Peyre and illustrated in his *Oeuvres d'Architecture de Marie-Joseph Peyre, Ancien Pensionnaire de l'Académie a Rome,* 1795 (pl. VIII).

Figure 29 (opposite): Syon House Gateway by Robert Adam, as illustrated in *The Works in Architecture of Robert and James Adam, Esquires,* 1778 (vol. I, I, pl. I).

Figure 30 (center left): Wimpole Hall Gate and Entrance Lodges, Cambridgeshire, by John Soane, 1791-94 (courtesy of the Trustees of Sir John Soane's Museum).

Figure 31 (pages 8 and 9): Rendering by Joseph Gandy including a model of Soane's Wimpole Hall Gate and Entrance lodges, c. 1815 (courtesy of the Trustees of Sir John Soane's Museum).

Figure 32 (above right): Canova's tomb of Pope Clement XIII showing reclining lions, 1783-92 (Art Resource).

the Venetian Rezzonico family. This well-known papal monument features two bereaved, reclining lions, the one on the right depicted asleep at the feet of a genius, the other awake beneath an allegorical figure of Religion [FIGURE 32]. Though Whitmore does not tell us which of the two feline statues he "copied" at Corfu,[57] if one closely examines contemporary images of the Palace—for instance the oil painting by Joseph Schrantz from 1830 [FIGURE 33]—it is clear that this figure lay facing east, on the right side of the statue of Britannia. The Rezzonico copy would thus have been of the wakeful lion, which faces in the same direction.

Whitmore does not mention the date of the statue's installation; however we may assume that it was in place in time for the Palace's official inauguration[58] in the spring of 1823. This was the year after Antonio Canova's death, which saw the realization by his students of his own sepulcher in the Basilica of the Frari in Venice.[59] Like his Rezzonico tomb, Canova's Frari monument also features a reclining lion, this one winged and emblematic of St. Mark, patron Saint of the Serene Republic [FIGURE 34]. This celebrated allegorical figure is very similar to the wakeful Rezzonico lion, differing principally in that it grasps a closed gospel of Mark, which symbolizes the decline of

Venice. The decision to reproduce the Rezzonico lion is likely to have been made by Whitmore soon after Canova's death, perhaps on the basis of its affinities with the popular figure from the sculptor's tomb (and presumably its more Britannic, wingless appearance), or the fact that Clement XIII was himself a native of Venice. In either case, Whitmore appears to have been deliberately alluding to the recent dissolution of the Serene Republic. Seated atop the paired Corfuote ship and bereaved Venetian lion—now stripped of its wings as Venice had lost its political and military power—the figure of Britannia was here represented as assuming the Republic's erstwhile role as protector of this small corner of the Greek world.

* * *

As this brief analysis of the Palace of St. Michael and St. George has attempted to demonstrate, Georgian architecture was characterized by more than a casual reliance on precedent, as some historians today advocate. Terms like neo-Palladianism and Greek Revival can be misleading in suggesting the artificial resuscitation of eclipsed or irrelevant cultures of building. In the complex eighteenth- and early nineteenth-century world of cultural and political expansion and rising

national awareness, antique modes of expression were not understood simply as aesthetic toolkits to be sifted for stylish results or the facile projection of status. If gradually less consulted, the Renaissance treatises were still accepted for the reasonableness of their proportioning systems and Greek forms were appreciated for their raw expressive qualities that evoked cultural origins, constructional logic, and political equability. At Corfu they were given national and ethnological dimensions and served to gently mediate and bind native Greek and British interests. In this respect, George Whitmore's Palace is a testament to the rich expressive potential contained within the classical tradition and deserves more than a passing mention in the history books. ❧

Richard M. Economakis is an Associate Professor of Architecture at the University of Notre Dame.

BIBLIOGRAPHY

Adam, R., *The Works in Architecture of Robert and James Adam, Esquires* (London, 1761).

Boswell, D., "A Grecian Architecture Revival: General Whitmore's Achievements," *Treasures of Malta*, III, 1 (Christmas 1996), pp. 39-45.

Campbell, C., *Vitruvius Britannicus, or the British Architect* (London, 1715-25).

Chandler, R., Revett, N., and Pars, W., *Ionian Antiquities* (London: Society of Dilettanti, 1769).

Clarke, T., "Britain in the Adriatic: English Regency Architecture in Corfu," *Country Life*, Sept. 10, 1938, pp. 252-256.

Colvin, H., *A Biographical Dictionary of British Architects: 1600-1840*, 4th Edition (London and New Haven: Paul Mellor Centre for Studies in British Art, Yale University Press, 2008).

Curl, J. S., *Georgian Architecture* (Devon: David & Charles, 2002).

Dimacopoulos, J., *George Whitmore on Corfu* (Greek Ministry of Culture, ICOM – Hellenic Committee, Athens, 1994).

Dimacopoulos, J., "Whitmore of Corfu," in *The Architectural Review*, vol. CLXVI, n. 994, December 1979, pp. 356-359.

Forte, J., *The Palace of St. Michael and St. George: An Anthology* (ANEDK, Dorrian Lambley Publishing & Design, Corfu, 1994).

Gibbs, J., *Rules for Drawing the Several Parts of Architecture*, (London, 1732).

Giles, F. (ed.), *Corfu: The Garden Isle* (London: John Murray Publishers, 1994).

Hourmouzios, S., "An English Palace in Corfu," *Country Life*, April 26, 1962, pp. 958-960.

Johnson, F. P., "The Kardaki Temple," *American Journal of Archaeology*, vol. 40, No. 1 (Jan. – Mar. 1936), pp. 46-54.

Johnson, J. (ed.), *The General: The Travel Memoirs of General Sir George Whitmore* (Gloucester: Alan Sutton Publishing, 1987).

John Soane, (London: Architectural Monographs, Academy Editions, 1983).

Mordaunt Crook, J., *The Greek Revival: Neo-Classical Attitudes in British Architecture, 1760-1870*, (London: John Murray Publishers Ltd., 1972).

Nicolson, N., "Corfu: the Palace Erected in Honour of St. Michael and St. George," *Great Palaces of Europe*, (New York: G. P. Putnam's Sons, 1964).

Paine, J., *Plans, Elevations and Sections of Noblemen and Gentlemen's Houses* (London, 1767).

Stroud, D., *Sir John Soane, Architect*, (London: Faber and Faber, 1984).

Stuart, J., and Revett, N., *Antiquities of Athens*, (London, 1762).

Watkin, D., *The Architect King: George III and the Culture of the Enlightenment*, (London: Royal Collection Publications, 2004).

Endnotes

1. Lieutenant Colonel (later General Sir) George Whitmore (1775-1862) was descended from a landed family in Shropshire. At the age of fourteen he became an army cadet, and in 1794 he was posted to Gibraltar as second Lieutenant, Royal Engineers, where he became First Lieutenant. After a stint in the Caribbean (1800-1802) and the Eastern District (1802-1811), he served in Malta as Lieutenant Colonel, R.E. (1813). In 1815 he accompanied Malta's Governor, Sir Thomas Maitland, on a first visit to Corfu and the Ionian Islands. He returned and remained in Corfu from 1816 until 1824, serving intermittently in Malta until 1829. He became General R.E. in 1854, probably retiring the same year.

2. Otto was made king of Greece by decision of the Great Powers in London in May 1832. His selection was approved in August 1832 by the Greek National Assembly, and the following year he arrived in Nauplion with a retinue of Bavarian advisers.

3. The Athenian buildings by Leo von Klenze, Friedrich von Gärtner, the brothers Christian and Theophilos Hansen, François, Boulanger, and Ernst Ziller are among the finest examples of European neoclassicism.

4. In this isolated corner of the Mediterranean, skilled labor was a scarce commodity. As Colonel Whitmore bemoans in his memoirs, "I had a sergeant of sappers for my house carpenter, a corporal of (ditto) for my clerk of works, and a Malta master mason who could not understand working drawings," (*The General: The Travel Memoirs of General Sir George Whitmore*, J. Johnson (ed.), Alan Sutton, London 1987, p. 58; hereafter referred to as *The General*). Language was a serious obstacle, as the workforce comprised numerous nationalities: "I think there were no less than 8 or 9 different languages spoken on it by the workmen, who rarely understood any alphabet but their own. How this Tower of Babel was ever completed under such disadvantages appears even to me wonderful" *(Ibid.)*.

5. Lieutenant-General Sir Thomas Maitland (1759-1824) was the third son of James Maitland, 7th Earl of Lauderdale. He served as Governor of Ceylon (1805-1811), Governor of Malta (1813-1824), and—simultaneously—Lord High Commissioner of the Ionian Islands (1815-1824).

6. With at least four accomplished classical buildings in Corfu to his credit, the term is quite justified. These works include the Palace of St. Michael and St. George, the Maitland Monument (an Ionic tholos situated in the public park to the south of the Palace), and the Mon Repos Palace on the Kanoni promontory to the south of Corfu; in his memoirs Whitmore also refers to his designs for the Ionian Academy (damaged in a WWII bombing raid and recently restored), and says that he dressed the exterior of a small Greek Orthodox church near the Palace—presumably the Panagia Mandrakina. The Anglican Church of St. George in the Old Fort (now a museum) is also attributed to Whitmore.

7. Whitmore's travel memoirs, published in 1987, have been an invaluable source of original information; his perspicacious, anecdotal writing style revealing a complex and sensitive personality capable of the most subtle allusions. *The General: The Travel Memoirs of General Sir George Whitmore*, J. Johnson (ed.), Alan Sutton, London, 1987.

8. Napoleonic forces occupied the formerly Venetian Ionian Islands between 1797 and the Treaty of Paris that was signed in 1815.

9. Maitland insisted on Maltese limestone, perhaps owing to the similarity of Malta's traditional honey-colored building material to England's fashionable Bath stone. Whitmore, however, was aware of this imported material's unsuitability, for as he says, "tho' it stands well in Malta (it) does not bear the damps to which Corfu is subjected in the winter season. The surface is attacked by vegetation and flakes off when the sun regains its power." (*The General*, p. 58. See also p. 83, where Whitmore laments the poor condition of the stone on a visit to Corfu after a ten-month absence). Along with the shipments of this stone came scores of Maltese stonemasons, whose descendants today number in the thousands and form the largest constituency in Corfu's thriving Catholic community.

10. The British governed the Ionian Island Republic as a Protectorate between 1815 and 1864, when the Republic was ceded to Greece as an "accession present" to King George I of the Hellenes.

11. *The General*, p. 56; see also Dimacopoulos, p. 50.

12. These monumental arches, more Janus than triumphal in that they occupy pedestrian intersections, bear the Greek inscriptions "Gate of St. George" (west) and "Gate of St. Michael" (east).

13. *The General*, p. 85.

14. Although Whitmore's awning was likely made of canvas (he does not describe it in detail in his memoirs), some façade-length metal examples from the Regency period survive, as at Grimston Park Hall, Yorkshire (1840), by Decimus Burton; Mordaunt Crook, fig. 134.

15. The Parliament Hall features a colonnaded Ionic pronaos with a small loft.

16. Forte, p. 26. Chiaroscuro panels were popular in Georgian interiors, as for instance over the niches in Robert Adam's Rotunda at Kedleston hall, Derbyshire (1760–1770).

17. Because of its circular shape, the Rotunda is lit by a single set of shuttered French doors that open onto the colonnade terrace. The two flanking sets of doors that are visible on the exterior are blind, and employed for the sake of elevational balance and consistency.

18. The landscaped Park of the Spianada extends about five hundred yards to the south of the Palace. Its name is derived from the Italian "spianata." When he refers to this public park, Whitmore makes use of the French equivalent "Esplanade," which term was common in English parlance for coastal promenades.

19. Dimacopoulos, pp. 33-34; see also Forte, p. 12.

20. *The General*, p. 53.

21. *Ibid.*, p. 56. See also Hourmouzios, p. 958.

22. "King Tom," as Maitland was known by his entourage, was a "whimsical eccentric who delighted in mocking and belittling his audience;" Forte, p. 38. On Maitland's tyrannical nature, see also Clarke, pp. 254-255.

23. Forte, p. 12.

24. Whitmore was responsible for the design of the Maitland Rotunda, a round Ionic colonnaded building designed in the manner of an antique tholos like the Temple of Vesta at Tivoli, and situated at the far end of the Park of the Spianada.

25. *The General*, p. 56.

26. *Ibid.*

27. Mordaunt Crook, p. 28.

28. *Ibid.*, p. 77.

29. *Ibid.*, p. 78.

30. Noted in Dimacopoulos, pp. 42-43.

31. *Ibid*, n. 66. At the Corfuote Palace, the Gallery's Corinthian and Entrance Hall Ionic orders appear to be superimposed according to Vincenzo Scamozzi's prescription, so that the Corinthian base diameters match the neck diameters of the Ionic columns below. Dimacopoulos (p. 51) suggests that Whitmore left the Ionic columns of the Entrance Hall unfluted in order to make them appear more robust and therefore capable of supporting the loftier space above. This was a common device in neoclassical architecture—see for instance the courtyard at the University Library in Helsinki by Johann Engel (1836).

32. Dimacopoulos, pp. 42-45, n. 62. Whitmore's interest in local antiquities is attested by his partial excavation in 1822 of the Doric Temple at Kardaki (unusual for its plain unarticulated frieze). The site is located on a promontory south of the town of Corfu that would later constitute the grounds of the Palace of Mon Repos, which Whitmore designed in 1828 for the second Lord High Commissioner, Sir Frederick Adam. Whitmore's findings were excerpted by W. Railton in "Description of the newly-discovered Grecian Temple in the island of Corfu, at Cardachio," published in the supplementary fifth volume of the *Antiquities of Athens* (1850).

33. Other obvious Hellenic details in the Palace include inverted olive wreaths derived from the Choragic Monument of Thrassylos in the spandrels of the colonnade archways, and a painted double guilloche band that runs along the cove of the Hall of St. George. Dimacopoulos (pp. 42-48) believes this pattern to be a deliberate reference to a terracotta sima from the sixth-century BC Temple of Artemis on Corfu, and suggests, on the basis of an identical guilloche that appears in the Duomo at Verona, that it was already known in the sixteenth century to the architect Michele Sanmicheli, who presumably observed the sima when he was engaged in the construction of parts of the Old Fort in Corfu. To reinforce the likelihood that Whitmore was aware of the Corfuote guilloche, Dimacopoulos points out that remains of the Temple of Artemis had again been uncovered by workmen in 1812, during the French administration of the island. The present author is aware of no record, however, confirming that the particular sima was unearthed during these excavations. The double-guilloche was a common motif in archaic Greek temple cornices, and was a fairly familiar Georgian decorative theme

when Whitmore was active on Corfu. Antique examples and adaptations of the theme are illustrated in publications by Piranesi, Gibbs, Nicholson, and numerous other contemporary pattern books and folios. Dimacopoulos' argument is nevertheless compelling (especially considering Whitmore's associative methodology), and must be regarded as a real possibility.

34. Dimacopoulos, pp. 45-46. Whitmore derived the profile of his Ionic base from the first edition of the *Ionian Antiquities* of 1769, which erroneously places the scotiae of the Temple of Athena at Priene in alignment with the column shaft. This awkward positioning of elements, which the Dilettanti originally assumed because the presence of flutes on the lower half of the torus suggested that they were intended to be seen in the round, was corrected in subsequent editions of the *Antiquities*. Dinsmoor (p. 222, n. 3), argues that the torus was meant to be entirely fluted, the lower half having been carved first because it would have been difficult to do so afterwards, the upper half never receiving the intended treatment. At the Palace, Whitmore alleviated the curious effect of the recessed scotiae by including plinths, which counterbalance the pronounced tori.

35. Dimacopoulos, pp. 45-46.

36. Hourmouzios (p. 959) notes the presence of fourteen columns in the Entrance Hall and seven doors leading from the Gallery, but does not associate this fact with a symbolic numerical referencing system.

37. Dimacopoulos, p. 34; Forte p. 12.

38. Dimacopoulos, pp. 53-56.

39. *Ibid*, pp. 45-46. Michele Sanmicheli is known to have constructed a number of buildings on Corfu, including the western ramparts of the Old Fort (1537), which were completed by his nephew Giangirolamo Sanmicheli.

40. *The General*, pp. 194-209.

41. *Ibid.*, p. 195.

42. *Ibid.*

43. Soon after his arrival on Corfu, Whitmore befriended the native sculptor Pavlos Prosalendis, who had been a student of Canova, and in whose circle he is likely to have met a number of Italian-educated Greek artists. Among these was a young architect whom he does not mention by name (Dimacopoulos, p. 29, thinks it may have been Gerasimos Pitsamanos), except that he was a rival for the initial design of the Palace: "a Greek who had studied architecture in Rome and drew his wholesale fancies from the Baths of Caracalla and the Roman palaces… This gentleman, however, disappeared when he found that his projects met no favour." (*The General*, p. 65). He also associated with Lord Guilford, an eccentric philhellene and polymath who founded the Ionian Academy, and Sir Frederick Adam, who eventually succeeded Maitland as Lord High Commissioner. Adam was the son of a cousin of the architect Robert Adam and is thought by Dimacopoulos (pp. 32-33) to have had some influence in the design of the Palace.

44. Hourmouzios, p. 960.

45. The Corfuote example has strong affinities with contemporary Regency examples like Nash's Caledon Hall (1812) at Co. Tyrone (Mordaunt Crook, figs. 127-128).

46. Watkin, p. 50, fig. 18.

47. *The General*, pp. 56, 57. Hourmouzios (pp. 958-959) repeats some of the dimensions, but does not derive proportional ratios out of them.

48. *Quattro Libri*, Pl. LI, LIII, LVII.

49. Gibbs, pl. LIV; see also Parissien, *Palladian Style*, p. 129.

50. Dimacopoulos, pp. 55, 56.

51. For instance, Robert Adam's entrance gateway and screen at Syon House (1760); Cooley and Gandon's Four Courts in Dublin (1776-1802); and P. Rousseau's Hôtel de Salm in Paris (1782-85). See also Dimacopoulos, p. 51.

52. Stroud, p. 149, fig. 100.

53. The question naturally arises as to how Whitmore could have come to view Soane's Wimpole project. An opportunity did in fact present itself in 1818, a year before commencement of work on the Palace, when Soane's draftsman, Joseph Gandy, exhibited his watercolor rendering "A selection of buildings erected from the designs of J. Soane, Esq., RA, between 1780 and 1815," at the Royal Academy in London. At the center of this striking image, which depicts scale models and framed renderings of buildings by Soane, the Wimpole archway and flanking lodges stand out prominently, glowing in the light of a lamp. Although the Colonel makes no mention in his memoirs of a visit to London in 1818, we must regard it as a strong possibility.

54. *The General*, pp. 56-57; Dimacopoulos, pp. 26-27.

55. Forte, p. 25.

56. *The General*, p. 57. The copy must have been substantially altered from the original, as it appears in contemporary renderings to have an erect head, unlike Canova's two Rezzonico lions.

57. Dimacopoulos (p. 25, fig. 17) seems to suggest that it is the sleeping lion on the right hand side of the Rezzonico tomb, but does not substantiate this claim.

58. *Ibid*, p. 40.

59. The Corfuote sculptor Pavlos Prosalendis, who was employed by Whitmore at the Palace and was known to have studied with Canova, may very well have participated in some manner in the execution of Canova's tomb. It is likely that the specific statue of the lion (and the copies of Canova's "Vesta" in the niches of the Rotunda) were in fact suggested to Whitmore by Prosalendis, on the basis of his familiarity with these artworks by the Italian sculptor.

Albert Simons

SOUTHERN SEVERITY AND THE QUIET CLASSICISM IN CHARLESTON

By Ralph Muldrow

Charleston, South Carolina is a gem of a city architecturally. Yet its setting was tarnished for ages after the Civil War. Even the rise of the "New South," with all its economic bravado, bypassed Charleston, like some curse intermingled with the cannon-fire that initiated the "War of Northern Aggression." But Charleston stood her ground, eking out a living while other "New South" cities like Savannah, Mobile, and New Orleans prospered as they partook of the colorful promises of the Northern Carpetbaggers. Charleston lumbered along, enchanted briefly with phosphates, until that faction escaped to Florida for better and cheaper enticements.

It was into this milieu that Albert Simons was born in 1890. The youngest of five boys, his father, Dr. Thomas Grange Simons, was a physician and a public servant who tried to encourage public health through the advocacy of proper sewers and infrastructure. Pictured here as a young man, Albert Simons appears to be contemplating his future goals [FIGURE 1]. Albert was about twelve years old when an extraordinary event came to town. The South Carolina Interstate and West Indian Exposition, commonly known as the Charleston Exposition, sought to evoke the architectural wonder that was the 1893 Columbian exposition in Chicago—the Great White City full of classical buildings. A New York architect named Bradford Gilbert deftly designed a similar cityscape of ornate classical buildings, complete with lagoons and a pavilion of fine arts. Such a cosmopolitan sight may have swayed the artistically talented Simons to long for training in the field of architecture.[1]

Albert Simons's uncle, William Martin Aiken, was a very successful architect who designed large, classical projects including what is now known as "The Old Post Office Building" in Washington, D.C. near the national mall. Aiken had studied architecture at M.I.T. and worked for H. H. Richardson and William Ralph Emerson. In Charleston, he had designed the gazebo in White Point Gardens.

Undoubtedly, Aiken's career must have influenced his nephew's decision to become an architect.

Albert Simons spent his first year of college at the College of Charleston, but then switched to the University of Pennsylvania, which had the famous professor of design, Paul Philippe Cret from France, as the vibrant Dean of Architecture. Cret brought the Beaux-Arts system of architectural design training to Penn, including the practice of ink and watercolor wash presentation drawings, and the very disciplined approach that included time-limited segments for student projects known as exercises "en loge."

Attending Penn at that special moment—when pedagogy met with visionary designs executed with great dexterity—allowed young Albert to excel. His achievements did not go unrecognized—his designs for an elaborate "Museum of Applied Science" were chosen by one of his professors, John Harbeson, to be published as illustrations in Harbeson's seminal book, *The Study of Architecture.*[2] Cret, in his own work and in his critiques, savored a spare palette. Simons' immersion into the rigorous studios taught by Cret resulted in drawings that seem to hark back to the restrained designs of Robert Mills, the early lowcountry architect of the First Baptist Church and the Marine Hospital in Charleston, who is known for the design of the Washington Monument and the U.S. Treasury Building. Robert Mills also assisted Thomas Jefferson with the redesign of Monticello.

Simons came to Penn as an admirer of Mills, only to find a living designer whose work and emphases were also directed towards an austere classicism. Paul Cret's later work in Washington included the

Figure 1 (above): Albert Simons.

Figure 2 (opposite): Robert Mills, The Fireproof Building, Charleston, 1822. Photograph by Charles N. Bayless, AIA (Historic American Buildings Survey, Prints and Photographs Division, Library of Congress).

Figure 3 (above left): Albert Simons, color pencil drawing of the Alhambra, Spain.

Figure 4 (above right): Albert Simons, watercolor of canal-side buildings, Venice.

Figure 5 (opposite right): Albert Simons, pencil sketch of the a frieze in the Roman Forum.

gem-like Pan-American Union Building and a more figuratively Deco building, the Folger Shakespeare Theater. Simons's preference of this severity for public projects appears to have its roots in the Regency architecture of Charleston, notably The Fireproof Building [FIGURE 2], in which Mills had a hand albeit under the watchful eye of William Jay, who was briefly but importantly the Clerk of the Works for the city of Charleston. The British-born Jay previously worked in London and had imbibed the spare classicism of architects such as Sir John Soane and John Nash.

Albert Simons spent eighteen months in Europe (1912-13) with the support of both the University of Pennsylvania and his uncle, William Martin Aiken. During his travels to England, France, Austria, Italy, Spain, Turkey, and other countries, he created wonderful travel sketches, many in watercolor, to fulfill the Beaux-Arts-instilled desire to learn through sketching great examples of architecture. His travel sketches included formal monuments and vernacular street scenes, quick portraits, and thumbnail caricatures. He traveled to Istanbul and made mesmerizing impressionist images of that exotic place. His color pencil drawings of the Alhambra are iridescently polychromatic and spatially dynamic. His view from a Venetian Gondola is rich in its depiction of brightly colored red-washed stucco walls and the canal. His depictions —of Roman houses, such as those at Pompeii, and Greek temples, such as the Parthenon—in layers of watercolor leave us a rich legacy of his travels [FIGURES 3-5].

After graduating from Penn and traveling around Europe, Albert returned to the States. During previous summers he worked for Evans, Warner and Bigger in Philadelphia. Upon his return from European travels and a stint with Atelier Hebrard in Paris, he joined the architecture firm of Lawrence Hall Fowler in Baltimore (1913-14) and worked on beautiful, historically-themed houses for the handsome subdivision called Roland Park. The firm designed well-studied houses, especially in the Georgian Revival mode. Simons was to keep in touch with Fowler throughout many years, and their correspondence included concern regarding "modern" versus traditional architecture. In 1915 and 1916, Simons was one of the first professors to teach architectural design at Clemson College.[3] He used some of the design assignments that he had himself done at Penn, and also taught descriptive geometry, shades and shadows, history of architecture, and appreciation of the Fine Arts.

From 1916 to 1917, the next brief but important role Albert Simons was called to play was that of a partner in Todd & Todd Architects, which became Todd, Simons and Todd, an architecture firm in Charleston. He then joined the military during World War I and ended up, among other things, painting camouflage to foil the enemy. He found time previously to draw houses and details that were part of the book *The Dwelling Houses of Charleston* for Alice Ravenel Huger Smith and her father. These studies allowed Albert Simons exposure to many great houses of Charleston and were invaluable to his contextual design career.

By 1920, when he was thirty years old, he joined forces with Samuel Lapham and created a firm that still exists under another name—The firm of "Simons & Lapham" lasted sixty years (much later joined by Jack Mitchell, James Small, and Dennis Donohue). The

Twenties roared, with wonderful traditional houses on the drafting boards, but also industrial, religious, educational and recreational structures, health facilities, public buildings, military structures, transportation buildings, and restorations.[4] Simons's firm did new houses especially in the Georgian Revival style, and designed additions to be seamless with existing buildings. Other structures for churches and commercial businesses were designed to fit with their context in a quiet and appropriate manner [FIGURES 6, 7, and 8]. One notable example of this is Simons' design for the addition of a classical choir and apse for the historic St. Philip's church [FIGURE 10].

He did design work for many of the plantation houses, which were often saved by wealthy northerners who hired Simons & Lapham to convert the old plantations into hunting retreats. Simons & Lapham also designed new plantation houses in South Carolina, including Chelsea Plantation near Ridgeland, and Windsor, near Georgetown. These he designed in a lowcountry style, understated and elegant. He also designed new homes in a new gated neighborhood called "Yeaman's Hall." Numerous northerners had houses built there, some by northern architects including James Gamble Rogers, and others by Simons & Lapham.

Oddly enough, the 1930s were good years for Simons & Lapham despite the Great Depression. Their most substantial commissions were the Gymnasium for the College of Charleston and the Memminger Auditorium next to the Memminger School downtown. The auditorium has a rectangular portico with Doric columns *in antis* [FIGURE 11]. Memminger Auditorium shares traits of this spare classicism with the College of Charleston gymnasium. It bears some semblance to the Paul Cret-designed Pan-American Union building in Washington, D.C., and is said to have excellent acoustics for instrumental performances.

The gymnasium was funded as a project of the depression-era Federal Emergency Administration of Public Works. Simons designed it with fine proportions and a scored, lightly-tinted rose-colored stucco. Like many such buildings of the 1930s, the overall building references the Roman bath configuration. The gym has engaged columns, a restrained severity in its moldings, and spare wall surfaces. These two buildings stand out as the most prominent buildings that Simons & Lapham designed in Charleston.

SMALL FRIEZE IN ROMAN FORVM

Adjacent to the Memminger Auditorium is a housing project designed by Simons & Lapham called the "Robert Mills Manor." It was one of the first Federal projects of its kind in the country. For these buildings, Simons & Lapham created very appealing structures with excellent materials, including tile roofs (copper over the front stoops) and brick that was carefully chosen to match the Charleston "grey-brick," so called because the unfired clay has a grey tint to it. Once fired, the "greybrick," becomes a warm reddish-brown color with flecks of iron in it. To provide such handsome housing was a real achievement, especially given the standard government housing—boxy and flat roofed—that came right on the heels of these fine, contextual buildings.

In addition to his outstanding career as one of the best and busiest architects in the lowcountry of South Carolina, Simons displayed amazing energy in serving the city in a wide number of ways. He was one of the founders of the historic district in Charleston, which was the first such district in the nation. It became a national model for other cities to maintain and protect their historic buildings. They also created the first board of architectural review in order to improve and monitor construction in the historic district.

Albert Simons was appointed to the architectural review board and served for 43 years, often giving design advice that helped make for a better historic district. He also served on the Planning and Zoning Commission for decades, pushing for planning on a regional scale.

During the depression, Simons, along with his cousin Samuel Stoney and his business partner Samuel Lapham, created two books: *The Early Architecture of Charleston* and *Plantations of the Carolina Lowcountry.* These were compilations of fieldwork done over the years; they are still in print and are both useful and visually delightful. Simons had been the regional head of the recently-formed Historic American Building Survey, and he personally created some of the exquisite measured drawings in those books.

He also was one of the team of four that surveyed and rated the architecture of the city, building by building, in order of importance and made it available to the public in book form in *This is Charleston* published in 1944 by the Carolina Arts Association. He participated in what is now known as the Charleston Renaissance in the 1920s through the 1940s. He joined very talented artists like Elizabeth O'Neile Verner, Alice Ravanel Huger Smith, and Alfred Hutty in sketching and doing etchings through the Charleston Etcher's Club. He was a member of the Society for the Preservation of Spirituals and designed their logo. He was a member of the Poetry Society as well, and was a leading force in both the Preservation Society of Charleston and the Historic Charleston Foundation.

Another important role Simons played in the community was that of an adjunct Professor at the College of Charleston. In reaction to H. L. Mencken's epithet that "the South is the Sahara of the Beaux-Arts," Albert Simons created a course in art appreciation which grew into a Department of Fine Arts and then a whole School of the Arts including Art History, Preservation & Planning, Music, Dance, Theater, and Arts Management.

Simons was aware of, but was not generally enamored with, the advent of modernism. In 1949 he wrote in a letter to Lawrence Fowler:

Having just come from a session of the jury of fellows where most of the best work submitted was definitely aligned with modernism, it was a pleasure to visit your library and renew my acquaintance with the great men of the past who have made architecture such an eloquent expression of the human spirit.

I have no quarrel with modernists, in fact, I admit that what they are doing is almost inevitable in this age which is almost wholly scientific. Much modern work is extremely dramatic, almost melodramatic in fact, but there is very little poetry of enchantment in any of it. I have no doubt that this deficiency will one day be restored. Then students will again seek the councils of the great men of the past and the study of their thinking will enrich our work with that sense of beauty now absent.

At the terminus of the central mall on the College of Charleston campus, Simons placed a double-height niche with colossal Greek Ionic columns attached to the main, original building on campus. Many are surprised that such a fine classical ensemble was designed and constructed in 1973. It looks like it has always been there, and that would be fine with Albert Simons, a quiet classicist whose work seems ubiquitous yet unobtrusive in this special place called Charleston.

Ralph Muldrow holds the Simons Chair in Historic Preservation and is Associate Professor of Art History at the College of Charleston.

Figure 7 (opposite top): Peoples Bank Building, Charleston.

Figure 8 (opposite middle): O. T. Wallace Building, Charleston.

Figure 9 (opposite bottom): Gas Station for Standard Oil, Charleston.

Figure 10 (left): Choir and apse, St. Phillip's Church, Charleston. Photograph by Charles N. Bayless, AIA (Historic American Buildings Survey, Prints and Photographs Division, Library of Congress).

Figure 11 (above): Memminger Auditorium, Charleston. Photograph by Ralph Muldrow.

Endnotes

1. Most of the information on Albert Simons for this essay was obtained from the Simons papers, which occupy some sixty linear feet of shelves at the South Carolina Historical Society; additional information was obtained from the Special Collections Department of the College of Charleston Library and from the South Carolina Room of the Charleston County Library.
2. John Harbeson, *The Study of Architecture* (Philadelphia: Pencil Points Press, 1927), p. 186, figures 244a and 244b.
3. Donald Drew Egbert, *The Beaux-Arts Tradition in Architecture* (Princeton: Princeton University Press, 1980) pp. 139-158.
4. Simons' choice of outstanding projects included the residence of Marshall Field III at Chelsea Plantation; The Paul D. Mills residence at Windsor Plantation in Georgetown County (1937); the Charles W. Coker residence at Hartsville, SC (1940); The City of Charleston Terminal Building at Charleston Municipal Airport; The University of South Carolina Law School Building at Columbia, SC; The University of South Carolina Law Building at Columbia, SC (1948); the W. W. Wanamaker residence at Orangeburg, SC (1948); the Charleston County Tuberculosis Hospital in Charleston (1951); St. James Church and Parish House at James Island, SC (1958); the Okeetee Hunt Club in Jasper County, SC; and the Charleston County Health Center, Charleston (1959). See Ernest Blevins, "Documentation of the Architecture of Samuel Lapham and the firm of Simons & Lapham." (Master's thesis, Savannah College of Art and Design, 2001), appendix E: Opinion on their best work.
5. From a letter to Laurence H. Fowler of Baltimore on February 16, 1949; from the Simons Papers at the South Carolina Historical Society.

The Splendid Inheritance of the Past
THE WRITINGS AND WORKS OF SIR REGINALD BLOMFIELD

By Katherine J. Wheeler

Throughout his long and prolific career as an architect and architectural writer, Sir Reginald Blomfield (1856-1942) understood history as a central component of architecture [FIGURE 1]. The practice of the "Mistress Art," as Blomfield called architecture, was the practice of history. Blomfield maintained that the ardent study of the past was the key to creating an architecture for the modern condition, and his invention of the "Grand Manner" was a careful compilation of architectural principles drawn from all styles. He was not, however, trying to turn back the clock of the progression of architectural style, and he embraced many of the changes in the profession at the time, including the development of professional organizations and formalized architectural education. The study of architecture's history was, therefore, more than mere imitation of its forms; history was an analytical study of the past to reach certain larger truths.

Blomfield was extremely prolific in both his practice and his scholarship; he wrote seventeen books and numerous articles and was active in a wide range of professional organizations. Blomfield was an early supporter of the Royal Institute of British Architects (RIBA), although he resigned from the organization for a brief period in 1892 as one of the 1892 Memorialists who protested the move toward architectural registration and promoted the ideal of the architect as an artist, not just a businessman.[1] He rejoined the Institute in 1905 and quickly rose through the ranks, serving and then chairing the Board of Architectural Education, becoming acting RIBA President when Leonard Stokes became ill in 1911, and was elected President of the Institute in 1912.[2] Blomfield went on to receive the Institute's highest honor—the Gold Medal—in 1913. The following year, he was elected a full member of the Royal Academy of Art, for which he had served as Professor of Architecture 1906-11; in 1919 he was knighted for his contributions to the architectural profession.[3]

Throughout his teaching, his practice, and his writings, Blomfield

promoted the relevance of the past to the present in two important ways: through the proper study and writing of architecture's history, and, more importantly, through the application of the lessons that could be drawn from history to the problems and needs of the present day. This application included the development of a historically-based modern architecture that he called the "Grand Manner," which moved away from a focus on historic detail to a development of principles of design and composition. His insistence on history at the core of architectural study and practice in his work *Modernismus* (1934) indicated his opposition to the architectural developments of continental modernism after World War I.

History played a critical role not only in the practice of architecture but also more broadly in the intellectual life of the late-Victorian period. Discoveries in the fields of geology and archaeology and the writings of Charles Darwin gave the Victorians a new sense of time as linear and continuous, instead of cyclical.[4] The nineteenth-century historian E. A. Freeman, for example, viewed and promoted history as a singular continuity instead of a series of discrete incidents, thus closing any sense of a temporal gap between the past and the present.[5] Historical novels were very popular and the highlight of foreign travel typically involved visiting historic—and architectural—sites. The Victorians actively reframed the past in the process of writing about it and created a rich and multi-layered history that was directly relevant to their own time. To paraphrase the scholar Frank Turner, the late-Victorians wrote about the past to write about themselves.[6]

Blomfield developed much of his attitude toward history from his time at Exeter College, Oxford, in the late 1870s.[7] While at Exeter, he studied the *Litterae Humaniores*—known as "Moderations" or "Mods," and "Greats," an intense course of study of classical literature and history.[8] Blomfield received a Second in Mods, which drove him to study harder and he achieved a First in Greats. A rigorous and demanding syllabus, Mods tested Greek and Latin literature and history, and Greats required translation and critique of major classical works in both Greek and Latin. These courses of study gave Blomfield the strong academic background, appreciation of history, research and writing skills, and critical approach that molded his later thinking, research, and publications.

Central to the study of Greats at Oxford was an approach to the classics not simply for itself, but as it related to contemporary life. The literary scholar William Shuter noted that Greats was intended to not only train young men in the classics but also to "train them to think critically about philosophic and ethical questions and to relate historically earlier to historically later stages of thought."[9] Blomfield held his First in Greats as one of his most important accomplishments, and took to heart its lessons of history. In his memoirs he stated: "Looking back on a long professional life, I still regard that school of Greats as the foundation of my career. More than that, the school of *Litterae Humaniores* gave me some further understanding of Humanism, and brought me into touch with a side of life that I might otherwise have missed completely."[10] It was ultimately, however, the application of the past to the issues of the present day that later allowed Blomfield to see and create relationships and continuities between time periods that he carried into his study and practice of architecture.

It was also at Oxford where Blomfield encountered the ideas of some of the most eminent historians and writers of the time, including John Ruskin. Although he criticized Ruskin for his ego as well as his ideas (and for attracting the attention of all the young ladies), Blomfield thought well of the other Oxford dons, and two professors made a particularly strong impression on him: Ingram Bywater (1840-1914), a professor of ancient Greek, and Henry Pelham (1846-1907) who taught classics at Exeter College from 1870-89.[11] Bywater was a friend of the writer Walter Pater, whose book on the Renaissance Blomfield "read eagerly."[12] Blomfield's connection to Pelham remained important throughout his life, and in the 1910s they worked together to found the British School at Rome, as Blomfield was President of the RIBA at the time.[13] Blomfield made a point in his autobiography that it was Pelham who "gave me a living interest in history which I have never lost."[14]

Upon graduation from Oxford, Blomfield worked in the architectural office of his uncle Arthur W. Blomfield (1829-99), a well-known Gothic revival architect. Although the younger Blomfield found the office work boring and the atmosphere stifling, he tried to learn as much as he could, drawing extensively on his academic experience. He noted: "My uncle was very good to me, and so far as his time allowed took unusual trouble to instruct me, but the fact was that in those days one had to acquire most of one's knowledge on one's own, and it was here that I found my training at Oxford invaluable."[15] Blomfield had begun to apply the skills and methods of history to a different profession, one that at the time was itself steeped in history as a source of inspiration.

In 1882, searching for a more formal architectural education, Blomfield began his studies at the Royal Academy of Art (RA) junior school in architecture, which at the time was under the direction of R. Phené Spiers (1838-1916). Spiers had studied at the Ecole des

Figure 1: Portrait of Reginald Blomfield by William Strang, 1894. ©The Trustees of the British Museum.

Beaux-Arts and returned to England with a skill in drawing and an interest in the adaptations of classical architecture practiced there.[16] The visiting critics at the RA in those years were primarily Gothicists, however, and included Alfred Waterhouse, G. F. Bodley, and G. E. Street; men whose presence minimized Spiers's classicizing influence. Blomfield quickly progressed to the senior school and won prizes at both levels.[17]

After a brief tour of France and Spain in 1883, Blomfield opened his own architectural office at 17 Southampton Street, London, upstairs from that of the young architect Edward Prior.[18] It was through Prior that Blomfield became part of the Richard Norman Shaw "family" of young architects, which also included Mervyn Macartney, Ernest Newton, Gerald Horsley, and William Lethaby. Prior also encouraged Blomfield to join the Art Workers Guild, which he considered to be "an honest and sincere attempt to find a common standpoint from which all the graphic and plastic arts and crafts should be approached."[19] Blomfield felt a great affinity with these other young men and the ideals of the Guild and remained friends with them even after a minor tiff caused him to stop attending the Guild's meetings.

In the early days of his office Blomfield, like many young architects, often lacked steady work. He used his time productively, however, and traveled around the English countryside and filled numerous sketchbooks with drawings of traditional English buildings, gardens, and architectural details. Later, while looking back at his sketches and notes, he would emphasize to students the study of architecture in person, not just from books. Based on these early analyses he began to write articles for architectural journals on a variety of topics from decorative ironwork to the works of Palladio. These articles formed the foundation for his first book, *The Formal Garden in England* (1892), in which he was the first to use the term "formal" to describe gardens of the English Renaissance.[20] In this work Blomfield presented a history of the English formal garden that promoted the architect as the primary designer of the garden, resulting in an outcry from landscape gardeners [FIGURES 2 and 3]. From this publication, Blomfield both received several commissions for additions and renovations to country houses and gardens and gained recognition as a knowledgeable source on English architecture and its history.

The same year, Walter Armstrong of Bell Publishers invited Blomfield to write a history of English architecture. Thinking the topic was too large, Blomfield proposed instead to address the period from Henry VIII to the end of the eighteenth century, which he defined as the English Renaissance.[21] Published in 1897, Blomfield illustrated the two-volume work, *The History of Renaissance Architecture in England,* with his own drawings as well as with photographs and also examples of historical drawings gathered from various archives. Both the architectural and popular journals praised the book, and it was immediately added to the book lists in the new schools of architecture and those of the Royal Institute of British Architects and was republished in several editions. The book cemented Blomfield's reputation as a scholar of the history of architecture. Key to the book's popularity was his ability to depict

the Renaissance in England as a period in which architecture exhibited specifically English characteristics, while still being part of a larger European tradition thereby creating a legitimate yet classical English style. Previous attempts to associate nationalism with an architectural style in England had focused primarily on English medieval architecture—both the early Anglo-Saxon and the later Gothic.

Drawing upon contemporary nationalist sympathies, Blomfield laid a course for a modern English architecture grounded in the principles of the English Renaissance. In the process he had created a history of architecture that was distinctly English as well as intellectual, modern, and professional, as exemplified in the progressive nature of the works of Sir Christopher Wren and Inigo Jones [FIGURES 4-7].[22] "The homely fancy, the lovable humility, as one might say, of its traditional art were laid aside; the art of this country was to be no longer an affair of happy instinct, but completely conscious, dependent on scholarship almost as much as on capacity in design. Henceforward abstract thought, and imagination under rigid restraint, were to supersede the poetry of mediaeval fancy."[23]

Inigo Jones was the pivotal figure in Blomfield's architectural history. It was on Jones' distinctly English interpretation of the Italian Renaissance that Blomfield fashioned his argument for a modern English architecture, an entirely new way to approach architectural design grounded in scholarship not just tradition.[24] Blomfield considered Jones' work to be "not inferior to the finest work of Palladio and the great Italian masters" and praised his use of proportions, his ability to conceptualize his work within a "large architectural idea," and, most of all, his scholarship.[25] He also saw in Jones the figure of the heroic genius, the singular individual capable of being both of the time and above it, that so appealed to the late-Victorian imagination.

Not impressed with most works on the history of architecture in his own time, Blomfield openly criticized them, noting that they had two major flaws.[26] Either they were simply lists of dates or technical information, which was of no use to the layman; or, they were a "vehicle for moral disquisition," which the artist could not use. Histories of

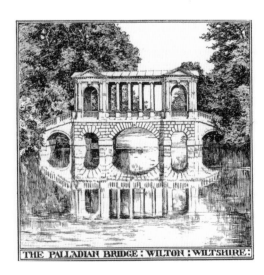

Figure 2 (far left): Palladian Bridge at Wilton House from R. T. Blomfield and F. I. Thomas, *The Formal Garden in England,* (1892).

Figure 3 (left): Terrace at Montacute House from R. T. Blomfield and F. I. Thomas, *The Formal Garden in England,* (1892).

architecture had to be more than dry facts or lessons on morality for the architect or layman to make use of them. For Blomfield, the study of the history of architecture had to be an objective critique of the evidence—both documents and buildings. Emotion, as evidenced in the writings of Ruskin, and conjecture, as in the writings of E. E. Viollet-le-Duc, were not appropriate to the practice of history. Blomfield recommended that architects study buildings in person whenever possible and that one could not simply rely on drawings or descriptions to fully understand the works [Figure 8].

In his own works Blomfield frequently took direct aim at other writers on architecture, both contemporary and historical, including Bernard Berenson, Leader Scott, E. E. Viollet-le-Duc, John Ruskin, A. W. N. Pugin, and Geoffrey Scott, among others. In an article on Palladio, for example, Blomfield criticized Berenson's analysis of the design of Italian Renaissance churches as "aimed almost exclusively at space composition" and "unhistorical" because it was a subjective "description of the effect which the architecture makes on Mr. Berenson's mind" and not a hard critique of the facts.[27]

Blomfield took the role of history in both the education and design of architecture very seriously, and he directed many of his publications to the training of young architects [Figure 9]. For example, he explained that he had written an article on Palladio because too many architects and students of architecture took Palladio's mythic reputation at face value without critically analyzing his work. Specifically, Blomfield wanted the young architect to understand Palladio's place in history—including how he got there, what came before him, what his

sources of inspiration were, his methods of thought and design, and the intellectual atmosphere of the time.[28] Blomfield concluded that although Palladio's treatise, the *Quattro Libri*, was important, an unquestioning approach to such a prominent architect would lead to pedantry, dullness, and "rigid dogmatism."[29]

Blomfield demanded an intellectual and analytical approach to history, not one of gathering architectural details or random revivals. Ultimately for Blomfield, the proper study of history required a more holistic and methodical analysis of the building itself, taking into consideration the plan and the construction foremost and the details only last.[30] This approach was a direct departure from the nineteenth-century focus on ornament as the core element of architectural style. Ornament also had figured prominently in the early RIBA examinations that drove many of the curricula of the first schools of architecture, with schools and museums creating collections of plaster casts of ornament from historic buildings of all styles for students to study. Blomfield himself had initially been trained this way at the Royal

Figure 4 (above left): Christchurch, Newgate Street, by Sir Christopher Wren (now destroyed), from R. T. Blomfield, *The History of Renaissance Architecture in England,* (1897).

Figure 5 (above center): St Stephen Walbrook by Sir Christopher Wren from R. T. Blomfield, *The History of Renaissance Architecture in England,* (1897).

Figure 6 (above right): The South Front, Wilton House, by Inigo Jones from R. T. Blomfield, *The History of Renaissance Architecture in England,* (1897).

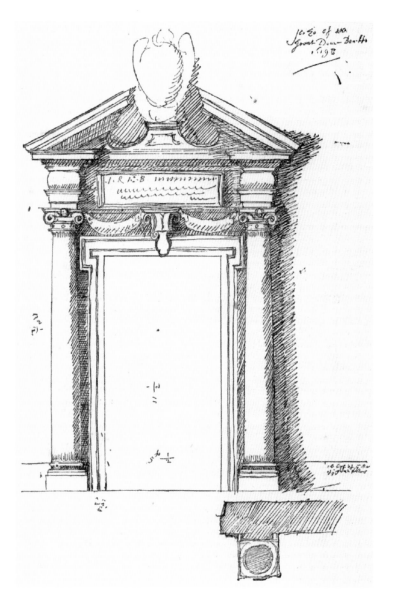

Academy and loathed what he called "Sketch-book architecture" noting that "the habit of collecting merely attractive details of carving, … [was] one of the most disastrous legacies of the Gothic revival [FIGURE 10]."[31] In his memoirs he noted: "The fact was that, owing to the disastrous misconception of architecture spread abroad by Ruskin and zealously advocated by Gilbert Scott, Street and the Gothic revivalists, students in my time were taught to waste their time on details of sculpture, the mason's craft in short, instead of using their brains on the critical and analytical study of buildings."[32] Ultimately what Blomfield did was to apply the standards and critical methods of classical history's long intellectual tradition to that of architectural history, which had a very short tradition and limited methodology. "Encyclopaedic knowledge is useful enough, but what is really priceless is the knowledge of good and evil, the power of analysis, the ability to cut through the crowds of facts and seize the essential point."[33]

Blomfield also used history in his development of a new "style." In *The Mistress Art* (1908) a collection of lectures given while he was a Professor of Architecture at the Royal Academy, Blomfield strongly promoted the "The Grand Manner." Essentially style-less, the Grand Manner was, however, linked to the "spirit" of architectural masterpieces of the past and reflected the "highest ideals of our art."[34] Blomfield was attempting to create a theoretical approach to architectural design using history *not* as the basis for a copying of architectural details of specific styles, but as the basis for developing larger, defining principles that he saw as independent of style, and whose understanding required a careful analysis of the monuments of the past. Blomfield synthesized these principles from examples throughout history, from ancient Egypt and ancient Greece to Imperial Rome and the English and French Renaissances. No single period or style was to dominate or be imitated, but each period held some aspect of the principles and therefore had some aspect from which architects could learn from the past and translate its "spirit" into an appropriate contemporary architecture.

The first of these principles was that the building should have a single overriding concept. "The central idea is predominant everywhere, it is never sacrificed to detail, but serenely maintains its sway, undisputed and irresistible."[35] The shift in focus from detail to overriding concept was radical, requiring a change of mindset away from an archaeological and eclectic approach to an architecture based on abstract and yet still historically-grounded principles. The second principle of the Grand Manner was scale. "Great size, or I should say the power of producing the effect of great size in orderly distribution, is one of the essential qualities of architecture. Short of that power I do not think any architecture can be called beautiful—at least it falls below the highest excellence of the art."[36] Blomfield illustrated the principle of great size with the architectural monuments of ancient Egypt, noting specifically their "monumental simplicity."[37] The "orderly distribution" of parts, the third principle of the Grand Manner, addressed not only the arrangement of rooms but also the building's relationship to its surroundings. Blomfield analyzed compositional strategies such as symmetry and the formation of hierarchies of elements.

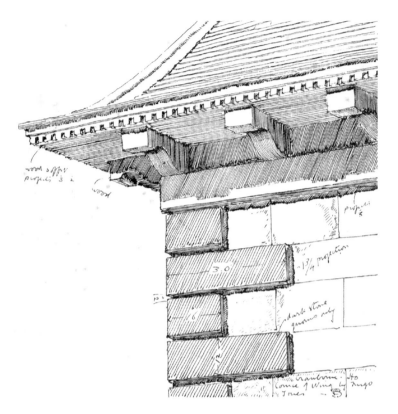

Blomfield's promotion of the Grand Manner aligned with a larger desire for a theoretical direction within the profession to link contemporary architecture with England's architectural traditions but without the direct imitation of any specific historical style or detail. Despite his insistence that it was astylistic, the Grand Manner reinforced the rise of interest in the architecture of the Ecole des Beaux-Arts, particularly as it had been interpreted in America and as it had been adopted by the newly-founded schools of architecture—most notably by the highly promoted Liverpool School of Architecture, under the aggressive direction of Charles H. Reilly. Ultimately, Blomfield thought that with the Grand Manner he was creating a viable and modern way to connect architecture's past fluidly to its present while giving the modern professional architect complete control of the project.

The precepts of the Grand Manner were also the foundation for Blomfield's own designs. For example in his design for the Quadrant, Piccadilly Circus, London, c. 1913, Blomfield set the buildings at a large, urban scale to define the public spaces and maintain a coherent composition through a single, unifying aesthetic [FIGURE 11]. Taking cues from Richard Norman Shaw's 1905 design of the Piccadilly Hotel, Blomfield drew on his knowledge of the architectural traditions of France and England to create a unified design. "My solution to the problem was to treat Shaw's building as the centre of one great composition, extending from Vigo Street to Piccadilly Circus on the south, with plain curtain façades east and west of the hotel, and pavilions at either end, with a suggestion of a return to Shaw's design in the Ionic columns."[38] The grand façades are appropriately scaled for the urban

Figure 7 (opposite top): The Banqueting House, Whitehall, by Inigo Jones from R. T. Blomfield, *The History of Renaissance Architecture in England,* (1897).

Figure 8 (opposite bottom): Study of a door, Whitehall, from R. T. Blomfield, *The History of Renaissance Architecture in England,* (1897).

Figure 9 (top left): Study of the eaves detail at Cranborne Manor from R. T. Blomfield, *The History of Renaissance Architecture in England,* (1897).

Figure 10 (top right): Stone carving, Chantry Chapel, Salisbury, from R. T. Blomfield, *The History of Renaissance Architecture in England,* (1897).

Figure 11 (above): Piccadilly Circus. Photograph by Katherine Wheeler.

space, with a three-part composition—base, middle, and top—unified along Regent Street by the street arcade and the heavy cornice line. The architectural details hint at a variety of historical references, but cite no specific building or period. Emphasizing the coherence of the urban space, Blomfield's solution was a series of buildings that maintained a consistency of height, detail, and material, allowing the buildings to function as a backdrop instead of each demanding individual attention.

Blomfield's design for the Menin Gate, Ypres, Belgium (1923-26), is also an excellent example of his use of the Grand Manner in his own practice [FIGURES 12 and 13]. Marking a major thoroughfare through the city, the monument is dedicated to the missing British who had fallen in the nearby battles during World War I. From the road, the Gate is reminiscent of a Roman triumphal arch, but without directly imitating it. A complex interweaving of brick masses and large classical elements articulated in stone, the monument is grand in scale and its great vaulted mausoleum captures the solemnity of the memorial through the spirit of the classical architecture of Imperial Rome. There is no single historical model, and Blomfield drew from his broad knowledge of classical architecture, from classical antiquity to French eighteenth-century neoclassicism, to create an architecture that would appropriately commemorate the fallen.

The Great War was a critical point of change in terms of how people viewed and interpreted history. In architectural circles, particu-

larly on the continent, the war marked a caesura between the past and present, disconnecting contemporary architectural ideals from the continuity of tradition.[39] This break with the past greatly disturbed Blomfield, and in his book *Modernismus* (1934) he critiqued the New Architecture, which he called "Modernismus" to differentiate it from the contemporary architecture of England which he considered to be legitimately "modern." Blomfield likened Modernismus to a disease that "has invaded this country like an epidemic, and though there are signs of reaction, its attack is insidious and far-reaching."[40] He argued against the New Architecture through critiques of books that he saw as promoting the new style in either architecture or the other fine arts. Highlighting writings by Manning Robertson, Geoffrey Scott, and R. H. Wilenski, Blomfield carefully constructed an argument that promoted a new architecture with a solid foundation on existing traditions.

It is an oversimplification of Blomfield's position, however, to state that his attack on Modernismus is because he perceived the new style as anti-historicist. He agreed with its rejection of the revivalism of historical styles, and even noted that it was possible that the constant publication of images of historical buildings in the journals had wrought this new style in "sheer exasperation."[41] Both Blomfield and the continental modernists were reacting to the same problems in contemporary architecture—in particular, the imitation of historical styles and the idea that ornament defined architecture, creating a too heavy dependence on the past. Blomfield argued that the New Architecture had lost the *intellectual* aspect of history; a history not to be copied directly but

to be learned from careful study as a design method through a process of thorough reading of the evidence (building or text), analysis, then synthesis. Without the study of history as a foundation in their education, young architects had taken a "short cut" and lost the understanding of the standards of beauty and the guidelines by which to judge quality. "The modern tendency to ignore this lesson of the past," Blomfield wrote, "is the opposite extreme to the exaggerated worship of 59 yrs ago. Both are equally futile."[42]

In addition to the rejection of revivalist copyism, there were other positive aspects of the New Architecture that Blomfield acknowledged. He praised the elimination of "meaningless" ornament and saw the interest in function—"purpose"—as a good but "wrongly conceived" guideline for architectural quality or beauty. In addition, he appreciated how the New Architecture was considered to be a "serious" art. But ultimately, the negative traits of the New Architecture outweighed the positive, and he vehemently attacked it from all angles.

Blomfield criticized both the New Architecture and the New Art for several other factors beyond their lack of a historical foundation. First, he criticized what he saw as a direct connection between the new approaches and Communism, but also what he saw as a lack of individualism in the role of the artist. It was this role of individual artistic genius that he so praised in Inigo Jones and Sir Christopher Wren, because it was through the individual genius that art could progress; therefore, to eliminate this creative individuality meant the stagnation of art. Secondly, Blomfield also critiqued the use of material as a deter-

Figure 12 (opposite top): Menin Gate, Ypres, Belgium. Crown copyright Ministry for Culture and Heritage, Wellington, New Zealand.

Figure 13 (opposite bottom): Menin Gate, Ypres, Belgium. Photograph by Andrew P. Clarke.

Figure 14 (left): Detail, Japanese Palace, Dresden, from R. T. Blomfield, *Byways: Leaves from an Architect's Note-book,* (1929).

Figure 15 (right): Gate Pier, Amesbury Abbey, by John Webb from R. T. Blomfield, *Byways: Leaves from an Architect's Note-book,* (1929).

mining factor in the creation of both art and architecture, noting that most of the early buildings of the New Architecture were not actually concrete, but brick with stucco and therefore were not "honest." But not all historical traditions were appropriate, and he found the influence of primitive art to be appalling as it turned against the tide of civilization's advancement.[43] Drawing a parallel to the architecture of the Baroque, as described by Geoffrey Scott in *The Architecture of Humanism*, the New Architecture was likewise too sensational and dramatic [FIGURES 14]. But here Blomfield also saw a ray of hope. He maintained that England had never fully adopted the Baroque style because it was "alien to English tradition and temperament," as was, he argued, the New Architecture.[44]

Blomfield insisted that the modern arts had not brought beauty but had instead wrought chaos. Twice quoting Aristophanes' *Clouds*, Blomfield wrote, "Chaos is King, having abolished Zeus. … standards of values and leading principles have been wiped out."[45] In the place of value and principles, the marketplace held control over the standards for the New Art, and for the New Architecture function became the single determinant of beauty. Instead of reflecting the standardization and mechanization of life, art, thought Blomfield, should be a refuge from it.[46]

After the publication of *Modernismus*, Blomfield suffused his subsequent works with an increasingly shrill ideological opposition to modernism. In his 1940 biography of his hero Richard Norman Shaw, for example, he often pursued tangents condemning modernism by juxtaposing it against Shaw's use of the past. "The deplorable practice of 'Free Renaissance,' as it was called forty years ago, the neglect or ignorance of the classical tradition, and the shirking of the serious study of the scholarship of architecture have led to the substitution of the theories of M. Corbusier and the practice of Russian and German architects for our national tradition. Our young men are in a such a desperate hurry they will have none of that 'gentle development' that 'grafting on the old stock' which, as Shaw said, is the only road to progress."[47] Likewise, he begins his history of the French Renaissance with "The idea that it is possible to break entirely with the past, turn one's back on it and begin again, as if it had never existed, is historically unsound, and movements which are based on this fallacy are foredoomed to failure."[48]

His contemporaries often credited Blomfield with trying to revive and maintain classicism in the face of continental modernism. Charles Reilly, for example, was convinced that "It was due to his influence, more than anyone else's, that the Orders, and all that they implied in big scale and simple shapes, were once again thoroughly studied [FIGURE 15]."[49] Blomfield called for a return to principles and close study of the past, which closely associated him with classicism and its revivals, but he never specifically promoted a blind imitation of classicism or any other style. "The spirit of classical architecture does not rest in orders and entablatures, but in a clearness of conception that controls the whole design from first to last, and excludes everything that is not essential to the expression of the dominant idea."[50] Yet the study of the past was still required to ascertain and analyze these greater principles. The past simply could not be left behind. "In the headlong

Figure 16: Pont du Gard, France, from R. T. Blomfield, *Byways: Leaves from an Architect's Note-book,* (1929).

rush of recent architectural design this has been forgotten, the cry has been for the clean slate, *'novae tabulae,'* and a fresh start from nowhere, as if there never had been a past, and this is where I think the 'Modernist' will find that he has made a fatal mistake. However hard he may try, he cannot rid himself of the past. The essential qualities of great architecture will always be the same, whatever form it may take, imaginative planning, fine composition, and just proportion."[51]

Despite Blomfield's conclusion that the principles of architecture could be found in the great examples of architecture from across the world [FIGURE 16], he still preferred the English tradition. "It was perhaps, fortunate that Wren never went to Italy, and that his stay in France was a matter of only a few months, for it left him essentially English in his outlook. The only architecture with which he was really familiar was the architecture of his own country."[52] Blomfield was striving for a continuity of tradition of not just architecture's history, but specifically of the traditions of England. Historian David Watkin has pointed out how Blomfield aligned this interest in English architecture with contemporary nationalist tendencies, by looking to the English Renaissance as a period for inspiration and development.[53]

To say that Blomfield simply promoted a return to history and tradition in architecture negates the complexities of his position. For Blomfield, the study and practice of history was fundamentally an intellectual endeavor where larger patterns and larger principles would emerge to guide the architect. Ultimately Blomfield's attempts to fend off the advances of continental modernism were not enough, and despite his many achievements, he has since been either forgotten or disregarded both because of his strong adherence to history as the root of a modern architecture as well as his vehement attacks on continental modernism. Nonetheless, he always held out hope for a modern architecture based on tradition that would answer contemporary questions and needs: "I shall not live to see it, but I nurse the unconquerable hope that out of this chaotic welter of experiment and failure our English tradition will again emerge chastised and fortified by adversity."[54] As he wrote in his *Memoirs* of 1932, "Deep down in our people there is an abiding sense of the continuity of things, which will in due course assert itself and will not tolerate the attempt to break utterly with the past. We of the present had to set our face forward, but only fools or madmen would ignore the experience of those who have gone before."[55] ❧

Dr. Katherine J. Wheeler is an Assistant Professor in the School of Architecture at the University of Miami.

Endnotes

1. "Architecture-A Profession or an Art?" *The Times*, March 3, 1891, p. 9. The Memorialists later published their own pamphlet of essays: Richard Norman Shaw and T. G. Jackson, eds., *Architecture: a Profession or an Art? Thirteen Short Essays on the Qualifications and Training of Architects* (London: John Murray, 1892).
2. Blomfield, *Memoirs of an Architect* (London: Macmillan & Co., Ltd., 1932), p. 148.
3. For a list of Blomfield's architectural and written works see R. Fellows, *Sir Reginald Blomfield: An Edwardian Architect.* (London: A. Zwemmer Ltd., 1985), Appendix 2, pp. 168-176.
4. John Clive, "The Use of the Past in Victorian England." *Salmagundi*, No. 68-69 (Fall 1985-Winter 1986), p. 64.
5. Norman Vance, *The Victorians and Ancient Rome* (Oxford: Blackwells Ltd., 1997), pp. 244-5.
6. Frank M. Turner, *The Greek Heritage in Victorian Britain* (New Haven and London: Yale University Press, 1981), p. 8.
7. Blomfield, *Memoirs*, p. 22. The scholarship provided £110 per year for his four years there. See also A. Stuart Gray, "Sir Reginald Blomfield," *Edwardian Architecture. A Biographical Dictionary* (London: Gerald Duckworth & Co., 1985), pp. 113-116.
8. Blomfield, *Memoirs*, pp. 29-30.
9. William Shuter. "Pater, Wilde, Douglas and the Impact of the 'Greats'", *English Literature in Transition 1880-1920*, v. 46 (2003), p. 250. Shuter cites exam questions from the Greats that often ask the student to cite influences of the past on later periods, indicating that they were to perceive and note continuities between past and present. See Shuter, p. 255.
10. Blomfield, *Memoirs*, p. 31.
11. *Ibid.*, pp. 28-29. Bywater was friends with Walter Pater, William Morris, and Swinburne, as well as a member of the Society for the Protection of Ancient Buildings. Pelham's lectures on Roman history attracted large audiences. He was a Liberal who promoted the education of women and the importance of research in education. See F. J. Haverfield, "Pelham, Henry Francis (1846-1907)," rev. Roger T. Stearn, in *Oxford Dictionary of National Biography*, ed. H. C. G. Matthew and Brian Harrison (Oxford: Oxford University Press, 2004), http://www.oxforddnb.com/view/article/35459 (accessed November 12, 2008).
12. Blomfield, *Memoirs*, p. 30.
13. *Ibid.*, p. 149.
14. *Ibid.*, p. 29-30.
15. *Ibid.*, pp. 34, 37.
16. *Ibid.*, p. 43.
17. *Ibid.*, p. 38.
18. *Ibid.*, pp. 44-5.
19. *Ibid.*, p. 55.
20. Reginald Blomfield, *The Formal Garden in England* (London: B. T. Batsford, 1892). See also Judith B. Tankard, *Gardens of the Arts and Crafts Movement* (New York: Harry N. Abrams, Inc., 2004), p. 17.
21. Blomfield, *Memoirs*, p. 79.
22. Reginald Blomfield, *A History of Renaissance Architecture in England 1500-1800*, 2 vols. (London: George Bell and Sons, 1897), p. 402.
23. *Ibid.*, p. 103.
24. *Ibid.*, p. 109.
25. *Ibid.*, p. 109.
26. Blomfield, *Studies in Architecture* (London: Macmillan & Co., Ltd., 1905), p. v.
27. *Ibid.*, pp. 61-2.
28. *Ibid.*, p. 47.
29. *Ibid.*, p. 71.
30. *Ibid.*, pp. 14-15.
31. Reginald Blomfield, *The Mistress Art* (London: Edward Arnold, 1908), p. 26.
32. Blomfield, *Memoirs*, pp. 33-34.
33. Blomfield, *Memoirs*, p. 31.
34. Blomfield, *The Mistress Art*, pp. 156-7.
35. *Ibid.*, p. 167.
36. *Ibid.*, p. 166.
37. *Ibid.*, p. 167.
38. Blomfield, *Memoirs*, p. 214.
39. Blomfield, *Modernismus* (London: Macmillan & Co., 1934), p. 1.
40. *Ibid.*, pp. v-vi.
41. *Ibid.*, p. 69
42. *Ibid.*, p. 1.
43. *Ibid.*, pp. 105-6.
44. *Ibid.*, pp. 45-6.
45. *Ibid.*, p. 121.
46. *Ibid.*, p. 117.
47. Sir Reginald Blomfield, *Richard Norman Shaw, R.A. Architect, 1831-1912* (London: B. T. Batsford, Ltd., 1940), p. 31.
48. Sir Reginald Blomfield, *Three Hundred Years of French Architecture, 1494-1794* (London: Alexander MacLehose & Co., 1936), p. 1.
49. C. H. Reilly, "Sir Reginald Blomfield," chapter in *Representative British Architects of the Present Day.* Essay Index Reprint Series (London: 1931; reprint New York: Books for Libraries press, Inc., 1967), p. 54.
50. Sir Reginald Blomfield, *French Architecture and its Relation to Modern Practice. The Zaharoff Lecture, 1927* (Oxford: Clarendon Press, 1927), pp. 16-17.
51. Blomfield, *Richard Norman Shaw*, pp. 69, 71.
52. Blomfield, *Six Architects* (London: Macmillan & Co, Ltd., 1935), pp. 173-4.
53. David Watkin, *The Rise of Architectural History* (Chicago: University of Chicago Press, 1980; reprint 1983). See also Anne Helmreich, *The English Garden and National Identity: The Competing Styles of Garden Design 1870-1914* (Cambridge: Cambridge University Press, 2002). For a broader analysis of "Englishness" see Peter Mandler. *The English National Character. The History of an Idea from Edmund Burke to Tony Blair* (New Haven and London: Yale University Press, 2006).
54. Blomfield, *Richard Norman Shaw*, p. 32.
55. Blomfield, *Six Architects*, p. 186.

Portfolios

Duncan G. Stroik, Architect LLC

South Bend, Indiana

ALL SAINTS CHURCH, DIOCESE OF COVINGTON
Covington, Kentucky

PROJECT TEAM:
Duncan Stroik, Thomas Dietz, David Heit, Stefan Molina. Clarisey Frank Architecture, Ltd., Architect of Record: Terry Frank.

ALL SAINTS CHURCH IS LOCATED ON A PROMINENT SITE IN THE COUNTRYSIDE near Covington, Kentucky. The region is developing quickly in a typical way and this church design seeks to offer a vision of the sacred to those living and working in the area. The major approaches to the church offer views of its rear gable or its layered façade giving the *domus Ecclesiae* great prominence. The church can be seen from major roads and highways. A grassy piazza creates a focus and gathering space for the church, as well as for the existing school and rectory. Parking is in areas proximate to the church as well as along a new street with an allée of trees designed for processions. The composition of the exterior and interior elevations references the classicism of northern Kentucky, as well as the architecture of the Catholic architectural tradition in general. The construction is brick and limestone exterior over a steel frame with concrete block for durability.

The front façade is articulated as a gate to heaven, and gives intimations of the composition of the holy place within. Carved limestone bas-reliefs over the doorways symbolize the sacramental life of the Church and her saints. A stained glass window of the Assumption is placed over the entry with the coat of arms of the Bishop patron, His Excellency, Robert William Muench, placed in the tympanum. The façade is crowned by a glorified cross. The main entrance into the narthex allows communication to a vesting sacristy, stairs, and bathrooms. The interior of the nave is articulated with paired pilasters and arches, a simple entablature, and a plaster barrel vault. Large thermal windows bring light in from above. The baptismal font is given honor by being placed within its own space, to the right of the entrance and symbolizing entry into Mother Church through the sacrament of baptism.

The interior holds 600 people plus ample standing room in the rear and the narthex. Seating is arranged in four rows of pews with a nave 58-feet-wide and 50-feet- tall. A generous choir loft allows for choirs of up to fifty people plus an organ and other instruments. An implied transept helps to articulate a spacious sanctuary and devotional shrines to the Blessed Virgin Mary and to the Sacred Heart. Within the sanctuary the marble altar is central with a tent-like baldacchino overhead. The baldacchino symbolizes the *epiclesis* of the mass and has within its soffit an image of the Holy Spirit. The ambo is also paneled and can be accessed from either the sanctuary or the nave. It is balanced by the presider's chair with images of Saints Peter and Paul placed overhead. Within the apse there is a screen of pilasters and a panelled wall with a crucifix surmounting the entablature. The tabernacle is placed at the center of the wall and can be accessed from the sanctuary or the Blessed Sacrament chapel in the rear. The main sacristy is to the left of the sanctuary and a secondary foyer to the right has exterior doors allowing for prayer and eucharistic adoration

to occur in the Blessed Sacrament chapel when the church is closed. A ramp in the front of the church as well as a ramp in the rear foyer ensure that the whole church is accessible to the faithful. The undercroft is planned for parish gatherings and houses mechanical and other functional areas. As the church is dedicated to All Saints both the exterior and the interior of the building have images of the "cloud of witnesses," especially those from modern times, which surround the faithful and help them in their worship.

SHRINE OF OUR LADY OF GUADALUPE
La Crosse, Wisconsin

PROJECT TEAM:
Duncan Stroik, Kathryn Schuth, Hans Roegele,
Stefan Molina, Jamie LaCourt. River Architects,
Architect of Record: Mike Swinghamer, Sherry Wall.

THE SHRINE OF OUR LADY OF GUADALUPE is
said to be one of the first major Catholic
churches built in a classical manner in over
fifty years. It is meant to be a place for the
faithful to come on pilgrimage and to foster
devotion to the Blessed Virgin under her title
of Patroness of the Americas. In the tradition
of pilgrimage churches, the Shrine is located
high upon a hill outside of the city with a
campanile and dome that is visible from afar.

Since it is a place for prayer and pilgrimage,
the Shrine is designed to accommodate flow
and movement, with seating in the nave for
the liturgy and large open side aisles for circulation and prayer. The Shrine is the vision of
His Excellency Raymond L. Burke, Prefect of
the Apostolic Signatura, and was solemnly
dedicated on July 31, 2008.

The interior of the Shrine is a cruciform
domical church inspired by great Counter-
Reformation examples such as the Gesù,
Sant'Andrea della Valle, and San Giovanni
Battista dei Fiorentini in Rome. These
churches represent the highest standard in
sacred architecture and were designed by
many of the same architects who worked on
St. Peter's in the Vatican. Monumental fluted
Corinthian pilasters and arches define the

nave and give it a monumental scale worthy of a temple to the Lord. The glazed Corinthian capitals symbolize the Mother of God and include cherubim who look toward the sanctuary. In between are symbols of Mary which are connected to the capitals with swags made of roses. The entablature above is inscribed with the names of the Virgin from the litany of Loreto such as *Rosa Mystica* and *Regina Martyrum* while her symbols are reflected in the stained glass windows below. Generous side aisles flank the nave and feature the six minor shrines dedicated to the Divine Mercy and St. Faustina, St. Maria Goretti, St. Peregrine, St. Gianna Beretta Molla, Blessed Miguel Pro, and St. Thérèse of Lisieux, placed to encourage specific devotion. Doric confessionals are placed in the side aisles immediately in front of the crossing. Ribs punctuate the vaulted ceiling and stained glass windows follow the life of the Virgin.

Images of four doctors of the Church, Saints Ambrose, Ephrem, John Damascene, and Cyril of Alexandria—who are known for their writings on the Blessed Virgin—reside within the pendentives that support the dome with its eight clear windows. The frieze of the dome features an inscription in Latin from John 2:4-5: *Et dicit ei Iesus quid mihi et tibi est mulier nondum venit hora mea, Dicit mater eius ministris quodcumque dixerit vobis facite* ["O woman, what have you to do with me? My hour has not yet come." His mother said to the servants, "Do whatever he tells you."] The dome is painted with blue and gold colors based on the sacred image. It shows the constellations as they appeared on December 9, 1531, the day that Our Lady of Guadalupe revealed herself to Juan Diego, while the lantern above has an image of the Trinity. Minor shrines with marble statues of St. Juan Diego and St. Joseph flank the sanctuary while the transept holds the major shrines of paired Composite columns dedicated to the Sacred Heart of Jesus and the Immaculate Heart of Mary.

The raised marble sanctuary is defined by an altar rail, steps, and an ornamented archway. The focus of the sanctuary is a *rosso francia* marble and gold baldacchino surmounting the *rouge du roi* marble altar. The altar, which is shaped like an empty tomb,

symbolizes the sacrifice of the mass as well as recalls the Ascension and the Assumption of the Holy One of God. Behind the altar is a five-foot-tall marble tabernacle above which is placed a reproduction made by the Vatican Mosaic Studio of the miraculous icon of Our Lady of Guadalupe. The frame of the image is gilded in Mexican silver. A mahogany ambo with bas-reliefs of the four evangelists and tester is placed against one of the piers of the crossing and a life-sized wooden crucifix hangs above the baldacchino. The bishop's mahogany cathedra is raised and placed behind the ambo with the celebrant's chair facing it on the opposite side of the sanctuary. The sanctuary frieze has the central prayer of the Rosary inscribed: *Ave Maria, gratia plena, Dominus tecum. Benedicta tu in mulieribus, et benedictus fructus ventris tui, Jesus. Sancta Maria, Mater Dei, ora pro nobis peccatoribus, nunc, et in hora mortis nostrae. Amen.*

An ambulatory surrounds the apse and connects the sacristy and bishop's vestry. The sacristy is a vaulted space with mahogany cabinets, gilded plaster moldings, Eucharistic iconography, and a small shrine to St. John Vianney, patron of priests. The bishop's

vestry is a smaller version of the sacristy with a shrine to Bishop St. John Neumann, patron of Bishops. The narthex at the entrance to the Shrine has a trompe-l'oeil mural of the story of Our Lady of Guadalupe painted by Anthony Visco. The substantial choir loft, located above the narthex, features a classical organ case constructed from mahogany. In the lower level there is planned a crypt chapel with an oratory for spiritual lectures and prayer as well as a Hall of Honor for donors and a foyer with shrines to the blesseds of the diocese. All of the architectural elements and furnishings in the Shrine were designed specifically for this house of prayer including the pews, light fixtures, cabinetry, and sanctuary furnishings.

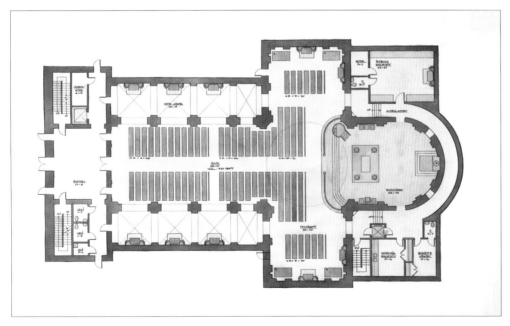

Our Lady of The Most Holy Trinity, Thomas Aquinas College Chapel
Santa Paula, California

Project Team:
Duncan Stroik, Stefan Molina, Hans Roegele, Kathryn Schuth, Antonio Bajuyo. Rasmussen & Associates, Architect of Record: Scott Boydstun, Jim Hanafin.

No end of human works is so great as the honor of God…for this reason magnificence is connected with holiness, since its chief effect is directed to religion or holiness.

— Thomas Aquinas, *Summa Theologiae*

Our Lady of the Most Holy Trinity chapel is prominently located at the head of the main quadrangle at Thomas Aquinas College. This central location reflects the central role of faith in the pursuit of wisdom. As *domus Dei*, the chapel is intended to offer a beautiful edifice for divine liturgy, for prayer, and to be an image of heavenly destiny. The design partakes of the broad tradition of Catholic architecture including the Early Christian, the Romanesque, the Renaissance, the Baroque, the Spanish tradition, and the churches of Southern California.

The three-story bell tower and dome can be seen from within the valley, and in particular from Ojai Road. Upon entering the campus, visitors see the chapel's curvilinear apse rising in front of them and can mount stairs up to a side terrace garden. Two octagonal corner pavilions, inspired by the *posas* built for catechesis by Spanish missionaries, provide a transition to the arcades of existing academic buildings.

The front of the chapel is on the college's main quadrangle with arcades providing covered access from the chapel to the academic buildings. The front façade is articulated by a limestone triumphal arch with fluted and spiral fluted Ionic columns. These frame the marble statues of St. Augustine, *Doctor Gratiae,* and St. Thomas Aquinas, *Doctor Communis,* the spiritual fathers of the college. Positioned above are four Corinthian pilasters that form a temple *in muris* punctuated by a central window. Within the triangular pediment two angels hold the col-

lege's coat of arms and a marble statue of Our Lady of the Most Holy Trinity surmounts the pediment. The lower frieze inscription, *Domina Nostra Sanctissimae Trinitatatis*, indicates the dedication of the chapel while the upper frieze quotes Rev. 12:1, *Et Signum magnum apparuit in caelo mulier amicta sole et luna sub pedibus eius et in capite eius corona stellarum duodecim.* The exterior has thick walls with a stucco finish, stone detailing, red tile roofs, and arched and circular windows.

Generous stairs and a broad terrace provide a gathering place and a location for outdoor ceremonies. The triumphal arch leads to a large porch or *exonarthex* with doric pilasters that support a heavy coffered vault. The main bronze doors have been designed to receive six bas-reliefs from the life of the Virgin with the "coronation" in the lunette above. The chapel has a nave, transept, and sanctuary in the shape of a cross, which can hold up to 400 people. Corinthian arcades made out of monolithic marble columns give it the character of an Early Christian basilica. The Corinthian capitals have an image of the Holy Spirit on their face. A giant order of Composite pilasters support a full entablature from which springs the vault of the ceiling with its ribbed supports and arched windows. The windows are high up in the nave and the aisles, symbolizing spiritual light. At the crossing, a segmental dome symbolizes the dome of

heaven with twelve circular windows in honor of the apostles. Large double pilasters give support to the dome with pendentives marked by symbols of the four evangelists. The side aisles provide places for procession and additional seating, and mahogany confessionals are placed at the center point of the nave.

The curved sanctuary is defined by a raised marble floor, an altar rail, and giant composite pilasters and arches. The main focus of the interior is on the pure white marble altar covered by a bronze baldacchino. Four solomonic columns on marble pedestals support a canopy, and angels holding wheat and grapes flank an image of Christ crucified. An octagonal marble and gold bronze tabernacle with an image of the redeemer is centrally located at the head of the chapel and a raised mahogany ambo with a sounding board is placed off to one side. To either side of the sanctuary are marble shrines with paintings of the Annunciation and the Baptism of Christ. Shrines in honor of the temptation of St. Thomas and the communion of St. Theresa of Avila are located at the end of the transepts. A sacristy and a work sacristy with mahogany cabinetry are located to either side of the sanctuary and are connected by a small ambulatory.

All images are used by permission of Duncan G. Stroik, Architect LLC. For an additional image see section opener on pages 44 and 45.

Cooper Johnson Smith Architects, Inc.

Tampa, Florida

REEDY CREEK FIRE STATION AND 911 CALL CENTER
Lake Buena Vista, Florida

PROJECT TEAM:
Don Cooper (principal architect), David Peterson (project manager).

THE GOAL OF THIS PROJECT was to create a functional, low-maintenance Fire Station, 24- hour 911 Call Center, and Sheriff's Station facility that meets the demanding requirements of the local emergency services division, but also provides a design that can be enjoyed by the frequent visitors to the area. The Bermuda-style architecture was chosen for its playful forms and monumental characteristics, as well as for its appropriateness to the Florida climate.

ARCHITECTURAL SOLUTION

The design consists of a several independent buildings forming a compound that is connected by a covered walkway surrounding an interior courtyard. A formal entry courtyard is provided at the front of the building for visitors and is flanked by three flags. Independent entrances are provided for individual agencies, which meet the programmatic requirements of the project. The use of deep-set windows and doors, shutters, covered walkways, thick masonry walls, and concrete roof tile creates a sense of strength and permanence, but also helps to make the buildings highly energy efficient. The final solution was celebrated by the client, the district, the agencies involved, and the end user.

All images are used by permission of Cooper Johnson Smith Architects, Inc.

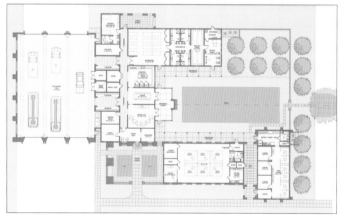

Purdum Residence
Holmes Beach, Manatee County, Florida

Project Team:
Don Cooper (principal architect), Angela Mayer, David Peterson and Jennifer Garcia.

THE INHERENT CHALLENGES OF THIS NARROW WATERFRONT LOT ON TAMPA BAY included the need to maximize waterfront views, the placement of the garage, and the creation of dual public frontages. The courtyard house typology *(H-plan)* provided solutions to these challenges by allowing the living spaces to spread across the water façade taking full advantage of views while setting the garage out of the way on the street frontage. The street front has a more fortified, solid, and secure expression with utilitarian spaces and garden walls forming a motor court with a delicate wood balcony presiding over the space. The side wings on the street side house the garage and golf cart storage, which are turned inwards to face each other rather than the street. This improves the public presence on the street and activates the semi-private motor court, which can accommodate multiple activities, public and private, formal and informal, for adults and children.

This courtyard typology is ideal for tropical coastal areas because the massing is broken up into narrow, linear wings that allow for cross-ventilation and natural sunlight, reducing the environmental impact and maximizing energy efficiency. As the main house divides the lot into one public and one private court, the side wings follow the edges of the property creating pleasant enclosed outdoor spaces while enhancing privacy and security for the home.

The two-story volume of the main house occupies the center of the lot with single-story side wings extending towards the water at the rear and towards the street at the front. The rear wings create an enclosed courtyard with a pool occupying the center overlooking the dock and the bay. A porch and gallery (two-story porch) protect the central Great Room and upper floor bedrooms from the elements and provide comfortable outdoor living spaces during inclement weather. These outdoor "rooms" can be enclosed with louvered shutters or curtains and used as "sleeping porches" to reduce the use of air conditioning during the more moderate times of the year. The waterfront façade has a more open, light, and airy expression to maximize views, natural sunlight, and ventilation.

The architectural vocabulary draws upon British Colonial precedents in the West Indies with masonry-stucco walls, a standing seam metal hip roof with a kick at the eaves, a wooden balcony supported by wood brackets on the more public street façade, and a wooden gallery atop hefty masonry columns framed with wood brackets on the more private waterfront façade. These features have been developed and refined over hundreds of years to accommodate comfortable living in the Caribbean and have evolved into a tradition of beautiful vernacular architecture that is, as a result, truly sustainable.

The covered outdoor spaces in conjunction with the protected courts, deep overhangs, and operable wood shutters are respectful of the context and climate, maximizes energy-efficiency, and minimizes environmental impact. The massing and layout of this house with its simple and flexible spaces can accommodate many different family types and lifestyles and can even change uses as the market demands.

All images are used by permission of Cooper Johnson Smith Architects, Inc.

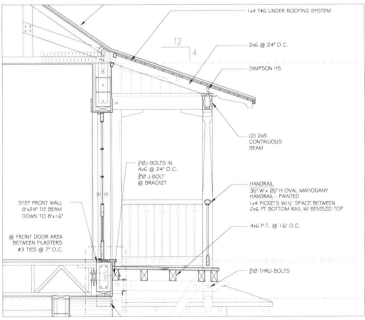

1x4 T&G UNDER ROOFING SYSTEM

2x6 @ 24" O.C.

SIMPSON H5

(2) 2x8
CONTINUOUS
BEAM

¾"Ø J-BOLTS IN
4x6 @ 24" O.C.
¾"Ø J-BOLT
@ BRACKET

STEP FRONT WALL
8"x24" TIE BEAM
DOWN TO 8"x16"

@ FRONT DOOR AREA
BETWEEN PILASTERS
#3 TIES @ 7" O.C.

HANDRAIL
3½" W x 2½" H OVAL MAHOGANY
HANDRAIL - PAINTED
1x4 PICKETS W/ ½" SPACE BETWEEN
2x6 PT BOTTOM RAIL W/ BEVELED TOP

4x6 P.T. @ 16" O.C.

¾"Ø THRU-BOLTS

Thomas Norman Rajkovich Architect, Ltd.

Evanston, Illinois

STUDIOLO FOR THE WARD RESIDENCE
Lake Forest, Illinois

PROJECT TEAM:
Thomas Norman Rajkovich

THE OWNERS OF AN HISTORICALLY SIGNIFICANT HOUSE IN LAKE FOREST, ILLINOIS required a design for a new two-story study and garden room to be appended to the original residence.

Drawing inspiration from the brilliant fictive oculus in Andrea Mantegna's *Camera degli Sposi* in the Palazzo Ducale in Mantua, the inventive top lighting in Sir John Soane's work, especially his own house at 13 Lincoln's Inn Fields and the Dulwich Picture gallery, and the structure of a Roman litter, the firm developed the design first in section. The objective was to gather light from the windows in the study on the second floor (above the level of adjoining dense landscape) and allow it to spill down into the garden room.

A fitted furniture element was introduced in the study, in the form of an octagonal, "donut-shaped" desk around an oculus which connects the two levels. The masculine Doric columns and pilasters of the garden room below support a beamed ceiling which, in turn, serves as the "carriage" for the desk—a tectonic assembly poetically related, both in conception and form, to a Roman litter. On the second floor, Ionic pilasters—appropriately maiden-like—carry more delicate beams, with the ceiling panels between painted sky blue, evoking an open pergola. The oculus permits the inhabitant to experience the upper and lower rooms simultaneously, in parallax.

Daylight entering the extensive perimeter fenestration of the second floor refracts through a glazed frame atop the oculus, allowing light from the study to illuminate the first floor. The light may be understood to represent knowledge obtained through

study, then shared. The furniture element that shapes the oculus has an essential and practical purpose in the study: it functions as a partner's desk, with seating at its ends and cabinet storage along the sides for the accommodation of computer components, a fax machine/printer, and lateral files.

At night, light from the first floor garden room radiates up through the glazing over the oculus and evokes the glow of a beacon within the study, visible from across the property through the second floor windows. Here, Karl Friedrich Schinkel's Cape Arcona lighthouse served as a precedent. Yet the heavy masonry bays of Schinkel's project (atop which sits a lantern light) are transformed into a delicate, trabeated timber structure, which houses the oculus "beacon."

The exterior of the structure is a simple, yet refined, essay in the classical. On the first floor, Doric piers and engaged columns are employed. The upper register combines Ionic engaged columns and Doric piers (whose cyma-profile echinus is drawn from the Baths of Diocletian's notoriously conflated order) carrying a common, denticulated Ionic entablature. There is the influence of Inigo Jones' Palladianism (particularly the Banqueting House façade) and the gravitas inherent in the compound articulation found in the Roman Baroque, notably at the exterior corners. The design thereby combines the openness of a classical columnar frame with a sense of solidity that is well-suited to the adjoining original house's stucco and masonry construction. Firmness, commodity, and delight each play their role.

All images are used by permission of Thomas Norman Rajkovich Architect, Ltd.

Pier Carlo Bontempi Architettura Civile & Disegno Urbano

Gaiano di Collecchio, Italy

Place de Toscane
Val d'Europe, France

Project Team:
Pier Carlo Bontempi, principal; Giuseppe Greci, project manager; Fabio Paoletti, design architect; Matteo Casola, engineer; Massimo Gandini, director.

The project is situated in France, 30 km east of Paris, in the new City of Val d'Europe, between a large commercial center and the Town Hall square. The scheme consists of a rectangular block of buildings at the heart of which is an elliptical piazza similar in dimensions to the Roman amphitheatre in Lucca, a fortified town in Tuscany.

The architecture of Place Toscane is inspired by the local architecture of the Ile-de-France, and designed with an architectural sensitivity and harmony that is distinctly Italian. A fountain at the visual focus of the square animates the environment with the cast shadow of its obelisk and the gurgling of its twelve jets of water running into two basins one above the other. Two wide passageways open into small courtyards where the space becomes more personal and private.

All images are used by permission of Pier Carlo Bontempi Architettura Civile & Disegno Urbano.

Cure & Penabad Studio
Khoury & Vogt Architects

Miami, Florida; Alys Beach, Florida

Oak Plaza
Miami, Florida

PROJECT TEAM:
Adib Cure and Carie Penabad;
Marieanne Khoury-Vogt and Erik Vogt

THE DISTRICT IN WHICH THIS INFILL PROJECT IS LOCATED is an older eighteen-block community located just north of downtown Miami. This neighborhood, long forgotten during the era of suburban sprawl, is now experiencing a dramatic urban renewal. Its revival can be largely attributed to an enlightened developer dedicated to creating a vibrant neighborhood for the city's design trades. Although it has already attracted leading designers and showrooms, the district has no identifiable center. Thus the desire for the project to define this center by creating its first public plaza.

The project thus encompassed five main objectives:

* Transformation of an existing parking lot into the first public plaza in the neighborhood.

* A new street to bisect an existing block, flanked by two galleried buildings.

* 12,800 square feet of new retail, office, and restaurant space.

* A new open loggia defining one edge of the plaza, offering the neighborhood an additional gathering space.

* Preservation of an existing 150-year-old stand of live oaks.

The site was originally occupied by a parking lot located underneath the stand of mature live oaks. A prerequisite of the project was the preservation of these trees as the centerpiece of the new plaza. The existing asphalt surface was replaced with native limestone, which will slowly weather under the shade of the trees. The edges of the plaza are defined by a thin retail building and adjacent monumental loggia, sheathed in iridescent mosaic tile.

Adjoining the plaza, a new street was created, which allows pedestrians to bisect the length of the existing block. The street provided an unprecedented moment for collaboration. At the onset of the project, the developer hired two independent firms to design new retail buildings on either side of the street. Rather than working in isolation, the architects chose to establish a dialogue in the belief that the best urbanism is produced collaboratively. The resulting street section, composed of flanking galleries that share common bays, fenestration, and lighting, is thus a unified and memorable space, a whole that adds up to more than the sum of its architectural parts.

A similar collaborative mode established a common strategy for the building façades on 40th Street. First floor storefronts are surmounted by open loggias at the second floor, each a variation on the theme of public display. The wider building develops a three-bay outdoor room, faced on its interior in brilliantly colored Cuban tile. The narrower building treats the building wall edges as a proscenium, with hanging metal curtains framing the loggia walls that cant back in forced perspective, an adumbration of the deep space beyond.

Although relatively small in scale, the project aspires to create a vision for the future design and construction of a city still in the making. In a place often defined by non-descript structures that seldom cohere into memorable streets or public spaces, it offers a distinct and coherent urban architecture illustrating a fundamental belief that architecture is first and foremost a civic art.

All images are used by permission of Cure & Penabad Studio and Khoury & Vogt Architects. Photography by Simon Hare.

Khoury & Vogt Architects

Alys Beach, Florida

SALES CENTER
Alys Beach, Florida

PROJECT TEAM:
Marieanne Khoury-Vogt and Erik Vogt.

SITUATED ALONG THE UPPER GULF COAST OF FLORIDA, the project is the first building to come out of the ground in a new 160-acre resort town that represents the latest in New Urbanist planning and architecture. It is intended to serve as both an information center and model house for the community, exemplifying the goals and aspirations of the town's founder.

The foremost design challenge was to establish an urban type and architectural syntax that would produce not only interesting houses but a harmonious urbanism for the town as a whole. Toward this end, the attached courtyard, or patio, and house, as found in the colonial architecture of Latin and South America, was decided upon as a primary architectural type for the residential program. Although the model house is detached, because of its commercial use, it exemplifies critical aspects of the type for future homeowners and architects. A single-room-width volume, which allows for cross ventilation, wraps and protects a private courtyard. The courtyard is lined with open galleries and will be landscaped with native trees, flowering plants, and climbing vines, protected from the salt sea air by high walls. A stone-paved stair leads to a roof terrace, overlooking the site and Gulf of Mexico.

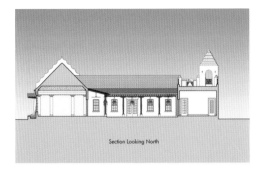

Section Looking North

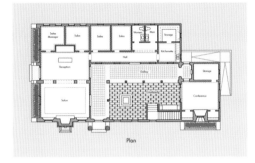

Plan

The architecture of Bermuda is the touchstone for the character of the building and the town. While the tautness and simplicity of its forms supports the making of a calm, relaxed urbanism, it also affords room for sculptural expression, as evidenced in the battered chimney, scalloped gables, and rooftop buttery.

These simple volumes and sculptural forms are unified by the choice of an all-white color palette, entrained in the stucco walls and lime-washed roofs. This strategy will be deployed throughout the town for private residences, so that the streets and squares they form will be rendered as harmonious public spaces, set off by a tropical landscape and an ever-changing play of reflected light.

All images are used by permission of Khoury & Vogt Architects.

Eric Watson Architect, P.A.

Tampa, Florida

Hardiman House
Tampa, Florida

PROJECT TEAM:
Eric Watson, AIA; Gar Barkman, RA; Grant Rimbey.

THIS NEW WATERFRONT HOME is a primary residence with an informal program of interior and exterior spaces for an active family who entertain frequently. The house is designed to take full advantage of the waterfront site and to provide a comfortable environment to enjoy indoor-outdoor living.

Arranged around an interior courtyard, the house is split into two primary building forms—a two-story section facing the bay, and a one-story section facing the street. This arrangement allows an abundance of sunlight into the interior and direct exterior access to all first floor spaces. The dispersed program, positioned in the one- and two-story sections on both sides of the courtyard, diminished the apparent size of the nearly 10,000-square-foot structure.

The house's Anglo-Caribbean style incorporates a mixture of traditional materials and details. The first floor concrete masonry exterior walls are finished in smooth stucco rendered as a solid base supporting a lighter second floor of wood-framed exterior walls, clad in rough-sawn cedar siding. Exposed rafter tails provide texture and strong shadows against the stucco walls. Cast stone elements such as the Doric columns and the entry architrave add refinement to the variety of traditional building details and materials.

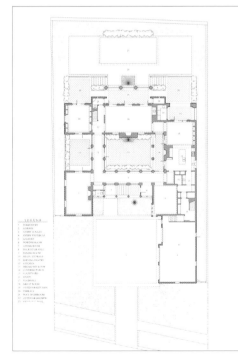

BAKER HOUSE
Seaside, Florida

PROJECT TEAM:
Eric Watson, AIA; Gar Barkman, RA.

THE BAKER HOUSE, LOCATED IN SEASIDE, FLORIDA, is a Palladian-inspired classical design. Recalling elements of "high style" classicism, as well as those of an informal beach cottage, the house is true to its classical origins yet tailored to its resort surroundings and southern location. The canonical Greek Doric porch exists comfortably with the abundant over-sized sash windows, rafter tails, and tin roof.

Located on a challenging pie-shaped lot near the town center, the symmetrical façade belies the informal interior arranged with living spaces open to each other as well as to the covered exterior porches. Single-story bay projections reconcile site geometries with the orthogonal main block and provide a sunny sitting area for the living room and a spacious master bathroom. Readily available exterior and interior finish materials and stock molding profiles kept construction costs in line while remaining true to the house's historical origins.

All images are used by permission of Eric Watson Architect, P.A.

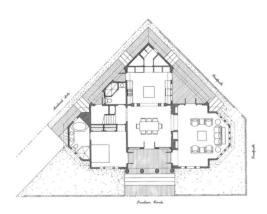

Thomas Gordon Smith Architects

South Bend, Indiana

CEDAR GROVE MAUSOLEUM COMPLEX, UNIVERSITY OF NOTRE DAME
Notre Dame, Indiana

PROJECT TEAM:
Thomas Gordon Smith and John P. Haigh.

THOMAS GORDON SMITH ARCHITECTS provided a master plan for a new Mausoleum Complex at Cedar Grove Cemetery at the University of Notre Dame. The project includes mausolea, a new office structure, gardens, reconfigured roads, and paths.

The goal of the project was to construct within a 150-year-old university cemetery new mausolea: durable, dignified structures that honor the dead. The contemplative gardens around the mausolea enhance the park-like atmosphere of the cemetery. The buildings are oriented in response to iconic views on campus.

The first two mausolea have been constructed and won a 2008 Brick Industry Association Award. Additional mausolea and a new welcome office cottage will complete the master plan.

All images are used by permission of Thomas Gordon Smith Architects.

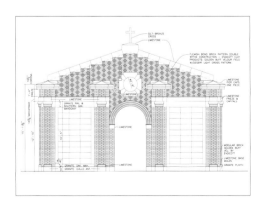

de la Guardia Victoria Architects & Urbanists, Inc.

Coral Gables, Florida

ALMERIA ROW
Coral Gables, Florida

PROJECT TEAM:
Maria de la Guardia and Teófilo Victoria, Principals; and Elizabeth Pereiro.

ALMERIA ROW IS A MULTI-FAMILY DEVELOP-MENT project built in Coral Gables, Florida. Design work started in 2004 and construction for the first phase of the project was completed in 2007.

The project consists of ten townhouses built on ten fee-simple parcels measuring on average 23' x 120'. The townhouses are each two stories high and range in size between 2,840 square feet and 3,037 square feet. The development introduces a new residential type to the city of Coral Gables. In a rare collaboration between city, owner, and architect the zoning code was changed to accommodate the characteristics of the "classic" townhouse common in London and New York. Because it is a fee-simple scheme each unit is built on its own parcel and shares a common wall. Almeria Row is neither a condominium unit nor a detached housing unit, but rather an attached single-family residence. The size of the parcel establishes a new minimum size parcel in the zoning code and allows for higher densities without relying on oversized apartment blocks. The proportion of width to height characteristic of the townhouse type, the repetition of the unit, and the proximity of the stoop to the sidewalk results in a street elevation which is at once familiar and out of the ordinary.

The townhouse is composed of two volumes connected by a courtyard. The first floor of the main volume consists of the public program of the house including the living room and dining room, kitchen and family room. The private functions of the residence, master bedroom and master bath, as well as a

second bedroom and bathroom are housed on the second floor. The second volume houses a two-car garage on the first floor with access to an alley behind the property. There are two additional bedrooms and bathrooms on the second floor. The bedrooms above the garage can be accessed from the courtyard by means of a separate set of stairs. This project recalls the traditional town home all while meeting the requirements of modern day living.

The constructive participation and collaboration among the patron, municipality, and architect were elemental in the success of the project. The importance and value of the commitment of these different parties to a common goal was, in fact, the most important lesson learned over the course of the project. Better and more sustainable housing options for the city and its urban residents are now achievable as a result of this mutual effort.

Prior to Almeria Row, fee-simple townhouses in Coral Gables were not included in the zoning code. As a result, the revision to the zoning code readdressed the front and rear setbacks for single-family residences and reduced the minimum size lot required for residential units by half.

The incorporation of townhouse zoning guidelines to the existing zoning resolution occurred at a time when the municipal government was under pressure to limit development and enlighten developers eager to introduce a residential type to the home market that offered a higher standard of urban living. The architects assisted in the revisions to the existing code and, with the incorporation of new legislation, worked to promote the building of a housing type that for decades and no apparent reason, had been excluded from the zoning resolution. Not only in Miami-Dade County, but throughout the country the townhouse had practically disappeared as a housing option despite the many excellent examples of townhouse neighborhoods in American as well as European cities. In Coral Gables the townhouse as an integral type of the urban fabric is in fact recovered from the original master plan designed by George E. Merrick and his architects. The master plan included entire residential districts where the townhouse was the prevalent housing type. Blocks were traversed by alleyways designated for utilities and service and were composed of 25' x 100' lots.

Almeria Row recovers a housing option which is as old and universal as the city itself. It reconsiders, as is common in traditional building, the type in new and contemporary circumstances. The incorporation of a court-yard, unusual to the townhouse, is an attempt to adapt northern European models to better suited Mediterranean examples. The work of the architect Mott Schmidt was an inspiration for Almeria Row. Other cultural sources such as the houses in the Moorish districts of Seville, Spain, offered an interesting evolution of the townhouse type due to their small but charming and luminous courtyards.

The project is characterized primarily by a traditional conception of composition and style in architecture. The use of a classical syntax built in cut stone imbues the building and the civic realm with a serene and elegant quality.

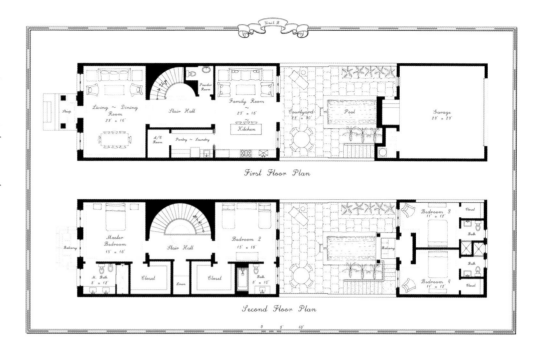

First Floor Plan

Second Floor Plan

Ca'Liza
New Providence, Bahamas

PROJECT TEAM:
Maria de la Guardia and Teófilo Victoria, Principals;
Anne Finch, Ricardo Lopez, Josh Arcurio,
Elizabeth Pereiro, Jose Venegas.

Ca'Liza, NAMED AFTER THE NEW BORN DAUGHTER OF THE PATRONS, is a single-family residence built on the shores of the Atlantic Ocean on the northern coast of the island of New Providence in The Bahamas. The site is approximately ten miles west of the capital city of Nassau. The design of the house was begun in the summer of 2005 and construction was completed in the spring of 2008.

The location and program of the project is consistent with the guidelines established by a regional master plan that promotes the preservation of the existing rural character of the western side of the island by relying on a traditional Bahamian urban pattern of concentrated building in villages and towns, allowing for large extensions of green open space to remain between the urban areas. The master plan relies on vernacular and colloquial building types to maintain architectural consistency and continuity not only in New Providence but also with the neighboring Family Islands.

In The Bahamas, architecture traditions in vernacular building as well as in works of civic significance have been greatly influenced by Palladianism. In Nassau, the Parliament buildings, the Supreme Court, and Governor's House, for instance, are neo-Palladian schemes, but Palladian influences are evident as well in the homes, large and small, along George and Queen Streets. This building tradition was first brought to Nassau by Loyalists from the Carolinas, but eventually it would become prevalent throughout the country, imbuing the laconic landscape of sand and brush of The Bahamas with a classical and enduring beauty.

Ca'Liza adheres to this tradition, typologically and stylistically, and pursues a familiar pictorial frame of architecture and landscape. The house, surrounded by a subtropical hammock of sea grape, palm, ficus, silk cotton, and gumbo limbo, sits on a

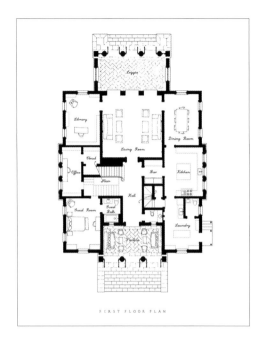

FIRST FLOOR PLAN

SECOND FLOOR PLAN

ridge overlooking the sea. It is approximately 6.000 square feet plus an attic floor. The public functions are housed in the first floor and the private rooms are in the second story with several more guest rooms in the attic. In addition, two carriage houses provide for a garage and staff quarters. The main house and carriage house are aligned along a central axis, which runs the entire length of the site and connects the deep green of the landscape with the turquoise hue of the sea.

The main house, clad in coralina limestone, has two fronts, one to the ocean and the other towards the hammock and the street. The ocean side is dominated by a two-tiered loggia composed of the Tuscan order at grade and the Doric order above. The portico on the land side is open below and enclosed above. Due to an enlightened zoning code, which measures building heights in terms of stories rather than dimensions, the house is cubic in volume, approximating the proportions and scale of a Palladian villa from the Veneto. Despite the vernacular character of the limestone and the shuttered loggias, the building nonetheless recovers an essential quality of the architecture of Andrea Palladio and inspires the name of the house in the Venetian manner, Ca'Liza.

DESIGN CHALLENGES
Even though Palladianism has been a prevalent building tradition in the history of The Bahamas, today knowledge of classical architecture has practically disappeared from building standards. For this project building crews had to be trained in classical composition and detailing, and the level of craftsmanship had to be improved. The owner of the house, Orjan Lindroth, a builder with a long-standing interest in recovering Bahamian traditions in the building arts, has jointly with his wife Amanda sponsored books, symposia, and conferences on preservation and traditional building and urbanism in The Bahamas.

All images are used by permission of de la Guardia Victoria Architects & Urbanists, Inc.

Eric Stengel Architecture

Nashville, Tennessee

TIME OUT FARM
Cornersville, Tennessee

This equestrian farm complex on 2,000 acres in Giles County consists of a main house; a caretaker's house; a barn with fourteen horse stalls, tack room, office, etc.; a hay barn; vehicle and farm equipment storage structures; pond dock; and a folly. The larger site design included several miles of riding trails, gates, and security.

Generally, all structures are horizontal lap siding in old-growth cedar painted white with green standing seam metal roofs; there is extensive use of timbers in all structures. The architectural vocabulary of the buildings is a simple "farm" vernacular. Some elements are detailed for function and meaning. For instance, the column hold downs at the barn are in black strap steel to resemble the bindings on a horse's legs.

All images are used by permission of Eric Stengel Architecture. Photo credit: Bob Schatz.

WHITESELL RESIDENCE
Nashville, Tennessee

This home was designed for a half-acre infill lot in an older Nashville neighborhood. It is intended to be a background building with clear and simple classical detailing that continues an age-old conversation about classical principles while being functional and practical for contemporary requirements. These efforts were in direct response to a rejection of the typical "builder's specials" with their embarrassing and childish use of materials and details. The brick pavilion in the front is detailed to reflect 1920s colonial revival houses, while the rear follows the idiom of late nineteenth-century farmhouse vernacular. The overall organizational concept is shown with the difference in materials—brick in front and siding behind—which is the notional result of a Georgian front being added to the "original" house by a subsequent generation.

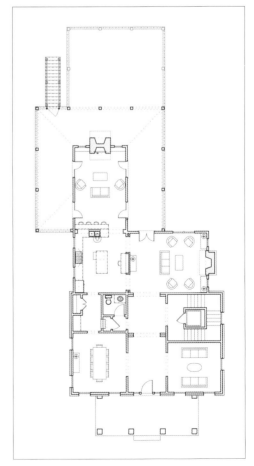

Fairfax & Sammons Architecture

New York City, Palm Beach, Charleston

PRIVATE RESIDENCE
Greenwich, Connecticut

THE CLIENTS are an aesthetically sensitive couple, interested in local history and architecture, who wanted to replace their 1980s wood-frame, contractor colonial with something more substantial. As they are collectors of Dutch paintings and Asian art, it seemed appropriate to design a house in the William and Mary style.

This idiom combined domestic influences from William of Orange's native country of the Netherlands with grander Baroque themes from France. It also included an exotic thread which, as a result of increasing trade with the Far East, exhibited a taste for oriental motifs heralding the beginnings of Chinoiserie. The house is based on the elegant Mompesson House, built in 1701 in Salisbury Close, England. It is a five-bay, six-room Palladian plan (rather than a more conventional center-hall, Colonial plan) with an added asymmetrical wing. Typical of the William and Mary style, it is built of red brick with white window trim and deep modillion cornice, and an entrance emphasized by a carved limestone portico. The load-bearing brickwork is in Flemish bond with brick quoins at the corners. The additional wing is a wood-frame structure, intended to recall the owners' previous house, which accommodates garages below and a family room above. This is designed with historical reference to early Connecticut architecture that typically has one paneled wall containing the fireplace. A wide-plank pine floor, painted an oxblood color, complements the room's vernacular style.

All images are used by permission of Fairfax & Sammons Architecture.

Fairfax & Sammons Architecture with Ben Pentreath

New York City, Palm Beach, Charleston

THE CRESCENT
Poundbury, U.K.

A NEW URBAN CRESCENT formed by groups of townhouses in a chaste Georgian style was commissioned and designed for the second phase of development in Poundbury, a model village for sustainable growth in Dorset, England, sponsored by The Prince of Wales. Poundbury has proved a remarkable phenomenon; a high-density development in open farmland on the edge of the market town of Dorchester, which demonstrates that it is possible to break the mold of character-less suburban developments and produce a plan for modern living that revives the best qualities of traditional urban townscapes.

Photograph by Ned Trifle

Photograph by Willie Miller

Robert A. M. Stern Architects

New York, New York

JACKSONVILLE PUBLIC LIBRARY
Jacksonville, Florida

PROJECT TEAM:
Partner: Alexander P. Lamis. Project Senior Associate:
Jeffery Povero. Project Associates: James Pearson,
Salvador Peña-Figueroa, George Punnoose,
Kim Siewlee Yap. Project Assistants: Daniel Arbelaez,
Jennifer Berlly, Ceren Bingol, Matthew Casey,
Thomas Fletcher, Mark Gage, Anthony Goldsby,
Jill Lagowski, Joshua Lekwa, Ernesto Martinez,
Mark Rodriguez, Mike Soriano, John Tulloch.
Interior Design Associates: Hyung Kee Lee,
Shannon Ratclilff. Interior Design Assistants:
Kasumi Hara, Kathleen Mancini. Landscape Design
Associate: Marsh Kriplen. Landscape Design Project
Manager: Michael Weber. Landscape Design Senior
Assistant: Ashley Christopher. Landscape Design
Assistant: Jennifer Burlly. Landscape Architect:
Nancy Jenkins-Frye, ASLA. Associate Architect:
Rolland, DelValle & Bradley.

A PUBLIC LIBRARY is the most democratic of institutions: it has the capacity to draw in the young and old, from every ethnicity and background. A great library must be much more than a depository for books or a facility for information exchange: it must be a great collective civic place. The firm's aspiration for the Jacksonville Main Library is to build a highly efficient, state-of-the-art facility that is also a great public place, with intimate and grand rooms, garden courtyards, conference areas, and cafes, all designed to attract the community and, by virtue of its exterior forms and interior spaces, to become a destination to which people will return again and again for education, inspiration, and a beautiful environment.

The design for the Jacksonville Main Library continues the city's rich tradition of civic buildings designed in a classical language adapted to the particulars of local climate and culture. Seen from Hemming Plaza and from Main Street, it presents an iconic civic appearance that renders the Library identifi-

able as a welcoming and ennobling public place. Facing Hemming Plaza, a generously-proportioned main entrance leads past a Cafe and Popular Library, each with large windows facing the street, to the Entry Hall and circulation desk, where a monumental stair rises through the building, connecting the various departments. The stair culminates at the Grand Reading Room, a place of civic proportions, 100 feet square and rising 46 feet to a handkerchief-vaulted ceiling, bathed in natural light from clerestory windows, with balconied windows overlooking Hemming Plaza.

At the second floor, readers and staff enjoy a courtyard with a fountain, around which are intimate reading areas.

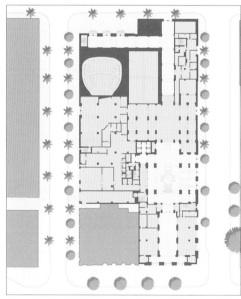

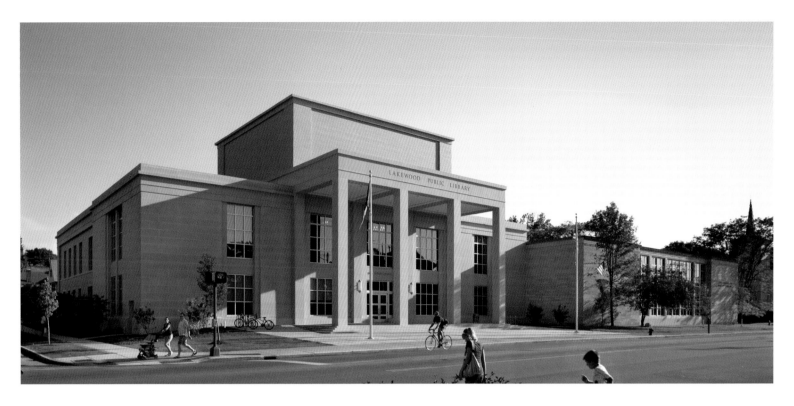

LAKEWOOD PUBLIC LIBRARY
Lakewood, Ohio

PROJECT TEAM:
Partner: Alexander P. Lamis. Project Senior Associate:
Julie Nymann. Project Associates: James Pearson,
Salvador Peña-Figueroa, Mike Soriano,
Kim Siewlee Yap. Interior Design Assistants:
Phillip Chan, Khania Curtis, Khara Nemitz,
Leah Taylor, Eric Van Speights, Jr. Landscape Senior
Associate: Michael Weber. Associate Architect:
CBLH Design, Inc.

THE RENOVATION of the 53,000-square-foot
Lakewood Public Library (Edward L. Tilton,
1916) and a 40,000-square-foot addition
created a well-organized state-of-the-art
library that is a great public place, with rooms
both grand and intimate, a destination that
attracts Lakewood's vibrant community in all
its diversity to return again and again for
education and inspiration.

The design continues Lakewood's rich
tradition of civic buildings in the classical
architectural language. The addition is
located to the east of the existing building; a
monumental entry porch provides a civic scale
that the current library lacks and enlivens

Detroit Avenue. From the entry porch, and
also from the second entrance from the parking lot, patrons move to a two-story skylit
lobby at the building's center. This central
lobby serves as an orientation point and opens
to the circulation desk, the popular materials
room, and the children's department, which
offers storytime, computer, and homework
rooms along with a double-height arts and
crafts room.

At the end of a main hall are elevators
and a grand stair with another skylight to
bring natural light down to the main level.
Upstairs are reading rooms, the general
collection stacks, and the technology center,
along with a large audiovisual department to
accommodate the library's fast-growing
collection of videos, CDs, and DVDs. The
paneled Grand Reading Room, located just
above the main entrance, is elegantly scaled—
50 feet long by 30 feet wide, and 30 feet
high—and furnished with wood tables and
carrels. Alcoves north and south offer
lounge chairs for casual reading. Hidden sky-
lights filter natural light throughout the
room. An intimate Quiet Reading Room is
located to the south, away from the bustle of
Detroit Avenue.

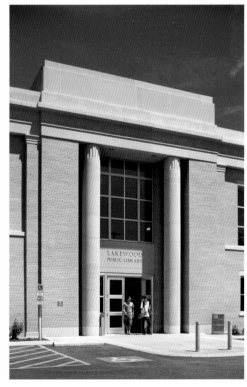

Baker Library | Bloomberg Center
Harvard Business School
Boston, Massachusetts

PROJECT TEAM:
Partners: Alexander P. Lamis, Kevin M. Smith, Graham S. Wyatt. Project Senior Associates: Melissa DelVecchio, Kurt Glauber. Project Associates: Enid DeGracia, Mike Soriano, Sue Jin Sung. Project Assistants: Giovanna Albretti, Flavia Bueno, Alexander Butler, Matthew Casey, Sara Evans, Thomas Fletcher, Mark Gage, Mark Haladyna, Jacqueline Ho, Donald Johnson, Edmund Leveckis, Dryden Razook, Ryan Rodenberg, Thomas Salazar, Mike Soriano, Suejin Sung, Brian Taylor, John Tulloch, Lindsay Weiss. Interior Design Associates: Hyung Kee Lee, Ken Stuckenschneider. Interior Design Assistants: Nadine Holzheimer, Khara Nemitz.
Landscape Architect: The Halvorson Company Inc.
Associate Architect: Finegold Alexander + Associates.

BAKER LIBRARY was designed by McKim, Mead & White and completed in 1927 as the centerpiece of the Harvard Business School campus. The renovation and addition reconceives the building as a 160,000-gross-square-foot center for research and group study, with greatly expanded meeting facilities, faculty offices and their support services, and archival storage for the Library's one-of-a-kind collection of historical business materials. Central to the reorganization is a second front entrance at what was originally the back of the building to address the reorientation of the campus to the south, making the building an easily accessible crossroads of the HBS campus.

The design provides for pedestrian movement through the building from north to south through the original portico and lobby, and secondary circulation from west to east, all on the first floor. The exterior façades and important interior rooms of the original building are restored and the original self-supporting stacks replaced with faculty offices, seminar rooms, and lounges. A skylit atrium brings natural light deep into the building and provides an informal meeting place for students and faculty.

The Baker Library | Bloomberg Center is RAMSA's second project at the Harvard Business School, following on the completion of the Spangler Campus Center in early 2001.

All images are used by permission of Robert A. M. Stern Architects. Photographs ©Peter Aaron/Esto.

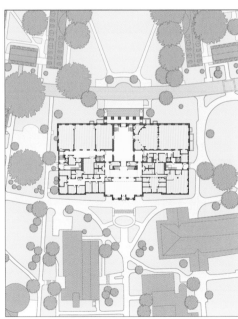

Sketchbooks
IMAGINATION AND THE SKETCH

By Richard W. Cameron

We were recently completing a large estate project for some wonderful clients in the Mid-Atlantic area, and after nearly four years of work I came across this quote from Mongiardino. It led me to think about the beginning of the project and the role that drawing and imagination play in the work with our clients.

I made many sketches at the outset of the project exploring ideas for the estate and for the main house, some of which encapsulated ideas that remain visible in the built work. Before our first formal meeting however, I made a series of presentation sketches in plan, elevation, and perspective to illustrate the proposed design. One of these drawings became—more than any other—the touchstone for the project (illustrated on page 87). As we proceeded to design and build the project all of us referred to this drawing at different times and for varied purposes (in conversations and decisions over the selection of building materials, design features, character, etc.).

As the project was nearing completion the owner told me that the thing he had found most satisfying about working with us was our ability to capture in sketches not only what the final result would look like, but also what it would feel like. He referred in particular to this drawing as the one that best exemplified this ability. "It looks and feels exactly like the house," he said.

There are actually many points of difference between the presentation sketches and the final building: the roof is a different color; there is no half-timbering on the gatehouse drawing—as there is in the final building; and many details are different or were refined. However, the thing I believe the client intended to say, which was central to the success of our working collaboration, is that the sketch looks like what

Occasionally the model intimidates the client. Then faith must be stronger than understanding, and only a vague intuition allows the work to begin favorably. But it is difficult for the client to understand the vision of the artist. Envisioning the finished work is not always easy for the architect, and it is almost always impossible for the client. Unlike the painting to be bought, or clothing, food, and the many other choices available to people—choices made on the basis of finished materials—the decision about the new house lies in the future, is based on credit, on the model (drawings), on agreements. The finished product is a surprise. Only faith can reward the client. After that critical moment is overcome, sometimes what emerges is the satisfaction of finding smooth solutions and natural resolutions to every uncertainty. The room responds to the client's way of life.

— Renzo Mongiardino, *Roomscapes* (1993)

he and his wife "imagined" the house was going to look like, and so in retrospect that fantasy house, and the house we built are in some fundamental agreement. This is why the sketch embodied not just the look of the house for them, but also the feeling it would have.

We were very lucky to have such wonderful clients with whom to work on such a large and long project, and the fact that they had that faculty of imagination was among the greatest gifts. Yet if there is a fundamental message I drew from the experience, it is this: when we sketch as designers, we dream, and we convey those dreams to paper.

The work of architecture that is in our head is transferred directly to the paper in an almost unconscious way. This is not to suggest that it is unstudied or that years of training and experience do not go into its making, but the hand-eye communication that translates to what the Beaux-Arts would have called the "parti" is direct and at its best captures the fundamental features and character of a design. In the best cases this is shared by everyone involved and acts as a guide to the project as it comes to fruition.

One of the reasons we draw everyday at the Ariel Atelier—and that we draw and sketch by hand specifically—is to practice and refine this ability. However adept we may become in the digital realm, this basic skill will continue to underlie the most successful designs and will always create the most productive working relationships with our clients. This is the fundamental principle that we continue to rely upon as we continue to build our design practice—capturing the essence of our designs for our clients with hand-drawn sketches.

Sketches and drawings by Richard W. Cameron and Jason Grimes.

Garden Front Portico

Detail of the Ravenwood capital

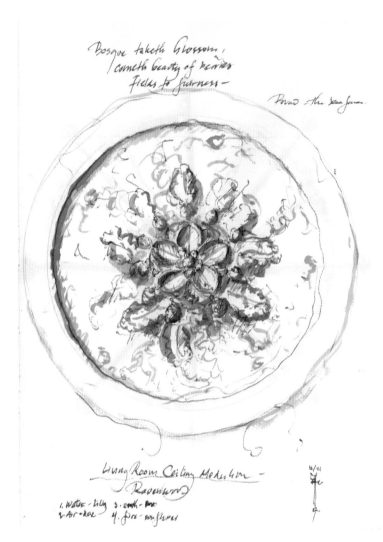

Ceiling ornament

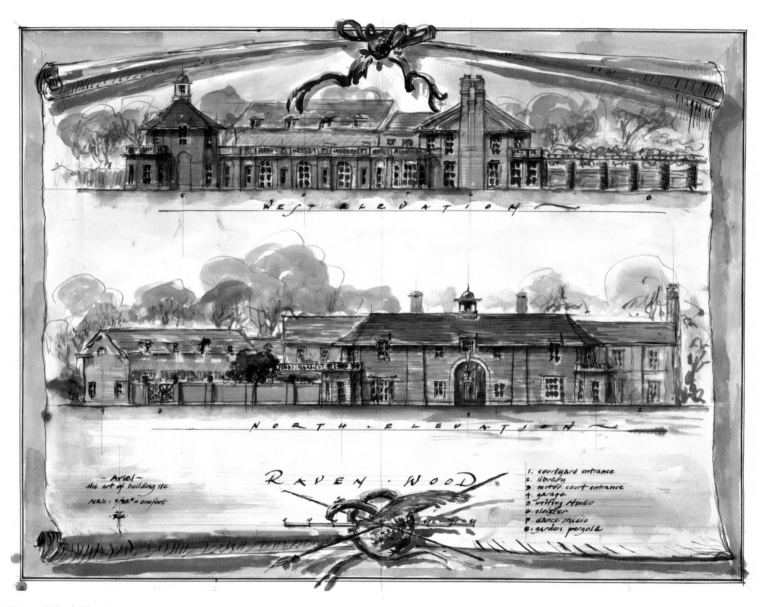

WEST ELEVATION

NORTH ELEVATION

RAVEN·WOOD

Ariel~
the art of building llc
scale: 3/32" = one foot

1. courtyard entrance
2. library
3. motor court entrance
4. garage
5. writing studio
6. cloister
7. dance studio
8. garden pergola

West and North Elevations

The Cabinet

Theater staircase

View of the Motor Court

The Theater

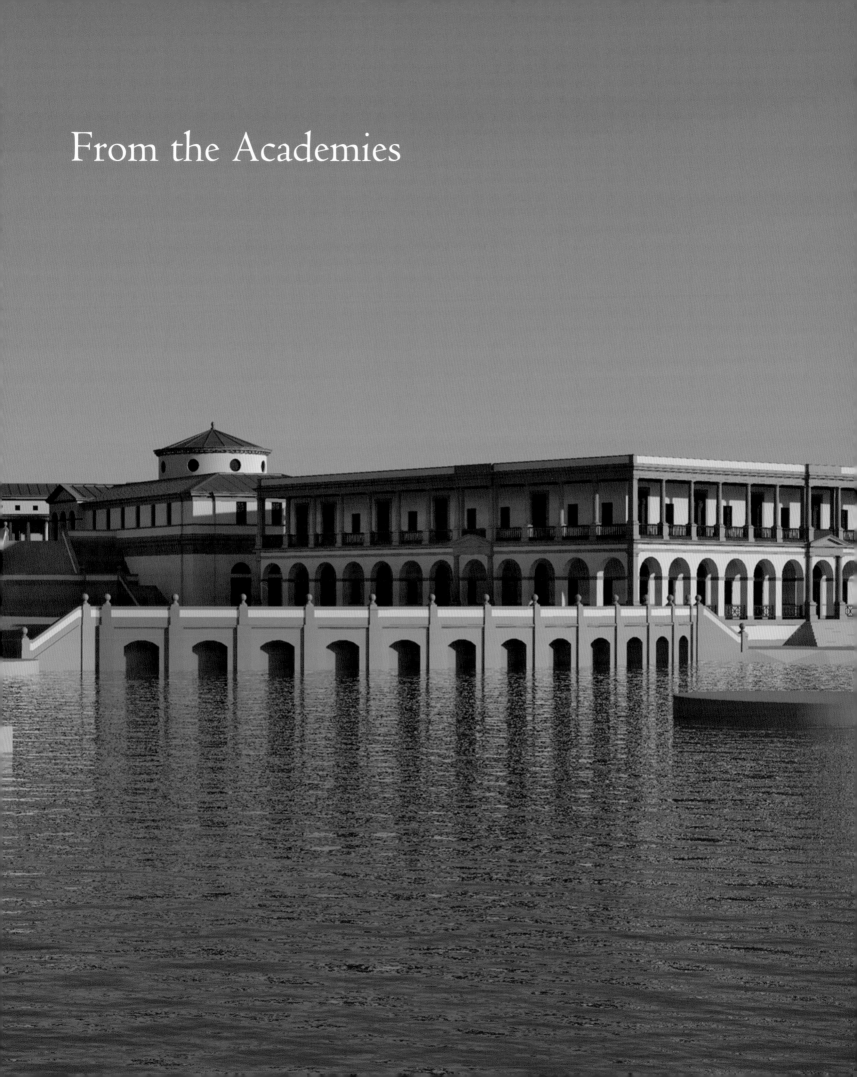

From the Academies

Founding Principles

CONTINUING INFLUENCE OF THE BEAUX-ARTS ON ARCHITECTURAL EDUCATION AT GEORGIA TECH

By Elizabeth Meredith Dowling

In 1885, the Georgia School of Technology received official authorization from the state legislature, but did not begin instruction until 1888. During the interim, construction of the first two campus buildings projected the equality of the "hand-mind" philosophy of the new technological training. Designed by the firm of Bruce and Morgan, the Shop Building (the "hand") and the Administration Building (the "mind") displayed similar prominent towers like many of the collegiate buildings the firm would design for Agnes Scott College, Clemson University, and Auburn University.

Of these two original campus buildings, the superior status held by the one representing the "mind" over that of the "hand" was subtly indicated by the greater mass of the Administration Building, which contained lecture rooms, chemical laboratory, a library, mechanical drawing rooms, a chapel, and offices. Engineering schools of the era combined scientific studies with physical hands-on shop-work where students produced saleable goods to provide financial support for their school. Georgia Tech would follow such a shop culture that elevated the status of physical labor alongside traditional academic

courses. A woodworking department, machine shop, forge room, and foundry existed in the Shop Building, with the last causing the fire that significantly damaged the building within the first decade of its existence. Items produced by the students included bookends, doorstops, and gates for mausoleums at Atlanta's Oakland Cemetery. At Georgia Tech's founding, the derogatory reference to the "North Avenue Trade School" was fitting. Although the authority to establish an architecture program was included in the initial bill, the only academic major offered was in mechanical engineering, and this would remain so until 1897 when majors in electrical and civil engineering were added to the degree offerings. Although an architecture curriculum did not arrive at Georgia Tech for two decades, the idea of improving the quality of architects and architecture in Georgia was promoted in the meantime. Both A. C. Bruce and Thomas H. Morgan, both of whom received their architectural training in the apprenticeship system, promoted the professionalization of architecture through higher education. In an article published in 1890, Morgan wrote that:

. . .the State University should provide a department of architecture presided over by an architect of known training in art, and skilled in construction. This field will then be open to the student. It is a profession with possibilities for greatness with requirements in skilled training second to none, and the systematic study of architecture in the State University would soon be seen in the better and most artistic character of our buildings.

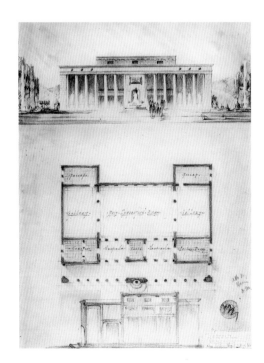

When the Architectural Program finally began in 1908, a tradition of training architects was more typical in the academic offerings of major universities. Formal architectural education had emerged in the United States in 1865 with the founding of Boston Tech, which was later renamed the Massachusetts Institute of Technology. By 1900, programs in architecture had also been established at Cornell University, University of Illinois, Syracuse University, University of Michigan, Columbia University, University of Pennsylvania, Columbian College (now George Washington University), Armour Institute (now Illinois Institute of Technology), and Harvard University. Architectural education did not reach southern colleges until 1907 when the first program in the region was founded at Alabama Polytechnic Institute, later renamed Auburn University. The following year, Georgia Tech's program and one at Tulane University were founded.

Figure 1 (far left): N. Sprague, A Memorial Museum, 1930. Courtesy of Van Alen Institute: Design Archive.

Figure 2 (left): C. Dubose, The Minis House, BAID Second Medal, 1928. Courtesy of Van Alen Institute: Design Archive.

Figure 3 (above): H. W. Phillips, An Architectural Motive to Terminate an Allée, BAID First Mention, 1930. Courtesy of Van Alen Institute: Design Archive.

All of these programs ultimately shared a common lineage—the Ecole des Beaux-Arts in Paris. Established in 1671 during the reign of Louis XIV, the French Académie Royale d'Architecture and its associated school was not the first of its kind, but it was the longest continuously developed mode of architectural education in the West, surviving until the student upheavals of 1968. In 1846, Richard Morris Hunt, the well-known architect of the Vanderbilt mansions and the Metropolitan Museum of Art, matriculated at the Ecole, which made him the first American to pursue formal academic training in architecture. Later, after establishing his office in New York City, he opened the first atelier to train his own employees in the design skills he had acquired in Paris. One of his students, William Ware, would later go on to translate this knowledge into the academic program of

Massachusetts Institute of Technology's architecture curriculum—the first such program in America. Our nation's colleges maintained a close association with the Ecole by hiring French studio critics, and, as will be discussed later, by providing students the opportunity to study in Paris. Intellectually the most profound influence on American education was the French critic who arrived in his new home ready to share the sophisticated culture, traditions, and architectural knowledge of Parisian life. By far the most famous of these French critics was Paul Cret, who was hired by the University of Pennsylvania in 1903 and continued teaching there until 1937. Cret's lasting influence on American architecture cannot be overstated. Not only did he produce many fine buildings around the country, but he also taught hundreds of future architects. One of the best known

today would be Louis Kahn. Although Georgia Tech did not have a French critic on its faculty, a student from Cret's earliest years, Francis Palmer Smith, became Georgia Tech's first long-term director of Architecture.

The actual initiation of the Architecture Program at Georgia Tech does not owe its start to the thoughtful deliberation of the college administration, but instead to an enthusiastic twenty-year-old civil engineering student named Earnest Daniel "Ed" Ivey (1887-1966). In 1907, Ed Ivey met with Georgia Tech President Kenneth G. Matheson (1864-1931) to discuss the creation of an architecture program. But, rather than actively supporting a new curriculum in architecture, Matheson placed upon Ivey the burden of finding a group of students interested in the subject. Ivey succeeded in finding twenty students who wanted to pursue this educational direction and the program was initiated in 1908. The first curriculum of the program emphasized the visual with classes in architectural drawing, descriptive geometry, elements of architecture, shades and shadows, and perspective—and this was just in the freshman year. More advanced classes were offered in freehand drawing, pen and ink rendering, and watercolor drawing. These artistic skills were balanced with courses in theoretical knowledge drawn from the history of architecture, historic ornament, archeology, and the history of painting. The practical side of architectural studies began in the freshman year with a full year of shop-work followed in the sophomore and junior years with courses in building construction, sanitation, structural mechanics, and professional practice. In the sophomore through senior years, a single study termed "design" was listed. In 1909, Francis Palmer Smith joined the Georgia Tech faculty fresh from his studies with his professor Paul Cret at the University of Pennsylvania. The character drawn from the Ecole-Penn connection remained with the program for the following decades. The concept of studio instruction, the types of projects offered, and the rendering techniques employed reflected an Americanized version of the Ecole approach. As in the French system, students began with small, less complicated building types and proceeded to those of greater complexity

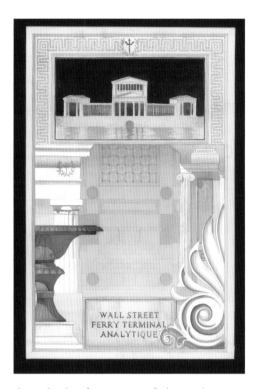

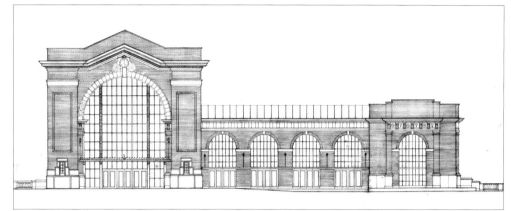

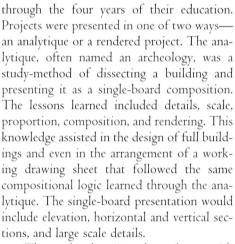

through the four years of their education. Projects were presented in one of two ways—an analytique or a rendered project. The analytique, often named an archeology, was a study-method of dissecting a building and presenting it as a single-board composition. The lessons learned included details, scale, proportion, composition, and rendering. This knowledge assisted in the design of full buildings and even in the arrangement of a working drawing sheet that followed the same compositional logic learned through the analytique. The single-board presentation would include elevation, horizontal and vertical sections, and large scale details.

The rendered project always began with an esquisse. The esquisse could be the end product and, if this was the case, it was usually named an esquisse-esquisse. The esquisse was created in twelve to twenty-four hours. The essential plan conception was thus established that would be developed in sections and elevations over the subsequent weeks. The value of this system was moving the student's efforts beyond the all-consuming search for the ideal plan, which is still so often the greatest pitfall today. Cret defended this method against modernist detractors by pointing out that a studio project is after all

only a method of learning and that there was as much to be learned in developing a bad plan as in spending an entire project searching for a perfect plan. With the concept set by an esquisse, the student could spend the full six or eight weeks exploring elevations, interiors, materials, and details. From as early as 1911, Georgia Tech's school had formed a relationship with the Beaux-Arts Institute of Design (BAID) in New York. This organization was established by men who had attended the Ecole and were devoted to improving the quality of American architecture. Their method was simple—the organization produced design programs that could be adopted for use in schools around the country. The most impressive work in a college studio or a private atelier was sent to New York for judging, and the best of these projects were given awards and were published in the BAID Bulletin. The concept survived from 1904 to 1956, and the process allowed visual comparison and juried competition between students in far-flung state schools and those in established, well-funded private universities.

Figure 4 (far left): David Pearson, Study of the Tempietto, Rome.

Figure 5 (above left): David Pearson, Fulton Ferry Terminal Project Analytique, MS in Classical Design 2008. Studio instructors: Michael Mesko assisted by Jonathan Lacrosse.

Figure 6 (top): Mike Watkins, Fulton Ferry Terminal Project, MS in Classical Design 2008. Studio instructors: Michael Mesko assisted by Jonathan Lacrosse.

Figure 7 (above): Jeremy Sommer, YMCA for Manila Naval Base, MS in Classical Design 2008. Studio instructors: Richard John assisted by Jonathan Lacrosse.

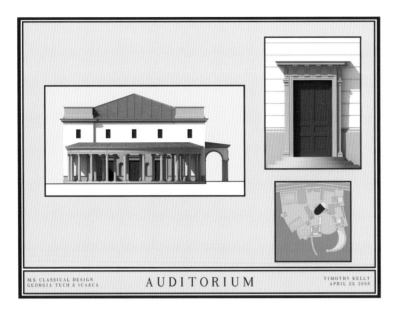

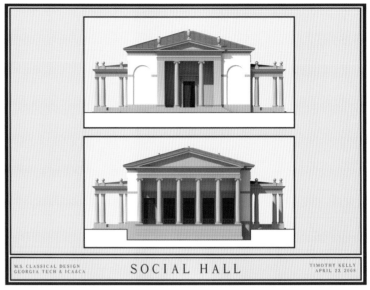

The value for a small public school in the south was immense. Georgia Tech had an established record of consistent and remarkable success. In 1939, a grand fete was held in Brittain Dining hall to receive the BAID prize for Georgia Tech architectural students having won the greatest number of prize-winning projects for the year. The New York architect John Mead Howells, co-designer of the Chicago Tribune Tower, gave the award. Through the years, the BAID name and funding changed, but the offering of competition prizes remained constant. The most widely recognized competitions administered by the foundation and its successors were the Lloyd Warren Fellowship-Paris Prize in Architecture and then later the Van Alen Prize. For each of these, many Georgia Tech students either won or placed with great frequency.

Although student work over the one hundred years in the Architecture Program changed in appearance reflecting the prevailing stylistic trends, the organization and many of the fundamental design principles have remained constant. Programs are issued, design instruction occurs in the studio over a period of weeks, concepts are created and developed, solutions are organized into formal presentations, and finally a jury of knowledgeable critics offers their opinions of the work. Over time, the popularity of various presentation media changes, but the love of

evocative drawings is always evident. The greatest potential change is associated with the introduction of the computer to the studio, but digital rendering is unrelated to style or period; it is merely another useful tool, that is, as long as it does not limit creative thought. The current eclecticism at the College of Architecture today reflects the diversity of worldwide architectural practice. The reemergence of design that promotes the development of traditional skills, such as hand sketching and rendering in pencil, ink, and watercolor, alongside the study of proportion and detailing, demonstrates that powerful design concepts continue to have relevance for clients in the twenty-first century. The desire to create beautiful, aesthetically pleasing buildings was the focus during the early decades of Georgia Tech's Architecture Program's instruction and continues as such today.

Art and Architecture in Greece and Italy
In 1993, I initiated the first College of Architecture summer foreign program with a five-week study of Italian art and architecture spanning from the ancient world through the Baroque seventeenth century. Based originally in Rome, but expanded to include Greece and Northern Italy, the instructional concept used the on-site study of architecture, museums, and urban spaces as the sole classroom. Students will forever recall living in the oldest

hotel in Rome, the Albergo Sole, built on the foundations of the theater of Pompey where Julius Caesar was assassinated. Beginning in 1994, Professor Douglas C. Allen joined the program assuming responsibility for the ancient Roman world. Using the material record of Rome, Ostia, Pompeii, Herculaneum, and Paestum, students from all disciplines at Georgia Tech learned of the profound debt Western civilization owes to the ancient Mediterranean world. This learning experience was expanded in 2006 when Professor Athanassios "Thanos" Economou joined the program and added depth to this study by clarifying the sources of Roman civilization in the ancient Greek world. Over the years, the program developed and I took charge of the Renaissance periods and moved the program northward to Florence, Siena, Venice, and Vicenza with periodic excursions to Assisi, Caprarola, Mantua, and Verona. Through the years, almost four hundred students from all majors at Georgia Tech have learned to appreciate urban life, Mediterranean civilization, and the vast beauty of the art and architecture of Greece and Italy.

Harrison Design Associates Visiting Scholar Program
In 2002, William H. "Bill" Harrison (B ARCH1971) and Gregory L. Palmer, principals in Harrison Design Associates,

commenced a gift leading to a $500,000 endowment in my honor and my area of specialization in traditional and classical architecture that is a shared interest of the firm. This significant gift marked only the second major endowment in the program's history. The firm of Harrison Design Associates is one of the largest practices in traditional design in the country with a total of four offices in Georgia and California. A portion of the endowment is used each year to bring in a variety of architects as visiting scholars to share their expertise with students through studio- and classroom-based instruction. From 2003 to 2007, the endowment sponsored five architects who offered courses in areas related to classical design. Eugene L. Surber, (BS ARCH 1961), taught a studio in the documentary measurement and compatible design. Anne Fairfax, principal with Fairfax and Sammons in New York, Charleston, and Palm Beach, taught a studio concerned with the study of local vocabulary in order to insert a building in a historic neighborhood. Gregory Saldana, president of Saldana Design & Preservation Inc., taught a course on measured drawings and archival research. Richard Sammons, principal of Fairfax and Sammons, taught an elective course on proportion that is the subject of an upcoming book on his research and application of proportion in design. Christine Franck, principal of Christine G. H. Franck, Inc., co-taught an elective course with Betty Dowling on ornament and historically inspired design. With the initiation of a master of science degree with an emphasis in classical design in 2007, the Harrison Visiting scholar assumed the role of studio instructor during the spring term for the new program. Richard John, assistant professor at the University of Miami, provided the first studio and in spring 2009, Michael Mesko, principal with MSM Design and Planning in New York, offered the second one in classical design.

Elizabeth M. Dowling, PhD, is a Professor of Architecture at Georgia Tech. The above account was written to mark the centenary of the school in 2008, which was commemorated by an exhibition and a book curated and edited by Prof. Dowling and Lisa M. Thomason.

Figures 8 and 9 (opposite page): Tim Kelly, YMCA for Manila Naval Base, MS in Classical Design 2008. For another rendering of this project, see the section opener on pages 92–93. Studio instructors: Richard John assisted by Jonathan Lacrosse.

Figure 10 (above): Paul Knight, Study of the Physics Building at Georgia Tech, MS in Classical Design 2009.

UNIVERSITY OF NOTRE DAME

Design I, First Year Graduate Studio, Spring 2009

INSTRUCTOR:
Richard Economakis

PROJECT: Art Gallery, Paris

For this exercise, first-year graduate students designed plans, sections, and elevations for a proposed art gallery in Paris, which offers a rich and challenging urban context. Students were encouraged to focus on space and the uses of poché, or the space within the structure of a building that is not accessible. French Baroque and neoclassical precedents were also closely studied.

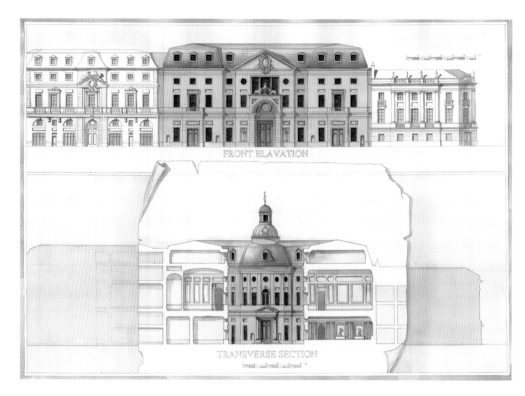

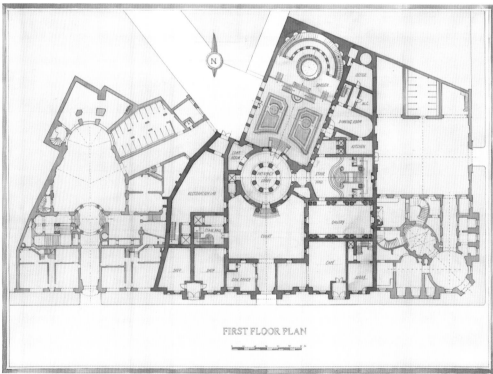

Figures 1 and 2 (above): Elevations and Plan by Leon Li.

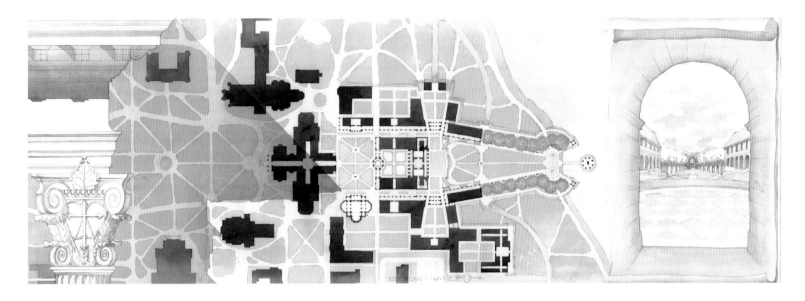

UNIVERSITY OF NOTRE DAME
Design I, First Year Graduate Studio, Fall 2008

INSTRUCTOR:
David Mayernik

PROJECT: Place Sacre Croix

This project called for a master plan for a sequence of public buildings and spaces between the Dome and St. Joseph Lake, University of Notre Dame. Graduate students under the direction of Prof. David Mayernik were asked to design a new series of spaces extending from the University of Notre Dame's Main Building or "Golden Dome" towards St. Joseph's Lake on campus. The primary building of this new ensemble was Le Mans Hall, housing Moreau Hall, which is to be coordinated with the Dome. It was expected that this building would both define positive outdoor spaces and allow for public circulation through the building at the ground level.

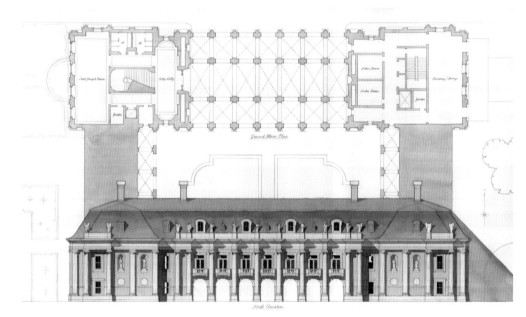

Figure 1 (above): Plan, detail, and perspective by Christopher Jamal Howard.

Figure 2 (below): Plan and elevation by John Mellor.

UNIVERSITY OF NOTRE DAME
Design VII, Fifth Year, Fall 2008

INSTRUCTOR:
Duncan Stroik

PROJECT: A New Quadrangle, Yale University
Yale University is one of the quintessential American campuses and has few rivals for the quality of its architecture, both traditional and modernist. It is located on the edge of one of the great American urban spaces; the New Haven Green with its three Protestant churches. For the first time in forty years, Yale is planning to add two new quadrangles to campus. Fifth-year University of Notre Dame School of Architecture students under the direction of Prof. Duncan Stroik were asked to design a new college in the classical tradition that looks as if it has always been there.

Figures 1 and 2 (above): Ronald Herr, watercolor perspective and elevation.

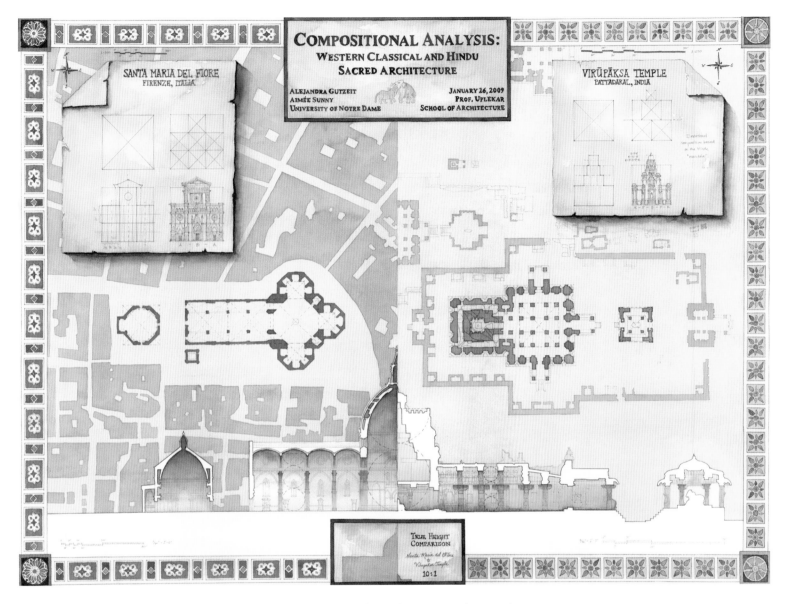

COMPOSITIONAL ANALYSIS:
WESTERN CLASSICAL AND HINDU
SACRED ARCHITECTURE

ALEJANDRA GUTZEIT
AIMÉE SUNNY
UNIVERSITY OF NOTRE DAME

JANUARY 26, 2009
PROF. UPLEKAR
SCHOOL OF ARCHITECTURE

SANTA MARIA DEL FIORE
FIRENZE, ITALIA

VIRŪPĀKSA TEMPLE
PATTADARAL, INDIA

TRUE HEIGHT
COMPARISON

10:1

UNIVERSITY OF NOTRE DAME

Design VI, Fourth Year Undergraduate Studio, Spring 2009

INSTRUCTOR:
Krupali Uplekar

PROJECT: Compositional Analyses of Classical and Non-Western Sacred Architecture; A Comparison of the Orders, Western Classical and Indian Vernacular.

Fourth-year students focus on analyses and comparisons in an unfamiliar cultural context. The intention is to demonstrate how an architect may bring his or her knowledge to bear on projects that require translation of basic principles from western classical traditions to corresponding but very different architectural traditions of another culture. Students learn more about western architecture, its substance, meaning, and principles through contrast and comparison.

Figure 1 (above): Compositional Analysis by Alejandra Gutzeit and Aimée Sunny.

YALE UNIVERSITY
Advanced Design Studio, Spring 2008

INSTRUCTORS:
Demetri Porphyrios
George Knight

PROJECT: Corfu Mixed-Use Development
Corfu, the northern most of the Ionian Islands, combines a most agreeable Mediterranean climate with luscious vegetation. The island has had a rich and variegated history—from ancient and Hellenistic Greece to Byzantium and the Eastern Roman Empire; and yet again from the Venetians to the British. All left their cultural, architectural, and urbanistic traditions on the island and most conspicuously on the City of Corfu. The city is an inspiring example of classico-vernacular architecture grafted onto the Venetian plan. The almost intact urban fabric of the city becomes a unique case study for both architectural character and urban strategies.

Close to the historic centre, in the vicinity of the port of ancient Korkyra—the reputed port of Ulysses—is situated the industrial site of the Desyllas Company. Since the second half of the nineteenth century the site has served as the company's headquarters and main manufacturing plant. Approximately twenty-five years ago, the Desyllas Company closed down and the site was bought for redevelopment by a group of investors who have appointed Porphyrios Associates as their architectural and urban design consultants.

Drawing on the urban and architectural precedents of Corfu and Venice, the studio proposes a mixed-use development project comprising residential, commercial, retail, and leisure. The studio also examines strategies of development for a site with present-day commercial requirements in the context of late nineteenth-century industrial listed buildings.

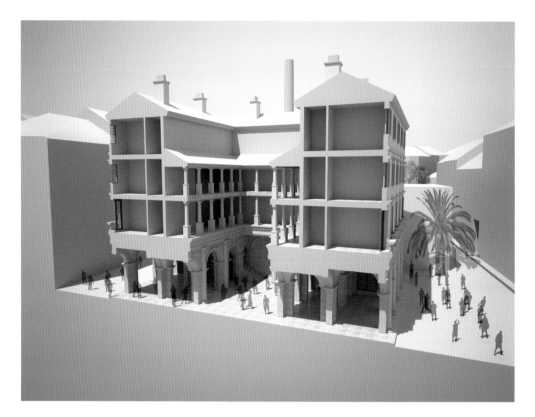

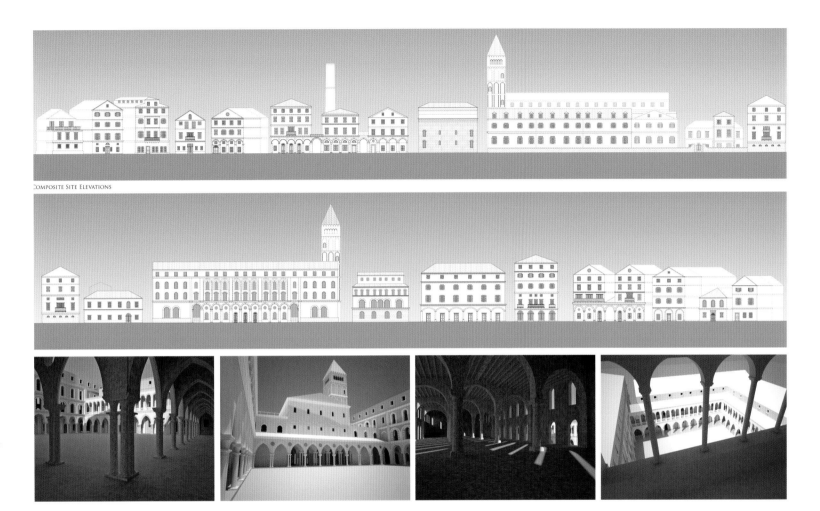

COMPOSITE SITE ELEVATIONS

Figures 1, 2, and 3 (opposite top and opposite bottom, and left): Jeff Geldart, Master plan and computer renderings.

Figure 4 (above): Gene Cartwright, Composite site elevations and plan.

JUDSON UNIVERSITY
Advanced Design Studios

Instructor:
Christopher Miller

Judson University's liberal arts character and the rich student interest in ethical service shape Judson's architecture program. The curriculum works to integrate the diverse approaches of its faculty (including a value in the history of architecture in contemporary practice) and the importance of cultivating the tradition of urban environments. At present, opportunities for students to explore classical architecture and traditional urbanism are found in summer European study, in a civic architecture studio, in watercolor instruction, in a substantial history and theory curriculum at the undergraduate and graduate levels, and in independent and thesis projects.

Figure 1 (above): Brian Mork, Analytique of Foellinger Auditorium.

Figure 2 (top right): Aaron Holverson, Elgin Railway Station Proposal.

Figure 3 (right): Nathaniel Brooks, Elgin City Hall Proposal.

Figures 4 and 5 (opposite page): Kevin Svensen, Elgin City Hall Proposal.

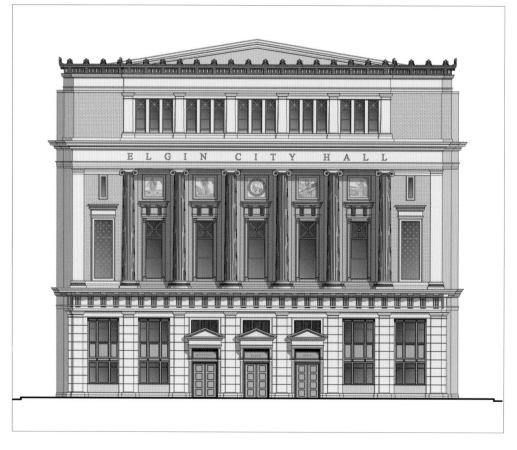

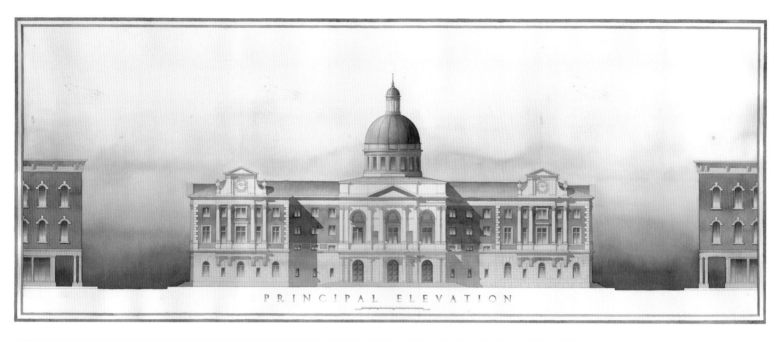

PRINCIPAL ELEVATION

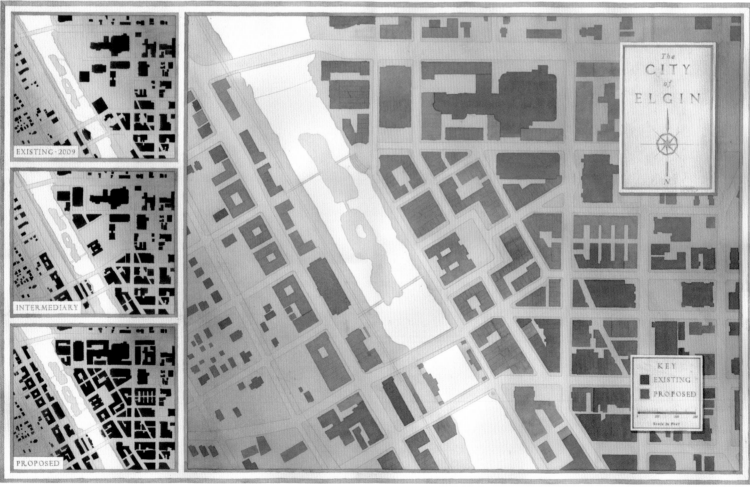

EXISTING · 2009

INTERMEDIARY

PROPOSED

The
CITY
of
ELGIN

N

KEY

EXISTING

PROPOSED

Scale in Feet

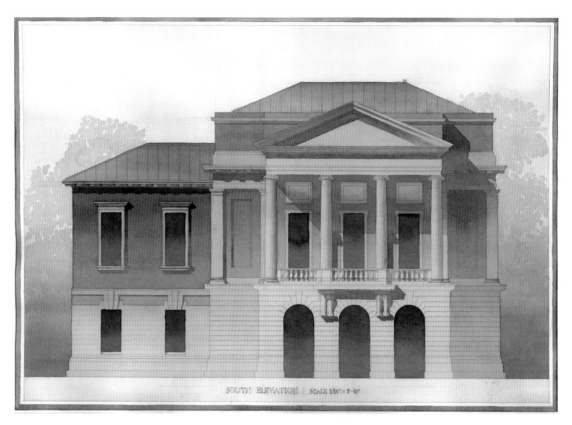

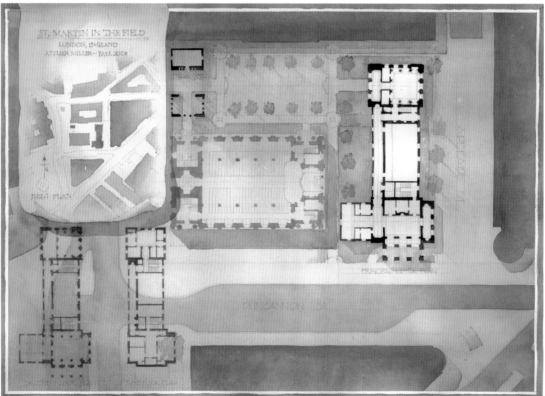

Figures 6 and 7 (above): Brian Mork, Judson University Advanced Design Studios. New Building adjacent to St. Martin in the Fields, London.

THE PRINCE'S FOUNDATION FOR THE BUILT ENVIRONMENT

The Prince of Wales's Summer School 2008: The Culture of Building

The goal of the Summer School is to promote the role of craft decoration in the broader building culture, develop craft sensibilities, and apply them to projects at various scales, from the design and execution of architectural ornament, up to urban interventions.

Through a series of lectures, workshops, drawing and building exercises, and field trips, Summer School participants gain an in-depth knowledge both of traditional building and repair techniques and how these have been, and can be, applied in the twenty-first century.

After an initial introduction to historic materials and a two-day drawing course, students studied the architectural and constructional development of Lincoln and Lincolnshire and had the opportunity to work together with Lincoln Cathedral's expert craft teams in the cathedral workshops to learn craft and conservation skills in the fields of masonry, joinery, leadwork, and stained glass. Study and drawing tours of local historic centers were also conducted. The program ended with a week-long live build project in Poundbury, Dorset.

The circular "Look-Out," sited close to the cricket pitch and medical center, is a place for young people to congregate on their own but within close proximity to other daily activity in Poundbury. The building of the shelter gave the apprentices, largely made up of stone masons and carpenters, the opportunity to gain invaluable practical experience from working closely with a master stone mason, Henry Rumbold, and master carpenter, Steven Finney. The Duchy of Cornwall fully supported the project, which was directed by Ben Bolgar, head of Design Theory & Networks, and Noel Isherwood, the Poundbury representative.

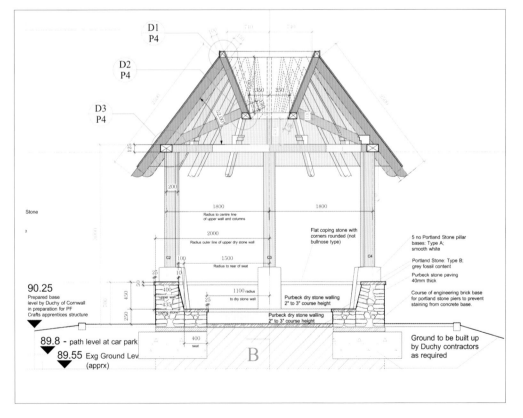

UNIVERSITY OF MIAMI

Upper Level Elective Studio:
Classical Language of Architecture

INSTRUCTOR:
Richard John

This studio departs from the usual format of a single design problem in order to study both the vocabulary (the orders) and the syntax (composition) of classical architecture through a number of smaller pedagogical exercises and esquisse problems. Students begin with the principles of composition, then study Paul Cret's method of program analysis before completing a Parallel of the Orders using original texts and treatises. After a façade redesign exercise based on Letarouilly, they undertake two projects: first a three-teacher village schoolhouse and then a YMCA for a Naval Base in Manila.

Figure 1 (top): John Melhorn, Manila YMCA.

Figure 2 (below): Wilhelm Nothnagel, Schoolhouse.

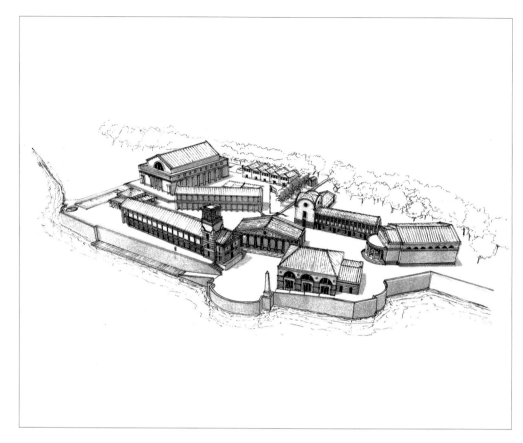

UNIVERSITY OF MIAMI
Seminar in Color Theory and Practice for Architects

Instructor:
Rocco Ceo

The course assignment was to design a small building in a garden or park to house a water pump and to determine the building's color palette and render it. Students were required to find a color palette that is balanced and harmonious based on the principles taught in the course. Inspiration for the color palettes were often site-generated by recording perceived colors of natural subjects at different times of day. They also worked to balance the color that was inherent in their proposed materials with applied colors.

Figure 1 (right): Katherine Pasternack, Elevations of a Pump house for Matheson Hammock Park (1931).

Figure 2 (below): Katherine Pasternack, Crab capital.

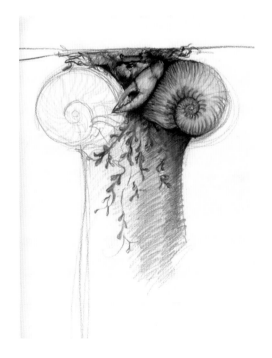

AMERICAN COLLEGE OF BUILDING ARTS

The American College of the Building Arts (ACBA) is dedicated to educating the next generation of building artisans and to preserving the building arts in a manner never before seen in America. Under the direction of experienced faculty, students have the opportunity to learn the skills needed to excel in their chosen field, and receive a quality liberal arts education. This combination of education, training, and access to highly-experienced faculty is available nowhere else in the United States. The College began in 1998 when a small team, led by John Paul Huguley, created the School of the Building Arts (SoBA) in Charleston, South Carolina. After the South Carolina Commission on Higher Education licensed the School in 2004, the name was changed to the American College of the Building Arts to reflect more accurately its place in the American educational hierarchy and the first students were admitted the following year. The historic graduation of the College's inaugural class occurred in May 2009 with Charleston Mayor Joe Riley giving the commencement address.

Freshman Drawing Class

INSTRUCTOR:
William Bates III

PROJECT: Study of the Orders
This exercise begins with a study of Claude Perrault's *Ordonnnance des cinq espèces de colonnes selon la méthode des Anciens* (Paris, 1683). Each student is given an order to replicate, studying not only the parts of that order, but also the method of the engraver in simulating texture, shade, and curvature with line weight and placement.

Figure 1 (far left): Graduating Class 2009: Moyer Fountain, Will Denton IV, James Murphy, Kyle Dooley, Adam All, Stephen Browning, and Shara Satterfield. Photograph by Jörg Meyer.

Figure 2 (top): ACBA students working on the restoration of Drayton Hall ceiling.

Figure 3 (left): Rob Stevens, Ink drawing after Perrault.

INSTITUTE OF
CLASSICAL ARCHITECTURE
& CLASSICAL AMERICA
Summer Program 2008

INSTRUCTORS:
Stephen T. Chrisman
Michael Mesko

PROJECT: Market Hall
The City Of New York and the Greenmarket Farmers Markets commissioned a permanent Market Hall building for Union Square. The Market Hall consists of two elements: a two-story Head House and an exterior colonnade or arcade. The Head House contains an information desk and restrooms on the first floor and Greenmarket offices on the second floor. The Head House is to be of masonry construction and utilize a full-height order on the exterior. Attached to the Head House is an exterior colonnade(s) or arcade(s), to be used for Market Stalls, also utilizing an order(s), and constructed of masonry columns, piers, or arches. Currently entirely open air, the new market hall will provide a sheltered environment within which the market may operate more conveniently during weather extremes. The course was treated as a design studio, during which each student was expected to develop an architectural design based on a charrette esquisse, prepare presentation drawings, and present the work in a final review with an invited jury.

Figure 1 (above): Joseph Skibba, Market Hall Project.

Figure 2 (bottom): Joseph DeSense, Market Hall Project.

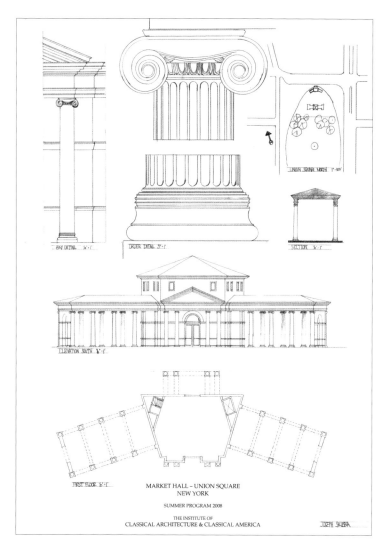

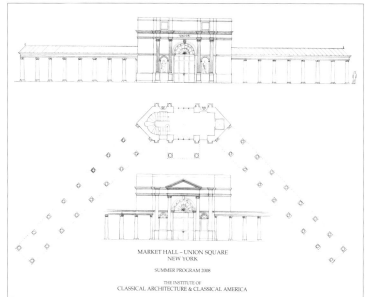

INSTITUTE OF CLASSICAL ARCHITECTURE & CLASSICAL AMERICA
Rome Drawing Tour 2009

INSTRUCTORS:
Michael Grimaldi
Michael Mesko
John Varriano

The ICA&CA selected instructors for their individual talents and knowledge. Each has a proven ability to teach effectively and, most importantly, their combined disciplines—history, fine art, and architecture—served to foster a meaningful appreciation for the enduring aesthetic achievements in Roman art and architecture. Tour highlights for the 23 participants included Ancient and Renaissance Rome, the sublime Hadrian's Villa, and the magnificent gardens of the Villa d'Este, as well as Rome's great collections.

Figure 1 (above): Richard Swann, Campidoglio capital.

Figure 2 (right): Kahlil Hamady, Villa Medici.

Figure 3 (top right): Kahlil Hamady, Acqua Paola.

Figure 4 (top left): Kahlil Hamady, San Giovanni.

Figure 5 (top left): Marvin Clawson, Acqua Paola.

Figure 6 (top right): David Pearson, Santa Maria Della Pace.

Figure 7 (above): David Pearson, Hadrian's Villa, Tivoli.

Figure 8 (left): Joyce Tsai, Four Rivers Fountain.

The Allied Arts

The Dangerous Path

LEONARD PORTER AND THE SINCERITY OF HOPE

By Denis R. McNamara

The "dangerous path" is what New York painter Leonard Porter (b. 1963) calls his decision almost two decades ago to commit himself to the renewal of classical painting. In looking beyond the Abstract Expressionism of his teachers, he took a great risk which today he half-jokingly calls "career suicide." But now with large commissions, accolades, and awards on his resume, Porter has emerged as a leader in the renewal of classical painting. Porter's work signals more than merely a nostalgic return to the past, but an intellectually sophisticated commentary on the return of hope after the cynicism of the twentieth century. For Porter, it is hope in the future that allows his return to the past, believing firmly that only when artists believe in the future will they see the value of the enduring tradition and the importance of painstaking craft.

"I am interested in making art that is intellectually compelling," Porter says, and, as a self-described painter of antiquity and classical mythology, the philosophical questions that arise from the ancient narratives energize his mind and find expression in his paintings. Porter's optimism pervades every aspect of his work, sending a message to the postmodern world that it is safe once again look to the past because the enduring lessons of history can still inform a developing future. Although partaking in traditional figurative painting, Porter's work remains distinct from what has come to be known as the Classical Realist School. He insists strongly on the use of grand historical narrative in his work rather than the personal or autobiographical, and tries to integrate his paintings into appropriate architectural settings. Moreover, the accentuation of elemental qualities of color and line allows him to engage an idealized specificity of idea without being limited to a narrow specificity of literal form. Here Porter's work reveals an interesting paradox. He insists on precision in narrative and historical accuracy in detail, yet his paintings display an idealizing tendency in their execution. Porter's figures stand outside of time, never looking like the modern-day model in period costume with shadows cast by studio lighting. Instead he favors the universalizing tendencies toward the abstract found in Greek vase painting, allowing the presentation of a world outside of earthly factuality.

For Porter, classical painting offers more than the glimmer of a beautifully-rendered surface, but evidences a sincere hope that has ennobled Western civilization with Greco-Roman ideas of freedom, justice, democracy, and human aspiration. He praises the "Goddess of Democracy" erected by Chinese students in 1989 when calling for human rights, where aspiration and promise found physical expression in a local adaptation of the Statue of Liberty. Here Chinese citizens found inspiration in an American monument that came from France and had roots in the ancient world. Students demanding civil rights could hearken back to the Greek notion of the polis and use the common artistic language associated with political freedom. For Porter, the "Goddess of Democracy" showed classical art at its best, and he calls it the best sculpture of the twentieth century.

THE DANGEROUS PATH

As with many of the first generation of new classical painters, Porter's artistic training in the mid-1980s was dominated by what he calls "orthodox modernism" of Abstract Expressionism at Rhode Island School of Design. As a young man desiring success in his field, he accepted the urgings of his teachers who constantly demanded that art privileges novelty over continuity. "'Break the rules' was the mantra," he says, and he remembers being impressed at first by a faculty member who suggested he try painting with his feet. He found the Gnostic mysteries in work by Picasso and Pollock fascinating because they always seemed just beyond the reach of intelligibility. In earning his Master of Fine Art from New York's School of Visual Arts, he began to see cracks in the hegemony of the prevailing theories. "We'd read the art magazines," he says, "take paragraph-long sentences, translate them into normal English, and then find out that what they were saying was really absurd."

Figure 1 (preceding pages): Tai-Yu Burying the Flower Petals, 2002, Oil on Linen 20 x 30 in. ©Leonard Porter MMII.

Figure 2 (opposite): Christ in Majesty, 2007, Oil on Canvas 192 x 117 in. Shuman Chapel, St. Andrew's Episcopal Church, Fort Worth, TX ©Leonard Porter MMVII.

Figure 3 (above): Landscape with Aeneas and Andromache, 1995, Oil on Linen, 36 x 54 in.
©Leonard Porter MCMXCVI.

Figure 4 (opposite): The Sacrifice of Iphigeneia, Work in progress, 2009, Oil on Linen,
67 x 108 in. Photograph by Jerry Zalez ©Leonard Porter MMIX.

In the early 1990s Porter came face to face with his desire to break the supreme taboo of his training. "The reason I was interested in art was because I loved beauty," he says, "and I liked things like order and hierarchy and rationality and humanism, and all of those things were not celebrated in contemporary art." In his further study, Porter came to a realization that what he calls the "modernist project" was about more than formalist taboos determining what can and cannot be painted on a canvas. The modernist project, he discovered, in its many facets, was a utopian project that failed, leading to postmodern nihilism and cynicism. With a surprising frankness Porter says: "I realized that my thoughts were not in line with the prevailing mood in the art world and I wanted to do something different. Porter repeatedly uses the word "sincere" to describe his method, which uses symbol, narrative, allusion, and the representation of three-dimensional space to say something straightforward, without idiosyncratic theories rooted in cynicism and irony. "I try to make a really good classical painting and that is anathema in the art world," he says. "It's a dangerous path because people can understand what I am doing, and it becomes much easier to criticize."

Porter's turn to classical mythology and traditional technique took time to develop. Because he decided to make paintings about beauty, hierarchy, and order, he looked at old master paintings, but, he says, "I had no idea how hard they are to paint and it took me a long time to learn how." At first, he was cautious about making the "sincere" image of a legible figural scene in space. He recalls in his early days painting clouds in the manner of Caspar David Friedrich with great relish, only to put a flat silver band around it with a white frame to merge it into the flatness of the wall. Looking back he says, "I realize that what

I really wanted to do was paint beautiful clouds and I was making up this scenario to allow me to indulge in beauty. Later, I said 'I don't care if the whole world tells me I can't do this, I'll just do it.'" Here began Porter's optimistic quest for sincerely presented, intellectually compelling subjects.

ANTIQUITY AND CLASSICAL MYTHOLOGY

The philosophical questions raised by the narratives of the ancient world formed a starting point for Porter's new direction in art. While Porter admires the technique of his colleagues who can "render a coffee can full of paint brushes in a traditional style that would satisfy Rembrandt's desire to render something as well," he is quick to add: "It's a coffee can! Who wants to put it on their wall? Give me a god or goddess or some important narrative!" Though he respects those who work hard to renew traditional methods, he continually asks the question: "what do you *do* with that technique?" His paintings rise beyond mere technique alone to engage the many themes that have fascinated the thinkers of western civilization. Porter's classical work therefore centers on the interaction of gods with humans, the founding of great cities, situations bonding people in common fate, and the human desire for better things.

Porter clearly prefers the Greek tradition with its dynamic intersection of myth and the recorded past, what he calls the "heroic age on the border with history" or "history at the time before history." Here he finds a rich potential in the drama where gods and people interact and deified humans become immortal, making the classical realm a nexus of the real and the ideal. From his earliest classical paintings, such as his 1996 *Landscape with Aeneas and Andromache* [FIGURE 3], Porter engaged the drama of the relationship described in Virgil's *Aeneid,* in which the pathos-laden Andromache serves as prophet speaking with Aeneas about the future of the new Troy, teaching him to focus on future greatness rather than former glory. It could stand as an ample metaphor for Porter's philosophy about the relationship between past, present, and future. Porter's work is decidedly not a servile revival or simple-minded retreat, but rather draws from the glory of past ages with a distinct emphasis on the present and future. By understanding paintings as "a creature of the mind" and not the eye alone, Porter avoids the pitfall of a vapid formalism. Instead he provides a density of meaning relevant to today's viewer in a language common to the greatest number of people, from the casual viewer who recognizes figures and landscape to the scholar of classics or philosophy. Some people are interested in stories, Porter argues, while others enter a painting through the understanding of individuals, human relationships, psychology, theory, or philosophy. For this reason, he argues, classical painting is indeed more accessible than paintings dependent on the highly idiosyncratic theories that dominate much of today's artistic production.

Porter's 2002 *Tai-Yu Burying the Flower Petals* [FIGURE 1], evidences this intellectually rigorous approach that sees the universal classical principles evident even in non-Western cultures. Drawn from the eighteenth-century Chinese novel, *Dream of the Red Chamber,* the painting's narrative depicts themes the intelligent and beautiful yet tragic figure, Tai-Yu, a reincarnation of the mythic crimson flower set next to

a divine stone. Tai-Yu's health is frail and her beauty fleeting, and seeing the many peach blossoms fallen to the ground, she suggests sweeping up the petals and burying them. In returning them to the earth, she prefigures her own death and burial. This meditation on the fragility of beauty and the briefness of life set amidst the larger narrative of Chinese court ritual and the intersection of the mortal and immortal caused Porter to believe it suitable for adaptation into the classical lexicon.

A more recent project, the *The Sacrifice of Iphigenia* [FIGURE 4], (in progress, 2009) reveals Porter's mature method and developed abilities. Human figures and strong architecture come to the fore, while layers of narrative and intellectual content are seen at work within a highly structured composition. The historical narrative itself provides the first level of compelling interest: the gods ask the Greek king Agamemnon to sacrifice his daughter, Iphigenia, in exchange for favorable winds for the military fleet. One sees here Porter's incorporation of themes like willing self-sacrifice and the inescapability of fate. The sacrificial procession reveals his accurate knowledge of detailed ritual as well as the emotional and intellectual questions involved in sacrifice:

family members lament the human loss while the wind gods wait in anticipation. But Porter does more than masterfully represent a mythic scene. He goes further to incorporate ideas on the nature and condition of humanity drawn from the early Greek poet Hesiod, who described the decline of humanity from the Golden Age through the current Iron Age. The Iron Age is characterized by "strife, sloth, and all manner of vices," and the Trojan War marks the "decline in intercession of the gods." But as Porter indicates, even as the state of man decays, the Golden Age remains as a source of inspiration.

Here again the relationship between the real and the ideal comes to the fore, as does Porter's insistent optimism. Porter intentionally displays Agamemnon and Iphigenia in archaic poses and dress, placing them in a circular floor pattern upon a pedestal, signaling their participation in the higher order of the more ancient time. Though Pandora sits at left with an open jar signaling the release of this chaos into the world, Porter makes clear that this is not a portrait of despair. In fact, Prometheus appears at the far left with fire to look inside the emptied jar for Hesiod's promised arrival of Hope. Porter writes: "Fueled by the concept of classical ideals and longing for a better world, man will always strive to better this imperfect one. With Prometheus' gift of fire and the potential for progress which it implies, the Golden Age of Antiquity becomes a source of inspiration rather than a figure of lamentation." *The Sacrifice of Iphigenia* [FIGURE 4] puts Porter's particular gifts on fine display. Technical mastery combines with primary, secondary, tertiary, and even quaternary narratives to make a lucid and rigorous commentary about the condition of humanity that draws deep from the elemental questions raised at the earliest days of Western civilization: humanity's lost dignity, glimpses of selfless nobility, and hope for an ever improving human condition.

NARRATIVE AND CHRISTIANITY

In a unique turn of events, Porter, a self-proclaimed atheist, has completed a number of works commissioned by Christian clients. In one sense it should not be surprising; Porter's portrayal of narrative regarding eternity, life, death, and interaction with the divine make him an ideal candidate for significant Christian painting. His first Christian commission came in 2002, when architects Michael Franck and James McCrery, who were then designing a new chapel for the Cathedral of St. Joseph in Sioux Falls, South Dakota, urged him to accept what he calls a "renaissance-like commission:" a mural nearly twenty-one feet wide and seven feet high composed of saints gathered around the seated Christ. Porter brought to his *Christ Enthroned with Saint and Angels* [FIGURES 5 and 6], the same intellectual intensity he brings to his works of classical antiquity, using a several-hundred-page brief from the client to delve deeply into the layered meanings of the figures and setting.

In this large mural, Porter maintained his narrative method, though he admits that working for a Christian congregation raised the project's level of intensity. Although very few clients today set expectations on the representation of Zeus, he knew that the viewers of this mural, including a community of nuns who held constant prayer vigil in the chapel, would have a living emotional and intellectual connection with the painting. "When it comes time to paint the face of Christ," Porter

Figures 5 and 6 (above and below): Christ Enthroned with Saints and Angels, 2004, Oil on Canvas, 89 x 248 in. Chapel of the Sacred Heart of Jesus, St. Joseph Cathedral, Sioux Falls, SD. All copyrights reserved.

Figure 7 (opposite): Detail of Christ Enthroned with Saints and Angels, 2004, Oil on Canvas, 89 x 248 in. Chapel of the Sacred Heart of Jesus, St. Joseph Cathedral, Sioux Falls, SD. All copyrights reserved.

says, "even if you don't believe it yourself, you know that your audience does and it is very important to them." Porter began the project with his "sincere" approach, respecting the client and the audience, treating the brief with respect to make a painting that could be celebrated and understood by a diverse and committed community.

Christ Enthroned with Saints and Angels forms the backdrop for the sanctuary in a small chapel dedicated to the Sacred Heart and used for daily Mass and perpetual Eucharistic adoration. Designed in conjunction with the classical architecture, the commission gave Porter a chance to work with the architects to create a harmonious whole. Motifs from the chapel's architecture therefore appear in the painting, merging heaven and earth. The mural centers on a beardless Christ displaying his Sacred Heart, sitting as victor over death atop his own tomb. The tomb's openings are in reality operating three-dimensional doors behind which the Eucharist is reserved, adding to the technical complexity of executing a painting, but establishing the relationship between real and ideal in an unusually intense way. The tomb of Christ is portrayed in paint, yet behind those painted doors is placed the sacramental Body of Christ, resting within the "tomb" of an earthly tabernacle.

While the eighteen saints and angels surrounding the figure of Christ recall the Italian *sacra conversazione* tradition, the composition shows a cruciform double narrative. The vast depth of field begins in the actual space of the chapel itself, where a floor pattern of grey, white, and red marble is imitated in the painting. A still life composition in the foreground alludes to the Passion and establishes a procession leading to the tomb, then Christ, and through to the landscape beyond. Saints and angels reinforce the movement to the center and a small-scale secondary narrative runs from right to left, allegorizing the life of a Christian devoted to the Sacred Heart. The landscape, inspired by the local Black Hills of South Dakota, is filled with symbolic detail: temple pediments with biblical scenes, broken calendars, and references to death, burial, and resurrection.

Porter's second large-scale mural, the sixteen-foot-high *Christ In Majesty*, 2007 [FIGURE 2], broached a similar subject in an entirely different way. Designed for an existing Gothic chapel in Fort Worth's St. Andrew's Episcopal Church, the image portrays water as the blood of the Lamb mentioned in the Book of Revelation in which heavenly beings are washed clean. Accordingly, water appears throughout the painting: Christ breaks through Friedrich-inspired clouds on a throne supported by images of the four evangelists, accompanied by fog, mist, multiple images of pouring, and the rainbow aureola that signifies the radiant combination of water and light. Seemingly weightless buildings, like the lighthouse as image of Christ, appear to float on the water as Christ walked on the Sea of Galilee.

Porter's design engages the narrative of purification through baptism and subsequent glorification in the Eucharist. At the lower right, a Bacchus-like figure pours wine into a chalice before a lamp stand, which incorporates the traditional eucharistic symbolism of the pelican plucking its own feathers to feed her young with her blood. To the side appear the "three Marys"—the Virgin, Mary Magdalene, and Mary the wife of Cleophas. The Virgin points to a mother and child

seated at her left in contemplation of the sacrifice of her own son, while the Magdalene points into the distance to a swallow in flight, a symbol of resurrection. "Hidden" images reward the viewer for close inspection, such as the architectural sculpture referring to The Washing of the Feet or the statues of Moses and Elijah in the throne, which recall their appearance with Christ on Mount Tabor at the Transfiguration.

Porter's small *St. Dominic and the Eighth Way of Prayer*, 2005 [FIGURE 9] again gave him the opportunity to focus upon the edge of human history and divinity, drawing upon the testimony at the canonization of the Spanish-born St. Dominic in 1234. In number eight of the saint's reported nine ways of prayer, Dominic was to said to enter an enclosed room for prayerful study and receive revelation on the meaning of scripture from an angel. Yet the members of the religious community Dominic founded were sent forth to teach, preach, and combat the Albigensian heresy centered in Albi, France. Porter adeptly combines the interiority of the saint's prayer with the external mission of preaching by displaying Dominic in an open loggia overlooking the Albi cathedral. The realism of the saint, whose face was modeled on Dominic's actual death mask, meets the Platonic perfection of the angel who bears a glass jug containing the *aquam sapientiae*, or water of wisdom mentioned in the antiphon from St. Dominic's liturgical feast. Small telling details again enrich the narrative. A dog's head on the base of the cross recalls the pun of the Latin word *Domini-canes* or "dogs of the Lord," while the bridge in the background shows a small figure leaving the town of Albi and its heresy, walking back toward Dominic. In one last numerological *tour de force*, Porter places Dominic atop a floor pattern composed of a blue square divided into nine sections surround-

Though Porter is now largely known for his figural works, his initial explorations in classicism began with the study of decorative ornamental painting, as evidenced by works as diverse as his 2002 *Wall Decoration in the "Etruscan" Style* [FIGURE 11], the *Betrothal Portrait of Thetis for Peleus*, 2003 [FIGURE 12], *Myths of the Zodiac on Twelve Dining Chairs* [FIGURE 13], and his many works on paper based on Greek vase painting. He returns frequently to the vase paintings for inspiration, where decorative linearity meets figural narrative. Porter's *Dream of Neoptolemus* [FIGURE 14] displays what he calls a dreamscape, which despite its complex content of sacrifice and war, maintains what he considers a pure, elemental quality and simplicity of line and color. These lessons appear to inform even Porter's most elaborate works, where clarity of expression and intellectual rigor are never lost in the complex interweaving of multiple compositional and intellectual elements.

Masterly craft, narrative richness, the zeal of a convert, and a relentless optimism distinguish Leonard Porter and his work. Several years ago, Porter made a small change on his website, removing a phrase stating that he "rejected his Modernist training." It now simply states that in 1991, he "began exploring classicism." What was once intertwined with rejection is now clearly about acceptance of what is good. He waits for a dream commission like a library's great hall to paint a full narrative of the Trojan War, where the decorative, narrative, and architectural themes can all come together, an opportunity that he believes will come when the culture embraces and supports this sort of unified vision. But until then, Porter paints, lectures, and teaches; his talents acknowledged with the Arthur Ross Award for Excellence in the Classical Tradition, which he received in 2006. "Hope is at the heart of what I do," Porter says. "I'm about the future and my work is about the future." Like many of the figures in his paintings, Porter's life as an artist is tied to the fate of being trained in the legacy of Modernism, yet his energy and optimism reveal his sense of free will: "The art world is a small place. If you don't like what you find there you can change it. It can be changed." A generation ago, proponents of the renewal of the classical tradition could only hope with William Morris for the "change beyond the change." Porter's work proves that now the time has come. ❦

Dr. Denis R. McNamara is Assistant Director and Faculty Member, The Liturgical Institute, Mundelein, Illinois.

Figure 10 (above left): St. Thérèse of Lisieux, 2008, Oil on Linen, 24 x 18 in. ©Leonard Porter MMVIII.

Figure 11 (opposite top left): Wall Decoration in the "Etruscan" Style, 2002, Oil on Canvas, 42 x 30 in. ©Leonard Porter MMII.

Figure 12 (opposite top right): A Betrothal Portrait of Thetis for Peleus, 2003, Oil on Canvas, 16 x 12 in. Private Collection, Washington, DC ©Leonard Porter MMIII.

Figure 13 (opposite bottom left): Myths of the Zodiac on Twelve Dining Chairs, 2003, Oil on Wood, 3 x 18 in. In collaboration with Brockschmidt & Coleman Decoration and Design. Private Collection, Wilmington, DE ©Leonard Porter MMIII.

Figure 14 (opposite bottom right): The Dream of Neoptolemus, 2008, Ink and Watercolor on Paper, 11 x 16 in. Private Collection, New York, NY ©Leonard Porter MMVIII.

ing a red octagon, signifying once again the eighth way of Dominic's nine ways of prayer.

Porter's contemplation of the relationship of the real and the ideal has made him, as a painter of classical antiquity, perhaps the most articulate painter of Christian themes working today. Though he does not see himself as primarily a painter of Christian art, his method serves the Christian client well, and he notes the welcome reception he and his work have had in Christian circles. Porter's work does for the Christian art world what it also does for the larger realm of Classical Realism: raises the bar for richness of form and depth of content. One might claim that Porter's Christian work has not yet found the spark resulting from the coming together of nature and grace that characterizes the Incarnation (with perhaps the one exception being his Zurbaran-inspired image of St. Thérèse of Lisieux [FIGURE 10]), but the paintings stimulate contemplation of the deepest questions of human nature relevant in both pagan antiquity and its contribution to the Christian worldview.

Grand Central Academy of Art

The Grand Central Academy of Art (GCA) at the ICA&CA was created by professional, exhibiting artists to offer classical training to serious students. The Academy offers a positive environment for classical instruction in drawing, painting, and sculpture. The GCA is home to the following programs: The Water Street Atelier, a program in classical painting; The Sculpture Atelier, a program in classical sculpture; The Hudson River Fellowship, a summer landscape painting school in the Catskill Mountains; and the GCA's Annual Classical Figure Sculpture Competition.

The goal of the Academy is to train a generation of highly-skilled, aesthetically sensitive artists in the humanist tradition. The program is built on the skills and ideas that have come from classical Greece and Rome, the Italian Renaissance, and through to the Beaux-Arts tradition of the nineteenth century.

Further, the mission of the Grand Central Academy is to offer a public place for the revival of the classical art tradition, to foster and support a community of artists in pursuit of aesthetic refinement and a high level of skill and beauty. The Grand Central Academy of Art is an integral part of the ICA&CA whose mission is the advancement of classical art and architecture in America.

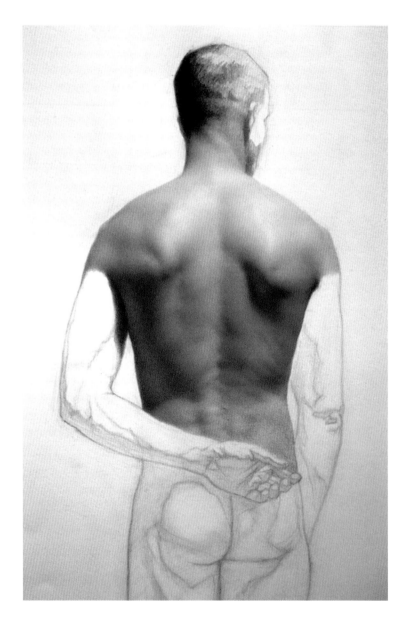

Figure 1 (above): "Michelle" by Greg Mortenson, 2009, Oil on Linen, 10 x 12 in. (3rd year).

Figure 2 (opposite): "Male Figure Study" by Angela Cunningham, 2008, Graphite on Paper, 18 x 24 in. (2nd year).

CAST DRAWING

Beginning core program students spend their first year in the Cast Hall learning to draw from the casts. Drawing from the antique cast, a classically rendered stationary object—using a limited palette under controlled light—teaches students to address the fundamental questions of composition, gesture, light direction, and value construction. Cast drawing encourages a slow, calm, thoughtful approach to gaining a deep understanding of the cast three-dimensionally. Students train to think sculpturally, to make more accurate decisions, and to create drawings that are true to life.

Students are required to draw each feature cast (ear, eye, nose, and mouth) and at least one head and figure. Each student works at his or her own pace, generally to the end of the first year to complete excellent examples of each.

Materials: Pad of paper with plate or vellum finish, kneaded rubber eraser, HB pencils, sharpener, razor or sand paper for sharpening pencils.

FIGURE DRAWING

Towards the end of the first year, students begin to draw the figure from life. Applying lessons learned by drawing the casts, they work on a series of linear figure drawings. The focus here is on accurate shapes, proportion, and dynamic gesture, without any finish or modeling. They move on to a series of drawings that show finished lines and clear resolution of detail. With their instructor's approval, students progress to drawing fully-finished, modeled figures in month-long poses.

Drawing the figure through a series of long poses, students learn to manage relationships creating an analogous balance that describes the three-dimensional experience on the flat page. As students gain fluency with the pencil, they will continue to utilize these principles in paint.

Materials: Pad of paper with plate or vellum finish, kneaded rubber eraser, HB pencils, sharpener, razor or sand paper for sharpening pencils.

Figure 3 (above): Cast Drawing, "Winged Victory" by Carla Crawford, 2009, Graphite on Paper, 18 x 24 in. (1st year).

Figure 4 (opposite top left): "Male Figure Study" by Colleen Barry, 2008, Oil on Linen, 18 x 24 in. (2nd year).

Figure 5 (opposite top right): Cast Painting, "Bearded Man" by Colleen Barry, 2009, Oil on Linen, 18 x 24 in. (2nd year).

Figure 6 (opposite bottom right): "Eggs with Spoon," by Elizabeth Ehmann, 2007, Oil on Linen, 10 x 12 in. (3rd year).

PAINTING

As students gain fluency with the pencil, they will continue to utilize these principles in paint. First, students work in grisaille (monochromatic painting in shades of gray) painting from the casts, copying master paintings, and then figures and portraits from life. Students showing facility in grisaille will begin using a color palette. Students must produce at least six finished, excellent month-long-pose figure paintings in color to show mastery.

Materials: a stretched lightly toned (neutral grey) primed linen, oil paints, a variety of small brushes in pristine shape suitable for small detail, medium filbert brushes, at least one large brush (hog hair or synthetic for large massing,) a wooden palette, a metal palette knife, mineral spirits or turpenoid, linseed oil, a kneaded eraser and a small, hand-held mirror.

SCULPTURE

A traditional emphasis on clarity of form, simplicity of action, balance, and harmony are woven through the sculpture program that includes meticulous copying of antique sculptures, rigorous study of anatomical figure structure (including a year-long study of écorché), and extensive modeling from life.

Painting core students are required to study sculpture alongside dedicated sculpture students. Likewise, sculpture students study cast and figure drawing and painting alongside painting students. While all students are required to model casts, half-life size figures, portraits, and an écorché, sculpture core students go on to model a life-size torso and figure.

Écorché is an advanced anatomical study of the human body as a whole. Students begin with an armature and sculpt the skeleton one bone at a time. Then the muscles are added layer upon layer as the human form is built up from the inside out. Study of the origin, insertion, and action of the muscles helps students develop an understanding of the body's overlapping forms and the portrayal of motion. Toward the end of the process, a live model is used to further the conception of the model's anatomy as a single system.

Materials: a figure, portrait, or écorché armature, 50 lbs. of water-clay (or oil-clay, red and green, for écorché), sculpting tools, water spray bottle, cotton rags and plastic bags.

Figure 7 (left): "Jessica" by Mark Porter, 2009, Water Clay, 33 in. (1st year sculpture student).

Figure 8 (opposite bottom left): "Nina" by Will St. John, 2008, Oil on Linen, 11 x 14 in. (2nd year).

Figure 9 (opposite top left): First-year student, Philip Salamone, working on final cast drawing, 2007.

Figure 10 (opposite right): Cast Painting, "The Boxer" by Angela Cunningham, 2009, Oil on Linen, 15 x 20 in. (2nd year).

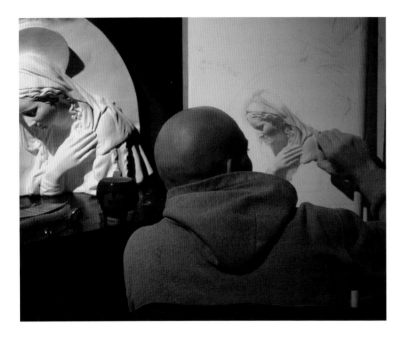

GCA's 2nd Annual Classical Figure Sculpture Competition

Furthering its commitment to the growing renewal of classical figurative art, the Grand Central Academy of Art conceived of a new figure sculpture competition in November of 2007. The first competition was subsequently held in June of 2008.

The second competition took place June 8-12, 2009, at the GCA's Sculpture Atelier. Twelve finalists, selected from sixty applicants, competed. The judges were Jacob Collins (New York artist and GCA director), Richard Cameron (ICA&CA co-founder and trustee, director of the Ariel Atelier) and Stuart Feldman (Philadelphia-based professional artist, sculptor, and teacher, and co-founder of the Schuylkill Academy of Fine Art).

The finalists, a mix of professional sculptors and talented students, competed together in the studio for 40 hours over five days to model a half-size figure from life. The model, likewise, held a beautiful standing pose, her outstretched arm holding an apple.

The prizes were awarded as follows:
Joshua Koffman of Philadelphia, PA, First Place, $10,000.
Kate Brockman of Philadelphia, PA, Second Place, $3,000.
Jiwoong Cheh of Brooklyn, NY (by way of Seoul, Korea), Third Place, $2,000.

To read about all the sculptors and to view competition photographs, please visit: http://grandcentralacademy.classicist.org/sculpturecompetition.html

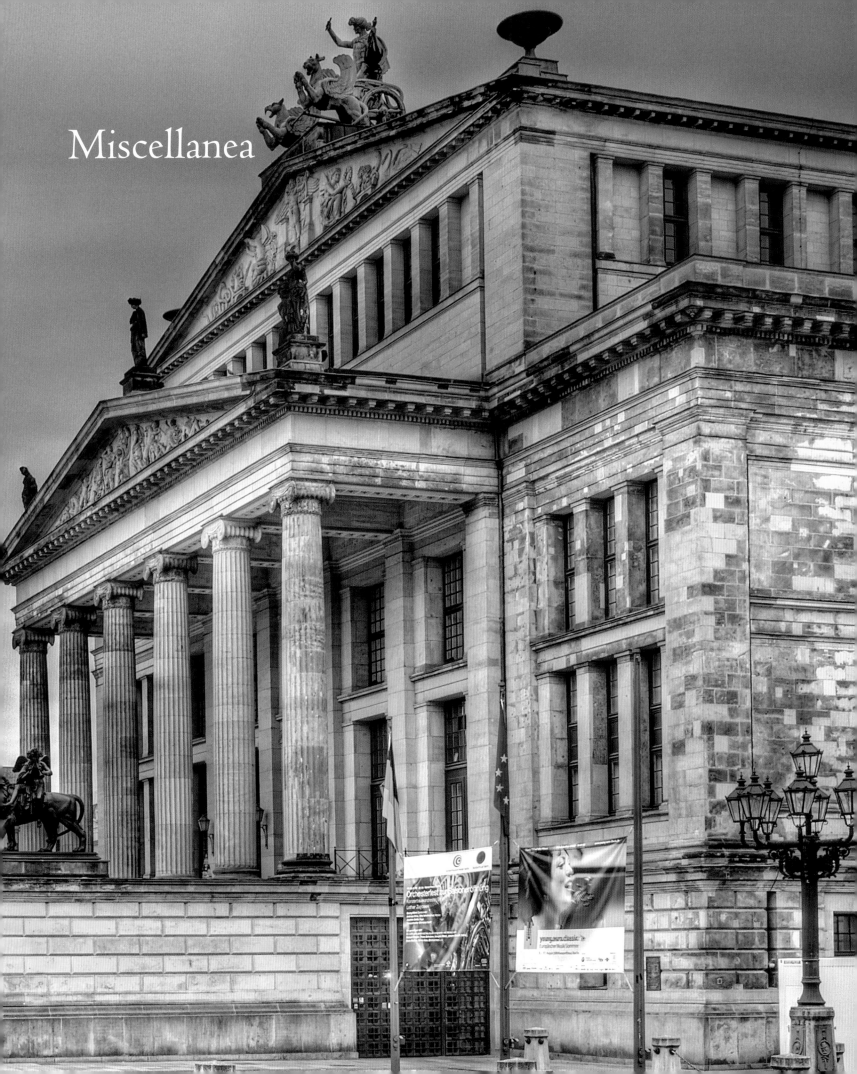

Miscellanea

The Poetics of Architectural Form in the Schauspielhaus of Karl Friedrich Schinkel

By Charles A. Barrett

Classical architecture has been described as the "Poetics of Order."[1] A central goal of the classical architect is to create an order out of the situation in which he finds himself. In organizing the complex and frequently contradictory set of needs and ideas with which he is confronted, he applies an apparatus of known forms and syntax, which organize these needs and ideas and remain in the finished work as traces of his cognitive process.

This apparatus consists of the orders themselves and the tradition of usage and interpretation that accompanies them. These orders are paradigms for the resolution of typical formal problems encountered by the architect and having to do with the identities of parts, their relationship to and influence upon one another, and their significance as a sustained allegorical model of the building—a "perpetuum carmen" in the words of Ovid.[2]

To say that the orders are paradigms of resolutions implies that they contain within them paradoxes—contradictions whose presence directs the design of the simplest of classical buildings. A simple example of this is the set of rules governing the disposition of the elements of the Doric frieze. They are:

- The face of the architrave and frieze must align with the neck of the column below.
- The triglyph at the end of the frieze, which ostensibly represents the end of a beam, must be placed at the corner and be one half module (one quarter the base diameter of the column) in width.
- The metopes, the flat panels that close the gap between the triglyphs, must be square and, according to most canons, one and one half modules (or three quarters of the base diameter of the column).
- The centers of the triglyphs must align alternately with the center of the column and the center of the span.

The fact that the column neck and triglyph are not of the same width means that one cannot satisfy all the rules at once.

A number of such resolutions can be noted. Vitruvius (Book IV) described the common practice (used in the Parthenon) of narrowing the intercolumniation in the terminal bays of a colonnade, allowing the proportions of triglyphs and metopes to be undisturbed and for the triglyph to be placed at the corner, but unfortunately not centered over the corner column. In certain archaic temples, the width of the triglyph is increased, allowing it to be centered and to reach the corner of the temple. Vitruvius himself recommends the displacement of the triglyph from the corner, keeping it centered over the terminal column. This dissociates the triglyph from the corner it is meant to articulate. The remaining distance between its edge and the corner is to be filled with a "semi-metope," in reality not half a metope but an L-shaped bent panel that, like Frank Lloyd Wright's "folded plane," fills in the corner physically but leaves it unarticulated and unstressed, suggesting openness.

None of these solutions achieves a non-contradictory, unambiguous result. Each is flawed. Yet in the larger reality of the building, a fault in the part can contribute to the resolution of the whole. This series of partial resolutions, rather than undermining the credibility of the order (as is suggested by the various ancient writers, such as Hermogenes, whom Vitruvius cites) creates a series of possible directions in which the study and practice of the order can be taken. In the scheme which narrows the terminal intercolumniation, the corner is made to appear denser (the solid to void ratio is higher) intensifying the ends of the colonnade. In the Vitruvian "solution" the unstressed semi-metope at the terminus of the frieze creates the ground work for an open corner.

Rather than defining the order ever more narrowly, as though perfected for every use, an icon out of context on a Beaux-Arts wash plate, we may see the order as an important source of architectural speculation and as the engine which generates architectural possibilities. The end result is an expanding canon, and a larger field for architectural activity. To complete the order, the architect must assess his needs and priorities and break any one of the rules (as the architect of every Doric building that has corners has had to do) and adjust the other forms to compensate and thereby achieve an image of the unity inherent in the building as a proposition.

Section opener (previous pages): Schauspielhaus, Berlin. Photograph by Wolfgang Staudt.

Figure 1 (opposite top): Anonymous, Schauspielhaus on the Gendarmenmarkt in Berlin, c.1821, Oil on Copper, 51.5 × 64.5 cm, The Hermitage, St Petersburg.

Figure 2 (opposite bottom): Perspective view of the Schauspielhaus, Berlin, from Karl Friedrich Schinkel, *Sammlung architectonischer Entwürfe* (Berlin: Wittich, 1828).

 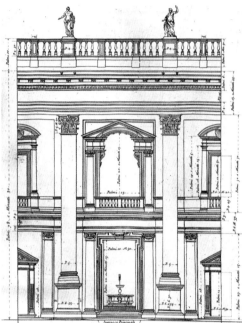

One of the earliest lessons one learns about classical architecture is that no architect uses an order straight from the book. While this is obviously an exaggeration, it is nonetheless true that classical architecture contains countless examples of orders adjusted to suit the purposes of their designer. These adjustments range from minor adjustments of proportion to the virtual invention of an order absolutely specific to its occasion. This phenomenon results from the interaction of Vitruvius' *Eurythmia* and *Symmetria* in the architectural project.

Eurythmia may be thought of as the idealized form of the individual part and *Symmetria* as the correspondence of the parts of an organic whole each carefully adjusted in identity, proportion, iconography, line quality (i.e., its shapes) and the character of light and shadow falling across its surfaces.

Most analyses of classical architecture focus on its systems of organization and classification. In the treatises it is normal to see a series of plates and / or descriptions of the orders one at a time or together in a spectrum from Tuscan through Corinthian or Composite. Thus the authors define the species of detail and proportion. Their

origins and iconography are described with some attention given to variation and occasionally to non-canonical orders.

Organizational schemes are presented that represent typical models for buildings and convey a basic sense of compositional goals for the building. Vitruvius, in Book III, for example, classifies temple types by three separate criteria: intercolumniation (the proportion of solid to void in the colonnade, expressed in terms of the base diameter of the column, i.e., picnostyle, eustyle, etc.), the number of structural repetitions in the width of the building (expressed in terms of the number of columns from side to side, i.e., tetrastyle, hexastyle, etc.), and plan type (i.e., a temple *in antis*, prostyle, dipteral, etc.), which conveys the relationship between the stylar and mural structures of the building, the placement of rooms, and hints at structure. From these we can derive grid patterns of plan and elevation of the sort that might have generated the idealized grid patterns illustrated by Cesariano and Serlio.

This necessary approach, which focuses on definition and overall scheme, is vital to imparting basic knowledge about architecture and its goals. This approach is somewhat less successful in conveying the subtleties of the decisions that an architect makes as he designs a classical building, and too often creates the impression of immutable forms cranked through a machine of organization attuned to set compositional goals from which emerges a predictable product.

In his lectures at Cambridge, Wittgenstein commented that "we teach / learn language by using it." We might, to use a simple example, refer to a dictionary for a basic definition of a word and its classification with regard to the parts of speech. But not until we have used the word and heard it used many times do we understand the sense and nuance of its meanings. Imagine then the complexity of a whole language.

In the study of the forms of classical architecture, we would gain considerably from a close understanding of usage. What is the significance of the forms of the Doric frieze? What are the governing principles of its arrangement? What problems emerge from the

---

Figure 3 (above): Michelangelo, Palazzo Nuovo, Campidoglio, Rome. Photograph by Marie-Lan Nguyen.

Figure 4 (above right): Central bay of Michelangelo's Palazzo Nuovo, Campidoglio, Rome, from Domenico de Rossi's *Studio d'architettura civile: opera de più celebri architetti de nostri tempi*, Vol. 1, (Roma: De Rossi, 1702).

Figure 5 (opposite left): Detail of a study for a Corinthian portico for St. Paul's Cathedral, London, office of Sir Christopher Wren (SP140).

Figure 6 (opposite middle): Detail of a study for a Corinthian portico for St. Paul's Cathedral, London, office of Sir Christopher Wren (SP141).

Figure 7 (opposite right): Detail of study for an Ionic portico for St. Paul's Cathedral, London, office of Sir Christopher Wren (SP50).

application of these forms and principles? What solutions are possible? Who has used them and for what purposes? All these questions lead to a better understanding of classical architecture.

Wittgenstein continued: "Language consists of propositions. A proposition is a picture of reality and we compare that picture with reality." We can view a building as a complex series of propositions, each of which asserts a relationship between the matter-of-fact building and the series of models by which we understand it. The goal then is to produce an allegorical relation between the two which, like Wittgenstein's "proposition," must convince us of its accuracy. This relation is in some ways similar to the *concetto* as described by Klein[3] or the "idea" as described by Panofsky,[4] both of which base the conception of the art work in a linkage between two or more schemes.

The completion of any building relies on the formation of a convincing poetic that intervenes between the scheme and the detailing and between the *Eurythmia* of the parts and the *Symmetria* of the whole to reveal in the project the unity underlying its many complexities.

Schema of the Schauspielhaus and its Antecedents

Although the Schauspielhaus is a neoclassical building in detail, massing, and architectonic goals, it is distinctly Renaissance in the organizational scheme of its elevation and sections. Its elevation consists of a raised basement supporting a giant order enclosing two minor superposed orders and surmounted by an attic pavilion [Figures 1 and 2].

Schinkel's use of the giant order had antecedents in the compositional schemes of a number of post-Renaissance buildings beginning with Michelangelo's twin palaces on the Campidoglio [Figures 3 and 4]. In Michelangelo's façades, the conceptual discrepancy between the two articulated stories and the implicit unity of the whole building was resolved through the application of a superimposed order of pilasters, which comprehends the entire height of the building.

Schinkel, however, did one thing that is very different. Before the Schauspielhaus, most façades with giant orders were carefully formulated to avoid certain problems inherent in the giant order scheme. If a building of two superposed orders were encased in a giant order, the capitals of the columns of the upper minor order collide uncomfortably with those of the columns of the major order. Further, each of the constituent orders would require an entablature in proportion to the height of its column.

The completion of both orders would require two entablatures of different sizes, one immediately above the other. Such formal redundancy would contradict the completion suggested by each order and subvert the equation of orders (i.e., two minor orders equals one giant order.) Conceptually, the upper minor order should resolve itself in the same entablature as the major order. Further, the spanning implications of the minor order capped with a roof are confounded by the weight of a second entablature apparently borne on them.

Another similar situation can be seen in a series of design studies for the façade of St Paul's Cathedral—made more than a century after Michelangelo's Campidoglio—by Hawksmoor and others in the studio of Sir Christopher Wren. In these drawings Wren's assistant attempted to articulate two minor superposed Corinthian orders in equation with a giant order the full height of the façade: Corinthian in the first scheme [Figures 5 and 6], and Ionic in the second [Figure 7]. He has aligned the tops of the capitals of the upper minor order with those of the major order. Immediately above, the entablatures of the

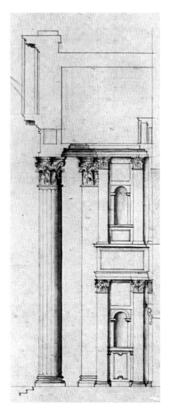

two orders run into each other. Since these entablatures are each in proportion to their respective orders, they and their constituent parts are of different heights. This produces an unsatisfactory connection, a collision rather than a continuity, between the two entablatures.

In the first design, the minor orders continue inside the portico of the giant order [Figures 5 and 6]. This means that the upper order would be incongruously surmounted by the entablature of the giant order, much too large in proportion. In section this problem has been addressed by substituting the architrave and cornice of the minor order on the interior of the portico. While this eases the problem of the minor order, it does so at the expense of the giant order which, inside of the portico, is surmounted by an extremely small architrave, too small, in appearance, to convincingly span between the giant order's columns. The inadequacy of the design is most fully revealed in the section of the entablature of the larger order, the identity and size of whose parts differ from its outer face to its inner face.

In a second scheme [Figure 7], the idea of continuing the upper minor order inside the portico has been dropped, eliminating the problem of the conjunction of the entablatures within the portico. But lost is the immediacy of the comparison between the giant order and the wall articulated by superposed minor pilaster orders. Because the the articulation of the minor order must cease as the wall passes behind the large order of the portico—the major organizing event of the design—it leaves unclearly stated the central idea of the composition: the insertion of the two minor orders into the giant order.

An effort is also made in this scheme to achieve a stronger linkage between the capitals of the large and small orders by substituting an Ionic giant order for the previous Corinthian. This permits an equation of the heights of the capitals of the small Corinthian and the large Ionic orders, and aligns their astragals and abaci. The strategy here is to make use of the different proportions of the Ionic and Corinthian in combination with their different sizes to produce equations and alignments of their parts. In this vein the architrave of the upper minor Corinthian order is equated and aligns with the top of the lower fascia of the larger Ionic architrave. The result is still compromised by the discontinuous entablatures above the columns. It is understandable that Wren abandoned the giant order (his aesthetic problems compounded by technical ones) for the simpler two-storied design that was executed [Figure 8].

These are inherent problems of the scheme, and they make clear the reasons for which Michelangelo did not fully articulate the inserted upper minor order of his palaces but rather implied them by means of their windows housed in columned aedicules fixed in the field of the recessed panel, whose edge subtly echoes the bay enclosure of the giant order. Carlo Maderno followed this common circumlocution (there are others) closely in his façade for Saint Peter's [Figure 9], and placed a full minor order only at the lowest level while reducing the articulation of the uppermost minor order to a window in a wall whose surface mediates between the capital of the giant order and the framed

Figure 8 (above): St. Paul's Cathedral, London. Photograph by Bernard Gagnon.

Figure 9 (left): Detail of façade of St. Peter's Basilica, Rome.

Figure 10 (opposite): Elevation of the Schauspielhaus, Berlin, from Karl Friedrich Schinkel, *Sammlung architectonischer Entwürfe* (Berlin: Wittich, 1828).

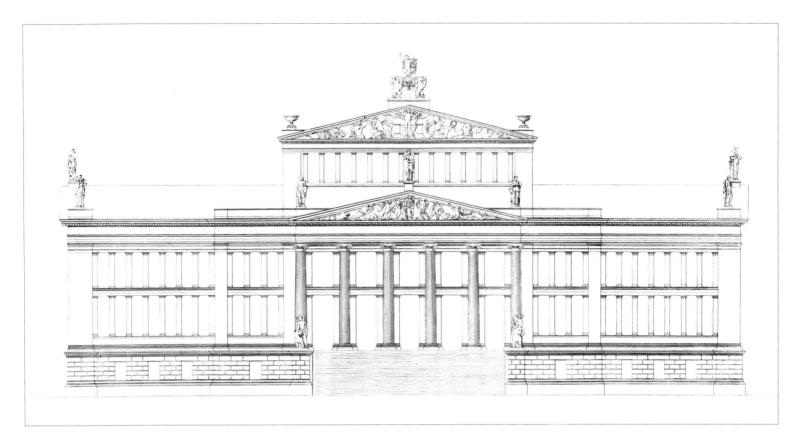

windows, thereby rendering a second entablature beneath that of the major order unnecessary.

This approach requires certain conditions, among them a Renaissance interpretation of classical architecture that understands a series of similarities between columns and walls and that permits them to exist conceptually in the same space in the form of a wall modulated by pilasters or engaged columns.

Working as he did in the period following and still dominated by Marc-Antoine Laugier's *Essai sur l'Architecture* Schinkel was no doubt unwilling to engage in such obvious conflations of wall and column.[5] The neoclassical distinction between column and wall and rejection of the forms that share characteristics of both, as well as the pursuit of the primacy of the column, required a consistent expression of trabeation—distinct from the wall—throughout, completely opposite in conception to Michelangelo's consubstantiation of the two structural elements. With the Renaissance solution unavailable, Schinkel was compelled to cope with the problematic insertion of two fully developed minor orders into his giant order. This, the adjacency of the crowning members of approximately coplanar giant and minor orders, is the fundamental problem posed by Schinkel's elevational scheme [Figure 10]. Its resolution depends upon Schinkel's creation of a bit of rhetoric, a figure of speech to allow the viewer's eye to pass unimpeded.

SCHINKEL'S APPARATUS AND RESOLUTION

The solution of this problem might, in many circumstances, have been inconceivable. Schinkel, however, in setting up the problem for himself, made certain choices of forms and conceptual structures that made possible his solution. Some comment on them and their origins will make his choices more understandable.

The five classical orders share a common formula for the representation of a building: a column, standing on an artificial ground plane known as the stylobate, bears a beam known as the architrave which, in turn supports a row of ceiling joists at a level called the frieze, which supports the projecting roof structure or eaves, known as the corona or cornice. The column can be broken down into base, shaft, and capital. A given order has a series of characteristic shapes, sequences of shapes, and ornaments which distinguish its parts, even when they appear alone.

In addition to columns, buildings have walls which can also bear the entablature (or parts thereof) of an order. In certain situations a column may exist cospatially with a wall. This confluence is marked by a pilaster or engaged column, fundamentally a flat column carved in relief at intervals along a wall. This situation occurs frequently in Roman prostyle temple forms in which a portico two or more columns deep is of the same width as the cella, the enclosed room that it fronts directly, and the colonnade continues along the side engaged in the cella wall [Figure 11].

In Greek sacred buildings where the pronaos is said to be *in antis* the cella (or naos) is fronted by an entrance porch (the pronaos) contained between two projecting walls called antae [Figure 12]. An architrave spans the opening between the projecting anta walls, resting on the ends of the antae and on the two or more columns between them. The ends of these walls, which bear the concentrated load of the architrave like the neighboring columns, are thickened slightly to reinforce them physically and visually. Finally, articulated bases and capitals give them the presence of columns. These additional articulations of the wall end, like the wall itself, are known as antae.

Schinkel rendered the Schauspielhaus in an Ionic order of Greek origin (specifically Attic), rather than Roman. Unlike the Roman orders upon which the architects of earlier works had based their designs, the Greek order permitted the use of antae rather than pilasters in those portions of his structure where mural and stylar structure coexist. This adoption by Schinkel of Greek antae was more than simply a fashionable substitution of a Greek form for a Roman one as were many other uses of the anta in his period. Many compositionally conservative buildings of the American Greek Revival treat it simply as an exotic ornamental treatment of a pilaster [FIGURE 13]. The anta suited Schinkel's purpose perfectly.

The pilaster and the anta are both forms born of the confluences and conflations of wall and column inherent in the act of building. They differ in two major ways. A pilaster is normally seen engaged in the faces of a wall and supported left and right by blank wall surface [FIGURE 14]. The entablature above continues to surmount other pilasters bound up in the same wall surface. The face of an anta, in contrast, occurs at the end of a wall, the entablature above spanning across a void to rest on freestanding columns [FIGURE 13]. In addition, their capitals and moldings are conceived differently. The pilaster capital and base are intended to replicate the design of those of the freestanding column of its order. The anta capital is conceived differently from that of the column, as its base is often differentiated from the column base [FIGURE 15]. The anta capital is, like an entablature, an affair of planes modulated by lines of horizontal moldings.

One significant gain for Schinkel is that, because the face of the anta is not normally supported at the sides by wall, he was not forced into a relief of columns and walls in the Renaissance manner and was able to use the column-like form of the anta free-standing to modulate the façades of his building. He was able to articulate the windows of his buildings as glass veils hung between the columns of a completely trabeated façade. In addition to easing the column/wall impasse of Schinkel's use of a Renaissance giant order scheme, his adoption of the Greek order made his solution of the problem of the giant and minor orders possible.

A cursory examination of Schinkel's elevation reveals that two entablatures are, after all, present at the top of the building with that of the upper minor order sheltered under the architrave of the giant order [FIGURE 16]. The minor order is completed by an entablature approximately in proportion. A close look at the corner shows the entablature of the major order resting upon the capital of the great antae at the corners of the building. The major order seems at rest and uncontradicted by the scale of the minor order. What has happened to the expected collision of the two orders of different scale?

Another look at the anta capital will reveal that its moldings run horizontally beyond the limits of the anta. Schinkel here quotes a common detail of Greek buildings [FIGURE 17]. The moldings of the anta capital continue horizontally to form a capital for the cella wall and intimate its column-like bearing capacity. A look at the base of the major order shows that the base of the anta, corresponding to its capital, also continues along the base of the low parapet upon which the minor stands. It is actually this anta capital that extends to form the entablature borne by the minor order, the end of which it articulates. This means that the capitals of the minor order, being below the entablature of that order, are also below the level of those of the giant order, thereby preventing the threatened collision.

The entablature of the minor order, extruded as it were from the capital of the major order, is separated from it by the fact that the face of the entire structure of inserted orders is set back a small distance from the face of the anta of the major order. The usual advantage of this in detailing is that all of the projecting moldings of the minor orders can be terminated by running them into the side of the major anta.

This common trick of the trade, a very basic tool in the practice of classical design, has been in use for thousands of years. Yet, it acquired

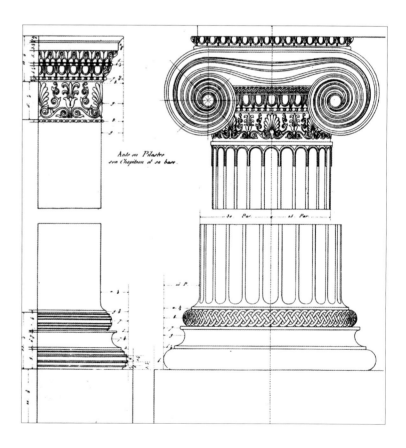

Figure 11 (opposite top left): Maison Carrée, Nîmes, France. Photograph by Flore Allemandou.

Figure 12 (opposite bottom left): Athenian Treasury, Delphi, Greece. Photograph by Sam Korn.

Figure 13 (opposite top right): Ithiel Town and Alexander Jackson Davis, Federal Hall, New York. Photographer unknown (Historic American Buildings Survey, Prints and Photographs Division, Library of Congress).

Figure 14 (opposite bottom right): Baldassare Peruzzi, Palazzo Massimo alle Colonne, Rome. Photograph by Richard John.

Figure 15 (right): Comparison of the column and anta of the Erechtheion, Athens, from Charles Normand, *Nouveau Parallèle des Ordres* (Paris: Firmin Didot, 1819).

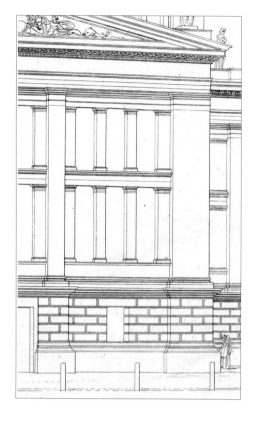

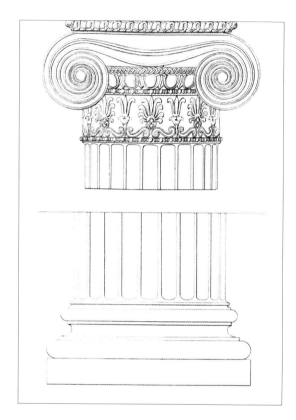

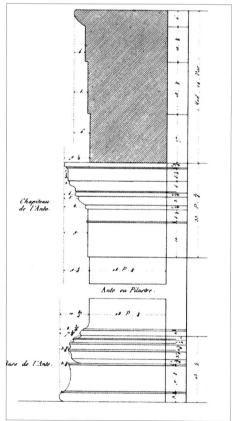

Figure 16 (top left): Detail of the Schauspielhaus, Berlin, from Karl Friedrich Schinkel, *Sammlung architectonischer Entwürfe* (Berlin: Wittich, 1828).

Figure 17 (top center): Temple on the Illissos river, Athens, from James Stuart and Nicholas Revett, *Antiquities of Athens* (London: John Haberkorn, 1762).

Figure 18 (top right): The order of the Schauspielhaus, Berlin, from Karl Friedrich Schinkel, *Sammlung architectonischer Entwürfe* (Berlin: Wittich, 1828).

Figure 19 (opposite): Detail of the anta capital of the Erechtheion, Athens. Photograph by Guillaume Piolle.

Figure 20 (far left): Anta capital of the temple on the Ilissos river, Athens, from Charles Normand, *Nouveau Parallèle des Ordres* (Paris: Firmin Didot, 1819).

Figure 21 (left): Detail of the corner anta of the Schauspielhaus, Berlin, from Karl Friedrich Schinkel, *Sammlung architectonischer Entwürfe* (Berlin: Wittich, 1828).

several new uses in Schinkel's building. This setback distinguishes the otherwise identical minor order entablature and major order capital from one another. It also creates a hollow beneath the entablature of the major order. This distinguishes the contiguous entablatures from one another with a show line heavy enough to outweigh those of any of their molding sequences and, by placing the minor entablature in shadow, gives emphasis to the hierarchically more important entablature of the major order.

But it is a very specific reference as well. While the columns of the Schauspielhaus portico are based on those of the Erechtheion on the Athenian Acropolis [FIGURE 18] as is the entablature (though Schinkel has added modillions below the cornice) the anta capital is not. Most Ionic anta capitals are formed of a neck articulated by a bead at its lower edge and at its top by two or more curved moldings, variously ovolo, hawk's beak, or cyma reversa [FIGURE 19]. Such an arrangement is hardly suggestive of a complete entablature, a sequence of two vertical planes divided by a molding and surmounted by a projecting cornice.

Schinkel has quoted a particular detail, the anta capital from the small Ionic amphiprostyle temple on the Ilissos river in Athens [FIGURE 20]. In the example (fortunately documented by James Stuart and Nicholas Revett before its destruction in the late eighteenth century) the bead molding that normally occurs at the bottom of the neck is placed about midway up the neck in a position making it very suggestive of the cymatium that normally divides architrave and frieze.

As evidence of the specificity with which Schinkel directed formulation of the detail to his compositional problem, it is interesting to note that the corresponding—and, at first glance, similar—detail at the entablature of the attic of the same building [FIGURE 21] is very differ-

ent. Here, Schinkel's problem was much simpler. Schinkel has articulated a single order, of somewhat smaller size than the two inserted minor orders below but necessarily raised on a podium wall in order to clear the pediment of the portico projecting below. His problem is to continue the major plan grid up from below, to continue the risalit[6] (a compositional term referring to accented articulation of the end of the elevation), which is marked below with the anta of the major order.

Presumably because of the irregularity of the base of this wall caused by its contact with sloping roofs, Schinkel marks the risalit with a pier free of the articulation of capital and base. What may seem to be a base at its bottom is actually no more than the continuation of the coping and curb of the parapet of the portico roof. The entablature is determined, not by these piers, but by the single small order, made up of antae as below.

The face of the order, unlike that of the minor order below, is in the same plane as the face of the pier. The junction of the pier and the order is articulated by a small reveal that continues down to the portico roof to separate the planar podium wall from the more three-dimensional pier.

CONCLUSION

Schinkel's Schauspielhaus, like every other building of merit, achieves a conceptual continuity only by virtue of resolutions of the smallest of details. Its design forms a poetic continuum of vision and reason extending from his most basic decisions of massing and concept, his identification of the dispositions and conflicts of elements, to his choice of apparatus and detailing of parts.

Schinkel's great theater would, beyond doubt, be a lesser work were it not for his subtle resolutions of detail, made explicit and significant through reference to the forms, syntax, and usage of the classical tradition. Is it not this tradition that, for better or worse, defined and directed the discourse of architecture even up to the present? Can we do other than gain from closer knowledge of it? ❦

In 1996, at his memorial service, Charles Barrett was described by Vincent Scully as follows: "lonely comrade; loyal friend; [he] was one of the most accomplished architectural draftsman of modern time. His creative imagination and his skill were boundless. Classical architecture lived again in his work. Whole cities rose up under his hands... It is in the memory of those he left behind and in the work they may do that he will build his stately mansions now." This essay was left unpublished at the time of Charles Barrett's death. —RTJ

Endnotes

1. Alexander Tzonis and Liane Lefaivre, *Classical Architecture: The Poetics of Order* (Cambridge: MIT Press, 1992).
2. Ovid, *Metamorphoses*, I.4.
3. Klein, Robert. "The Theory of Figurative Expression in Italian. Treatises on the Impresa." in *Form and Meaning* (New York: Viking Press, 1979), pp. 2-24.
4. Erwin Panofsky, *Idea: A Concept in Art Theory*, trans. J. J. S. Peake (Columbia: University of South Carolina Press, 1968).
5. Marc-Antoine Laugier, *Essai sur l'architecture*, (Paris: Duchesne, 1753).
6. Cf. the terms Ressaut in French and Risalto in Italian.

The New Canon

By Andrés Duany

The current renaissance of traditional architecture must be seen not as a single event, but as a process. A first generation restored the old and sturdy citadel which is the discipline of the classical language. The current generation can continue to unfurl beautiful banners from the ramparts, in the hopes that all will recognize its virtue—or it can sally to take territory by force. There is too much territory forlorn by American design. I do not allude to the bits held by modernism, but to the vast areas held by mindless production builders, by the green gadgets that pass for environmental buildings, by the nauseating plan books, by the junk-space of civic buildings, by the junk-products at Home Depot, by the hapless mobile home industry. These are blights on our physical and cultural landscape that can be redeemed only by traditional designers. This is risky I know. We could jeopardize the impeccable reputation of the citadel; but we could also show the place that traditional architecture can hold as nothing else can.

In this quest, we must be as courageous as the generation of pioneers. Bob Stern, Alan Greenberg, Tom Beeby, Rob Krier, Dimitri Porphyrios, and Thomas Gordon Smith all risked their good names by entering the wilderness of postmodernism. But see what they gained on the other side: the architecture now so confidently rewarded with the Driehaus Prize.

The best proof that architecture has been well and truly recovered in that heroic thirty-year campaign is that it can be dependably taught. Classicists today can be as good as their masters even while still young. I am aware that the rigor of the classical canon enables this instruction. I am also aware that the discipline of the orders was the compass that guided architecture out of postmodernism. But in teaching the orders today we should take care that students not become overly dependent on bookish authority. They must not learn the fear of being caught "incorrect." The measure should be what Lizz calls "plain old good architecture." After all, we are building primarily for the commons, not the patrons.

Will this generation bore deeper into refinement and elitism, or will it endeavor to spread classical architecture outwards to a broad, democratic, indeed populist, future? Will they continue reprinting ever more esoteric treatises, or will they write new ones conceived to serve, not the sixteenth or even the twentieth century, but the future which is upon us?

To explain what I mean, please permit me a rudimentary example. How can there be a viable canon of architecture that is incapable of producing an opening wider than it is high—by that I mean a horizontally proportioned intercolumniation? We cannot be effective today if we cannot even deal with a simple barn opening or a porte-cochere. And that is just one problem. We must confront the necessity of expanding the classical canon if it is to engage the twenty-first century.

I would propose a new ethos—one no longer dedicated to the polishing of the classical canon of Vitruvius, Palladio, and Vignola, but to supplementing that canon. Because this process cannot be allowed to devolve into neo-postmodernist dissipation, it should still be based on the authority of masters and masterpieces. First we must transcend the closed historic treatises, to rescue that which was discarded in the reductive process of writing them. Then we must recover to our side those transitional nineteenth- and twentieth century architects who have been assigned to the modernist camp—where they reside as the foundation of their authority—when they are, in fact, the last great flowering of classicism.

Take Frank Lloyd Wright. You could see the Prairie School as the beginning of the fall, but you could also see it as the last of the Greek Revivals. Wright was among those who, instead of the Parthenon and all of its proprieties, took the Erechtheion and all of its freedoms, to extract a contemporary architecture. If the Erechtheion—its dynamic massing and multiple columniations, its agile engagement with topography, its free repertoire of moldings, its localized symmetries and rotated approaches, its complex, multi-leveled interior, its contradictions and unresolved tension—is classical, then Wright is certainly among the great masters of classicism. Wright must be on our side if we are to take the territory of the twenty-first century.

Another master of the canon would be Jože Plečnik, who knew the classical language perfectly. Like Shakespeare, who found literature in moribund Latin and bequeathed it in native English with vitality to spare, Plečnik shows us the workings of what my brother Douglas calls "the vernacular mind." Not "the vernacular," which is a style, but the vernacular mind, which is the way of folk art. It is the ability to compose from memory and circumstance, to work sequentially through anything and everything, with craft but not perfection. The folk tradition, which Plečnik brought to classicism, is the essential tool, I think, to withstand the withering that the twenty-first century will impose upon us. Léon Krier knows it. Look at his American buildings at Miami, and at Seaside and Windsor. What lessons do they hold? Not one of them is correct in the canonical sense, and yet they are canonical buildings. And so I would also bring into the canon the work of Léon Krier.

An expanded canon would include newly drawn plates alongside Vignola's: the orders of masters such as Gilly, Soane, Thompson, Tony Garnier, Perret, Hoffman, Loos, Asplund, Piacentini, Terragni, Stern, Graves, Porphyrios, Rob Krier. This treatise would claim an enormous amount of new territory for classicism.

A portion of this Driehaus Award will be applied to such a treatise. We are almost there. We have only to climb one last Everest.

The above remarks were made on the occasion of the award of the 2008 Driehaus Prize to Elizabeth Plater-Zyberk and Andrés Duany. The illustrations opposite, by Javier Cenicacelaya and Iñigo Saloña, are from the planned treatise referred to above.

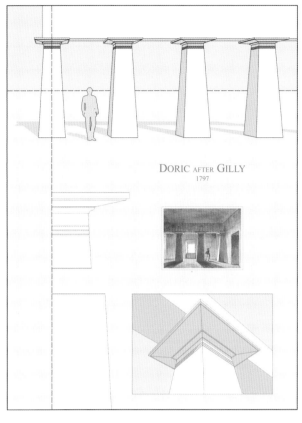

DORIC AFTER GILLY
1797

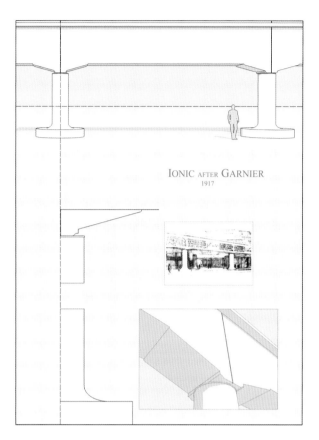

IONIC AFTER GARNIER
1917

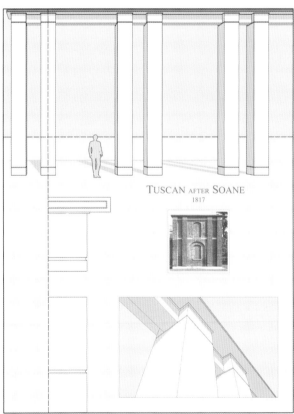

TUSCAN AFTER SOANE
1817

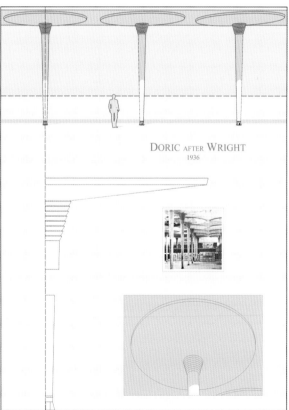

DORIC AFTER WRIGHT
1936

In Pursuit of the Antiquities of Athens and Ionia:

THE TRAVELS OF RICHARD CHANDLER, WILLIAM PARS, AND NICHOLAS REVETT IN ASIA MINOR AND GREECE IN 1764–66

Following the success of the publication of the first volume of James Stuart and Nicholas Revett's The Antiquities of Athens *in 1762, the Society of the Dilettante resolved to fund a further expedition, this time not just to Athens, but also to Ionia, the ancient territories along the eastern shores and islands of the Aegean sea, which now fall within the boundaries of present-day Turkey. On this second journey, Revett was accompanied not by Stuart, but by an Oxford philologist and ancient historian, Richard Chandler, and a topographical painter, William Pars.[1] The important drawings made by Pars on this trip were subsequently engraved to illustrate the second volume of* The Antiquities of Athens *and the two volumes of* Ionian Antiquities *in 1769 and 1797. Their popularity and significance was such that Paul Sandby was given permission to publish sepia aquatints of Pars' watercolors before the Society donated the originals to the British Museum in 1799. While the monochrome reproductions of these early views of the Parthenon, Erechtheion, and other ancient sites are familiar from* The Antiquities of Athens, *the original watercolors have rarely been exhibited and almost none have been published in full color.[2] To accompany the selection of William Pars' drawings reproduced here, some brief excerpts have been chosen from Richard Chandler's journal of the trip,[3] which vividly bring to life the challenges facing this first archaeological expedition into Asia Minor.* —RTJ

THE ACROPOLIS, ATHENS[4]

The acropolis, asty, or citadel, was the city of Cecrops.[5] It is now a fortress, with a thick irregular wall, standing on the brink of precipices, and enclosing a large area, about twice as long as broad. Some portions of the ancient wall may be discovered on the outside, particularly at the two extreme angles; and in many places it is patched with pieces of columns, and with marbles taken from the ruins. A considerable sum had been recently expended on the side next Hymettus, which was finished before we arrived. The scaffolding had been removed to the end toward Pentele,[6] but money was wanting, and the workmen were withdrawn. The garrison consists of a few Turks, who reside there with their families, and are called by the Greeks *Castriani,* or the soldiers of the castle. These hollow nightly from their station above the town, to approve their vigilance. Their houses overlook the city, plain, and gulf, and the situation is pleasant, but too airy, and attended with so many inconveniences, that those who are able, and have the option, prefer living below, when not on duty. The rock is lofty, abrupt, and inaccessible, except the front, which is toward the Piraeus; and on that quarter is a mountainous ridge, within cannon-shot. It is destitute of water fit for drinking, and supplies are daily carried up in earthen jars, on horses and asses, from one of the conduits in the town.

The acropolis furnished a very ample field to the ancient virtuosi. It was filled with monuments of Athenian glory, and exhibited an amazing display of beauty, of opulence, and of art; each contending, as it were, for the superiority. It appeared as one entire offering to the Deity, surpassing in excellence, and astonishing in richness. Even Pausanias seems here to be distressed by the multiplicity of his subject. But this banquet, as it were, of the senses has long been withdrawn, and is now become like the tale of a vision. The spectator views with concern the marble ruins intermixed with mean flat-roofed cottages, and, extant amid rubbish, the sad memorials of a nobler people; which, however, as visible from the sea, should have introduced modern Athens to more early notice. They who reported it was only a small village, must, it has been surmised, have beheld the acropolis through the wrong end of their telescopes.

THE PROPYLAIA (*Figure 1*)

The acropolis has now, as formerly, only one entrance, which fronts the Piraeus.[7] The ascent is by traverses and rude fortifications, furnished with cannon, but without carriages, and neglected. By the second gate is the station of the guard, who sits cross-legged under cover, much at his ease, smoking his pipe or drinking coffee; with his companions

Figure 1: William Pars, *The Propylaia, Athens*, 323mm x 448mm, Watercolor. ©Trustees of the British Museum.

about him in like attitudes. Over this gateway is an inscription in large characters on a stone turned upside down, and black from the fires made below. It records a present of a pair of gates.

Going farther up, you come to the ruins of the propylea, an edifice which graced the entrance into the citadel. This was one of the structures of Pericles, who began it when Euthymenes was archon, four hundred thirty-five years before Christ. It was completed in five years, at the expense of two thousand and twelve talents. It was of marble, of the Doric order, and had five doors, to afford an easy passage to the multitudes, which resorted on business or devotion to the acropolis.

The Propylea have ceased to be the entrance of the acropolis. The passage, which was between the columns in the centre, is walled up almost to their capitals, and above is a battery of cannon. The way now winds before the front of the ancient structure, and, turning to the left hand among rubbish and mean walls, you come to the back part, and

to the five doorways. The soil without is risen higher than the top of the two smaller. There, under the vault and cannon, lies an heap of large stones, the ruin of the roof.

The temple of Victory,[8] standing on an abrupt rock, has its back and one side unincumbered with the modern ramparts. The columns in the front being walled up, you enter it by a breach in the side within the Propylea. It was used by the Turks as a magazine for powder, until about the year 1656; when a sudden explosion, occasioned by lightning, carried away the roof, with a house erected on it, belonging to the officer who commanded in the acropolis, whose whole family, except a girl, perished. The women of the Aga[9] continued to inhabit in this quarter, but it is now abandoned and in ruins.

The pediment of the temple of Victory, with that of the opposite wing, is described as remaining in 1676; but on each building a square tower had been erected. One of the steps in the front of the Propylea

Figure 2: William Pars, *The Parthenon, Athens,* 360mm x 552mm, Watercolor. ©Trustees of the British Museum.

was entire, with the four columns, their entablature and the pediment. The portico, to which the five doorways belonged, consisted of a large square room, roofed with slabs of marble, which were laid on two great marble beams, and sustained by four beautiful columns. These were Ionic, the proportions of this order best suiting that purpose, as taller than the Doric; the reason it was likewise preferred in the pronaos of the temple of Victory. The roof of the Propylea, after standing above two thousand years, was probably destroyed, with all the pediments, by the Venetians in 1687, when they battered the castle in front, firing red-hot bullets, and took it, but were compelled to resign it again to the Turks in the following year. The exterior walls, and in particular a side of the temple of Victory, retain many marks of their hostilities. Pausanias was really, or pretended to be, ignorant to whom the equestrian statues before the wings of the Propylea belonged. One of the pedestals, which remains, will supply this deficiency. The whole is immured, except the front; which has been much battered by cannon-shot; and on this my companions, while busied in measuring and drawing, discovered some Greek letters, high above the ground. After

repeated trials, in which I was assisted by a pocket-telescope, I procured the inscription, which may be thus translated; "The people have erected Marcus Agrippa, son of Lucius, thrice consul, the friend of Caius."

THE PARTHENON *(Figure 2)*

It is not easy to conceive a more striking object than the Parthenon, though now a mere ruin. The columns within the naos have all been removed, but on the floor may be seen the circles, which directed the workmen in placing them; and at the farther end, is a groove across it, as for one of the partitions of the cell. The recess erected by the Christians is demolished, and from the rubbish of the ceiling the Turkish boys collect bits of the mosaic, of different colours, which composed the picture. We were told at Smyrna, that this substance had taken a polish, and been set in buckles. The cell is about half demolished; and in the columns which surrounded it is a large gap near the middle. On the walls are some traces of the paintings. Before the portico is a reservoir, sunk in the rock, to supply the Turks with water for the purifications customary on entering their mosques. In it, on the left hand, is the rubbish of the pile, erected to supply the place of a column; and on the right, a staircase, which leads out on the architrave, and has a marble or two with inscriptions, but worn so as not to be legible. It belonged to the minaret, which has been destroyed.

It is to be regretted that so much admirable sculpture as is still extant about this fabric should be all likely to perish, as it were immaturely, from ignorant contempt and brutal violence.[10] Numerous carved stones have disappeared; and many lying in the ruinous heaps, moved our indignation at the barbarism daily exercised in defacing them. Besides the two pediments, all the metopes were decorated with large figures in alto relievo, of which several are almost entire on the side next Hymettus. These are exceedingly striking, especially when viewed with a due proportion of light and shade, the sun rising behind the mountain. Their subject is the same as was chosen for the sandals of Minerva, or the battle of the Centaurs and Lapithae. On the frieze of the cell was carved, in basso relievo, the solemnity of a sacrifice to Minerva; and of this one hundred and seventy feet are standing, the greater part in good preservation, containing a procession on horseback. On two stones, which have fallen, are oxen led as victims. On another, fourteen feet long, are the virgins called Canephori, which assisted at the rites, bearing the sacred canisters on their heads, and in their hands each a taper; with other figures, one a venerable person with a beard, reading in a large volume, which is partly supported by a boy. This piece, now inserted in the wall of the fortress, is supposed to have ranged in the centre of the back front of the cell. We purchased two fine fragments of the frieze, which we found inserted over doorways in the town; and were presented with a beautiful trunk, which had fallen from the metopes, and lay neglected in the garden of a Turk.[11]

The marquis de Nointell, ambassador from France to the Porte in the year 1672, employed a painter to delineate the frieze;[12] but his sketches, the labour of a couple of months, must have been very imperfect, being made from beneath, without scaffolding, his eyes straining upwards. Mr. Pars devoted a much longer time to this work, which he executed with diligence, fidelity, and courage. His post was generally on the architrave of the colonnade, many feet from the ground, where he was exposed to gusts of wind, and to accidents in passing to and fro. Several of the Turks murmured, and some threatened, because he overlooked their houses; obliging them to confine or remove the women, to prevent their being seen from that exalted station. Besides views and other sculptures, he designed one hundred ninety-six feet of bass-relief in the acropolis.

THE ERECHTHEION (Figure 3)

We proceed now to the cluster of ruins on the north side of the Parthenon, containing the Erechtheum, and the temple of Pandrosos, daughter of Cecrops. The ruin of the Erechtheum is of white marble,

Figure 3: William Pars, *The Erechtheion, Athens,* 310mm x 547mm, Watercolor. ©Trustees of the British Museum.

the architectural ornaments of very exquisite workmanship, and uncommonly curious. The columns of the front of the temple of Neptune are standing with the architrave; and also the skreen and portico of Minerva Polias, with a portion of the cell retaining traces of the partition-wall. The order is Ionic. An edifice revered by ancient Attica, as holy in the highest degree, was in 1676 the dwelling of a Turkish family; and is now deserted and neglected; but many ponderous stones and much rubbish must be removed, before the well and trident would appear. The former, at least, might probably be discovered. The portico is used as a powder-magazine; but we obtained permission to dig and to examine the outside. The doorway of the vestibule is walled up, and the soil risen nearly to the top of the doorway of the Pandroseum. By the portico is a battery commanding the town, from which ascends an amusing hum. The Turks fire from it, to give notice of the commencement of Ramazan, or of their Lent, and of bairam, or the holydays, and on other public occasions. The Pandroseum is a small but very particular building, of which no satisfactory idea can be communicated by description. The entablature is supported by women, called Caryatides.[13] Their story is thus related. The Greeks, victorious in the Persian war, jointly destroyed Carya, a city of the Peloponnesus, which had favoured the common enemy. They cut off the males, and carried into captivity the women, whom they compelled to retain their former dress and ornaments, though in a state of servitude. The architects of those times, to perpetuate the memory of their punishment, represented them, as in this instance, each with a burden on her head, one hand uplifted to it, and the other hanging down by her side. The images were in number six, all looking toward the Parthenon. The four in front, with that next to the Propylea, remain, but mutilated, and their faces besmeared with paint. The soil is risen almost to the top of the basement on which they are placed. This temple was open or latticed between the statues; and in it also was a stunted olive-tree, with an altar of Jupiter Herceus standing under it. The Propylea are nearly in a line with the space dividing it from the Parthenon; which disposition, besides its other effects, occasioned the front and flank of the latter edifice to be seen at once by those who approached it from the entrance of the Acropolis.

TEMPLE OF POSEIDON, SOUNION[14] *(Figure 4)*

We now approached cape Sunium, which is steep, abrupt, and rocky. On it is the ruin of the temple of Minerva Sunias, overlooking from its lofty situation the subject deep, and visible from afar. We often lost, and recovered again, the view of this beautiful object; sailing on a wide canal, between Attica and Macronisi, or *Long Island.* This was called anciently Helene, because, it was said, Helen had landed on it in her way to Lacedaemon, after Troy was taken. It ranges, like Euboea, before the continent, and belonged to the Athenians; but was of little value, being rough and desert. It was reckoned about sixty stadia, or seven miles and a half, long; five miles from Sunium, and as many from Cea, which lies beyond it.

The waves, on our arrival near the promontory, broke gently, with a hollow murmur, at the foot of the rock beneath the temple. At the entrance of the shining gulf was a little fleet of Hydriote vessels,[15] eight in number, coming out with white triangular sails. We anchored within the cape in the port of Sunium, near three hours before mid-day; and landing, ascended to the ruin. Meanwhile our sailors, except two or three who accompanied us, stripped to their drawers to bathe, all of

Figure 4: William Pars, *Temple of Poseidon, Sounion,* 237mm x 473mm, Watercolor. ©Trustees of the British Museum.

Figure 5: William Pars, *The Gymnasium at Alexandria Troas,* 300mm x 550mm, Watercolor. ©Trustees of the British Museum.

them swimming and diving remarkably well; some running about on the sharp rocks with naked feet, as if void of feeling; and some examining the bottom of the clear water for the echinus, or sea-urchin, a species of shell-fish common on this coast, full of prickles like a chesnut, and now in perfection, the moon being nearly at the full.

The temple of Minerva Sunias was of white marble, and probably erected in the same happy period with the great temple of Minerva, called the Parthenon, in the acropolis at Athens, or in the time of Pericles, it having like proportions, though far inferior in magnitude. The order is Doric, and it appears to have been a fabric of exquisite beauty. It had six columns in front. Nine columns were standing on the south-west side in the year 1676, and five on the opposite, with two antae or pilasters at the south end, and part of the pronaos. The number is now twelve, besides two in front and one of the antae; the other lying in a heap, having been recently thrown down, as we were informed, by the famous Jaffier Bey, then captain of a Turkish galeote, to get at the metal uniting the stones. The ruin of the pronaos is much diminished. The columns next to the sea are scaled and damaged, owing to their aspect. We searched diligently for inscriptions, but without success, except finding on the wall of the temple many modern names,[16] with the following memorial in Greek, cut in rude and barbarous characters, but with some labour: *Onesimus remembered his sister Chreste.* The old name Sunium is disused, and the cape distinguished by its columns, Capo *Colonni.*

THE GYMNASIUM AT ALEXANDRIA TROAS[17] *(Figure 5)*

The Christian religion was planted early at Troas. In the beginning of the fifth century, the bishop, Silvanus, was required to deliver a vessel from a demon, which was believed to detain it, as it could not be launched. It was intended for transporting large columns, and was of great size. Going down to the beach, he prayed, and taking hold of a rope, called on the multitude to assist, when the ship readily obeyed him, and hurried into the sea. But the churches have been so long demolished, that the traces of them are uncertain.

The desolation of this place was begun, and probably completed, before the extinction of the Greek empire. Many houses and public structures at Constantinople have since been raised with its materials. We found only a few inconsiderable remnants of white marble by the principal ruin, where formerly was a vast heap. Some pieces in the water by the port, and two large granite columns, were perhaps removed to the shore to be ready for embarkation. The magazine is yet far from being exhausted. The name Troas was not become obsolete in the year 1389.

We were employed at Troas chiefly in taking a plan and two views of the principal ruin.[18] We dined under a spreading tree before the arcade; and on the second day had just resumed our labour, when we were almost reduced to fly with precipitation. One of the Turks, coming to us, emptied the ashes from his pipe, and a spark of fire fell unobserved in the grass, which was long, parched by the sun, and inflammable like tinder. A brisk wind soon kindled a blaze, which withered in an instant the leaves of the bushes and trees in its way, seized the branches and roots, and devoured all before it with prodigious crackling and noise, and with a thick smoke, leaving the ground black, and the stones hot. We were much alarmed, as a general conflagration of the country seemed likely to ensue. The Turks with their sabres cut down boughs, and we all begun buffetting the flames, which were at length subdued; the ruins somewhat retarding their progress, and enabling us to combat them more effectually. The struggle lasted about an hour, and a considerable tract of ground was laid waste. Close by was an area with dry matted grass, where no exertion could have delayed the fire, but in a moment it would have acquired the mastery, and must have ravaged uncontrolled, until repelled by the wind. The janizary signalized his prowess in this engagement. The sun shone exceedingly hot, and we were all covered with smoke and smut.

In the evening we returned to the vineyard, and found our cook, with two or three of the Turks, busy in a hovel, roasting a kid on a wooden spit or stake. We sat down with our Jew and janizary, and the flesh proved excellent. Our table was a mat on the ground, beneath a spreading vine. Our men formed a like group at a little distance from us. Soon after we fell asleep, and the starry heaven was our canopy.

THE THEATER AT MILETOS[19] (Figure 6)

Miletus is a very mean place, but still called Palat or Palatia, *the Palaces*. The principal relic of its former magnificence is a ruined theatre, which is visible afar off, and was a most capacious edifice, measuring in front four hundred and fifty-seven feet. The external face of this vast fabric is marble, and the stones have a projection near the upper edge, which, we surmised, might contribute to the raising them with facility. The seats ranged, as usual, on the slope of a hill, and a few of them remain. The vaults, which supported the extremities of the semicircle, with the arches or avenues in the two wings, are constructed with such solidity as not easily to be demolished. The entrance of the vault or substruction, on the left side, was filled up with soil; but we examined that next the river; one of our Armenians going before us with a candle in a long paper lantern. The moment we had crept in, innumerable large bats began flitting about us. The stench was hardly tolerable; and the commotion of the air, with the apprehensions of our attendant, threatened us with the loss of our light. After we had gone a considerable way in, we found the passage choked with dry filth, and returned.

The whole site of the town, to a great extent, is spread with rubbish, and overrun with thickets. The vestiges of the heathen city are

Figure 6: William Pars, *The Theater at Miletos,* 296mm x 471mm, Watercolor. ©Trustees of the British Museum.

Figure 7: William Pars, *Temple of Apollo, Didyma*, 299mm x 469mm, Watercolor. ©Trustees of the British Museum.

pieces of wall, broken arches, and a few scattered pedestals, and inscriptions, a square marble urn, and many wells. One of the pedestals has belonged to a statue of the emperor Hadrian, who was a friend to the Milesians, as appears from the titles of saviour and benefactor bestowed on him. Another has supported the emperor Severus, and has a long inscription, with this curious preamble: "The senate and people of the city of the Milesians, the first settled in Ionia, and the mother of many and great cities both in Pontus and Egypt, and in various other parts of the world." This lies among the bushes behind the theatre. Near the ferry is a large lion in a couchant posture, much injured; and in a Turkish burying-ground another. These were placed on graves, or perhaps before a building for ornament. Some fragments of ordinary churches are interspersed among the ruins; and traces remain of an old fortress erected upon the theatre, beneath which is a square enclosure, designed, it seems, as a station for an armed party to dispute or defend the passage of the river. Several piers of a mean aqueduct are standing. The fountain named from Biblis, with the scene of the stories concerning her passion, was in the territory of Miletus. A marble quarry, if

I mistake not, is discernible on the mountain, which bounds the plain on the left hand, at a distance toward the sea.

THE TEMPLE OF APOLLO AT DIDYMA[20] *(Figures 7 and 8)*

The temple of Apollo was eighteen or twenty stadia, or about two miles and a half, from the shore; and one hundred and eighty stadia, or twenty-two miles and a half, from Miletus. It is approached by a gentle ascent, and seen afar off; the land toward the sea lying flat and level. The memory of the pleasure which this spot afforded me will not be soon or easily erased. The columns yet entire are so exquisitely fine, the marble mass so vast and noble, that it is impossible perhaps to conceive greater beauty and majesty of ruin. At evening, a large flock of goats, returning to the fold, their bells tinkling, spread over the heap, climbing to browse on the shrubs and trees growing between the huge stones. The whole mass was illuminated by the declining sun with a variety of rich tints, and cast a very strong shade. The sea, at a distance, was smooth and shining, bordered by a mountainous coast, with rocky islands. The picture was as delicious as striking. A view of part of the

Figure 8: William Pars, *Didyma*, 180mm x 210mm, Watercolor. ©Trustees of the British Museum.

heap, with plates of the architecture of this glorious edifice, has been engraved and published, with its history, at the expense of the society of Dilettanti.[21]

We found among the ruins, which are extensive, a plain stone cistern, covered, except an end, with soil; many marble coffins, unopened, or with the lids broken; and one, in which was a thigh bone; all sunk deep in earth: with five statues, near each other, in a row, almost buried. In the stubble of some Turkey wheat were a number of bee-hives, each a long hollow trunk of wood headed like a barrel, piled in a heap. An Armenian, who was with me, on our putting up a hare, to my surprise slunk away. This animal, as I was afterwards informed, is held in abomination by that people, and the seeing it accounted an ill omen.

The temple of Apollo Didymeus seeming likely to detain us some time, we regretted the entire solitude of the spot, which obliged us to fix our quarters at Ura. Our Armenian cook, who tarried there with our baggage, sent us provisions ready dressed, and we dined under a shady tree by the ruins. Our horses were tied, and feeding by us. Our camel-leader testified his benevolence and regard, by frequent tenders of his short pipe, and of coffee, which he made unceasingly, sitting cross-legged by a small fire. The crows settled in large companies round about, and the partridge called in the stubble.

At our return in the evening to Ura, we found two fires, with our kettles boiling, in the open air, amid the huts and thickets. A mat was spread for us on the ground by one of them. The Turks of Ura, about fourteen in number, some with long beards, sitting cross-legged, helped to complete the grotesque circle. We were lighted by the moon, then full, and shining in a blue cloudless sky. The Turks smoked, talked, and drank coffee with great gravity, composure, and deliberation. One entertained us with playing on the Turkish guitar, and with uncouth

singing. The thin-voiced women, curious to see us, glided as ghosts across the glades, in white, with their faces muffled. The assemblage and the scene was uncommonly wild, and as solemn as savage.

The attention and knowledge of our guests was wholly confined to agriculture, their flocks and herds. They called the ruin of the temple an old castle, and we inferred from their answers to our inquiries about it, that the magnificence of the building had never excited in them one reflection, or indeed attracted their observation, even for a moment. Our discourse, which was carried on by interpreters, not very expert in the Italian language, soon became languid and tiresome; and the fatigues of the day contributed to render repose and silence desirable. We retired after supper to one of the huts, which was near the fire, and, like the rest, resembled a soldier's tent, being made with poles inclining, as the two sides of a triangle, and thatched with straw. It was barely a covering for three persons lying on the ground. The furniture was a jar of salted olives, at the farther end. Our men slept round the fire, and watched some hours for an opportunity to shoot the bull, which twice came near the huts, allured by the cattle. He then changed his haunt, removing to a thicket at a distance, where we frequently saw him, or heard him roar. The weather as yet was clear and pleasant, and the sun powerful. We drooped with heat at noon, but at night experienced cold, and in the morning our thatch was dripping with wet.

The disorders which began to prevail among us required a speedy exchange of the thickets for some lodging less damp and chilly. We renewed our journey, after two entire days, with satisfaction; leaving the temple at eleven, on a Friday, and travelling nearly south-eastward over low stony land covered with tufts or bushes. Before us was the mountain anciently called Grius, a high craggy range, parallel to mount Latmus; then stretching from the Milesian territory eastward through Caria as far as Euromus, which was on the seacoast, and once a place of some consequence.

ARCH AND TOMB AT MILAS[22] *(Figures 9 and 10)*

Mylasa, or Mylassa, was the capital of Hecatomnus, king of Caria, and father of Mausolus. It has been described as situated by a very fertile plain, with a mountain rising above it, in which was a quarry of very fine white marble. This being near, was exceedingly convenient in building, and had contributed greatly to the beauty of the city, which, it is said, if any, was handsomely adorned with public edifices, porticoes, and temples. The latter were so numerous, that a certain musician entering the market-place, as if to make proclamation, began, instead of, *Hear, ye people,* with, *Hear, ye temples.* The founders of the city were censured as inconsiderate in placing it beneath a steep precipice, by which it was commanded. Under the Romans it was a free city. Its distance from the sea, where nearest, or from Physcus, opposite the island of Rhodes, was eighty stadia, or ten miles. It is still a large place, commonly called Melasso. The houses are numerous, but chiefly of plaster, and mean, with trees interspersed. The air is accounted bad; and scorpions abound, as anciently, entering often at the doors and windows, and lurking in the rooms. The plain is surrounded by lofty mountains, and cultivated; but was now parched and bare, except some spots green with the tobacco plant, which was in flower, and pleasing to the eye.

Figure 9: William Pars, *Arch at Milas*, 296mm x 471mm, Watercolor. ©Trustees of the British Museum.

Our first inquiry was for the temple, erected about twelve years before the Christian era by the people of Mylasa to Augustus Caesar and the goddess Rome, which was standing not many years ago. We were shewn the basement, which remains, and were informed the ruin had been demolished, and a new mosque, which we saw on the mountain-side, above the town, raised with the marble. The house of a Turk occupying the site, we employed the Hungarian to treat with him for admission; but he affirmed we could see nothing; and added, that there was his haram, or the apartment of his women, which was an obstacle not to be surmounted. It had six columns in front, and the whole number had been twenty-two.

On the hill, and not far from the basement of the temple, is a column of the Corinthian order, standing, with a flat-roofed cottage, upon a piece of solid wall. It has supported a statue, and on the shaft is an inscription. "The people have erected Menander, son of Ouliades, son of Euthydemus, a benefactor to his country, and descended from benefactors." The Turk, who lived in the cottage, readily permitted a ladder to be placed on the terrace for measuring the capital, which was done as expeditiously as possible, but not before we were informed that

several of the inhabitants murmured because their houses were over-looked. Besides this, two fluted columns of the Ionic order remained not many years since.

Beneath the hill, on the east side of the town, is an arch or gateway of marble, of the Corinthian order. On the keystone of the exterior front, which is eastward, we observed a double hatchet, as on the two marbles near Myus. It was with difficulty we procured ladders to reach the top; and some were broken before we could find three sufficiently long and strong for our purpose. The going up, when these were united, was not without danger. The aga had expressed some wonder at our employment, as described to him; and seeing one of my companions on the arch,[23] from a window of his house, which was opposite, pronounced him, as we were told, a brave fellow, but without brains. We desired him to accept our umbrella, on his sending to purchase it for a present to a lady of his haram, who was going into the country. By the arch was a fountain, to which women came with earthen pitchers for water, and with their faces muffled.

We saw a broad marble pavement, with vestiges of a theatre, near the Corinthian column. Toward the centre of the town we observed a

Figure 10: William Pars, *Tomb at Milas,* 297mm x 471mm, Watercolor. ©Trustees of the British Museum.

small pool of water, and by it the massive arches of some public edifice. In the court of the aga's house was an altar much ornamented. We found an altar likewise in the streets, and a pedestal or two half buried, with pieces of ancient wall. Round the town are ranges of broken columns, the remnants of porticoes, now, with rubbish, bounding the vineyards. A large portion of the plain is covered with scattered fragments, and with piers of ordinary aqueducts; besides inscriptions, mostly ruined and illegible. Some altars dedicated to Hecatomnus have been discovered.

About a quarter of a mile from the town is a sepulchre, of the species called by the ancients *distega,* or *double-roofed.* It consisted of two square rooms. In the lower, which has a doorway, were deposited the urns with the ashes of the deceased. In the upper, the relations and friends solemnized the anniversary of the funeral, and performed stated rites. A hole made through the floor was designed for pouring libations of honey, milk, or wine, with which it was usual to gratify the manes or spirits. The roof is remarkable for its construction; but two stones are wanting, and some distorted. It is supported by pillars of the Corinthian order, fluted, some of which have suffered from violence,

being hewn near the bases, with a view to destroy the fabric for the iron and materials. The shafts are not circular, but elliptical; and in the angular columns square. The reason is, the sides, which are now open, were closed with marble pannels; and that form was necessary to give them a due projection. The inside has been painted blue. This structure is the first object, as you approach from Iasus, and stands by the road. The entrance was on the farther side, the ascent to it probably by a pair of steps, occasionally applied and removed.

Going down from this building, and turning from Mylasa, westward, you have the mountain on the right hand, and come, in about an hour, to another sepulchre. This is cut in the rock, high up in the side, near the top, and very difficult of access. Within the doorway on each side is a seat or bench, on which, it is likely, the urns were placed; and beyond is a smaller camera, or arched room. Over the entrance, without, is carved in basso relievo a facade; two Tuscan pillars between two pilasters, with an entablature and pediment, and a door. The slope of the mountain has been covered with innumerable sepulchres. In this the Swiss, as he told us, had persevered, digging for three nights, hoping to find some hidden treasure.

CONCLUSION: "Embark for England"[24]

On leaving Athens it was our purpose, after refreshing at Zante, to proceed to Ithaca, Cephallenia, and Corfu, the countries of Ulysses and Alcinous; and from the latter island to Brindisi and Naples. We were compelled to abandon that plan by the difficulty of procuring from Leghorn so large a sum of money as was necessary, and, besides other considerations, by the infirm state of health under which we laboured. The consul accepted our bills for three hundred Venetian zechins; of which near one hundred and thirty were remitted to Mr. Paul the consul at Patrae, who had most readily and obligingly supplied us to that amount. Our return to England was resolved on, and we waited impatiently for the ships expected from Venice; whither it is required that all vessels go before they lade with currants at Zante.

During our residence in the city, the house of a person who had fled from justice was razed to the ground by a party of soldiers; and the body of a state-prisoner, one Balsamachi of Cephallenia, who had been sent in irons from Constantinople, was exposed for a day on a gallows. He succeeded us in our apartments in the Lazaretto, and, when his quarantine expired, was privately strangled there, conveyed in a boat across the harbour, and suspended in the morning early; a paper hanging on his breast, inscribed with his name, his country, and crime in capital letters.

Some smaller vessels, which arrived, brought us intelligence that the *Roman Emperor,* captain Lad, and the *Sea-horse,* captain James, for London, were preparing to sail from Venice. We agreed for a passage, and put our baggage and provisions on board the *Roman Emperor,* but were induced to remand them; and then fixed our hopes on the *Sea-horse.* That ship tarrying elsewhere, we embarked in the evening, on Sunday, September the 1st, New Style, 1766, in the brig *Diligence,* captain Long, carrying five men and two boys, bound for Bristol. After a stormy and perilous voyage we anchored in King-road on the 2nd of November; but the *Sea-horse* was lost at Scilly on the 11th of the following month. ❦

Endnotes

1. Pars' brief career was best summed up by his friend and fellow artist Thomas Jones who lamented his death thus in November 1782: "He was appointed by the Dillettante Society to accompany Dr Chandler and Mr Revett as Draughtsman in their journey to Greece-He afterward travelled with Lord Palmerston, over Switzerland, Part of Germany and Ireland in the same Capacity-And this habit of life, notwithstanding his affected Protestations to the Contrary, certainly gave him an inward bias in favour of Landscape, though brought up to Portrait-He executed his tinted Drawings after nature, with a taste peculiar to himself-And though, in a fit of the Spleen, he would sometimes curse his fate, in being obliged to follow such trifling an Employment; as he called it-it was with the greatest Difficulty his Friends could detach him from this favourite Study, and persuade him to apply to Portrait painting-in which line there was now a fair Opening-He took our advice at last, and the Success he met with justified our Opinion-but-Poor Pars! his good fortune came too late to do him much Service-I shall only add that though he was rather hasty and sometimes indeed Violent in his Temper-He was a Warm and sincere friend-Adieu Dear Pars! Adieu." See A. P. Oppé, ed., "Memoirs of Thomas Jones, Penkerrig, Radnorshire," *Walpole Society,* 32 (1946-8).
2. Some were published in black and white in R. Chandler, *Travels in Asia Minor 1764-1765,* edited and abridged by Edith Clay (London: British Museum, 1971). All the drawings by William Pars reproduced here are ©Trustees of the British Museum.
3. Richard Chandler, *Travels in Asia Minor and Greece* (Oxford: Clarendon Press, 1825). Punctuation, though not spelling, has occasionally been modernized; ellipses have not been indicated.
4. *Idem,* Vol. II, Chapters 8-11.
5. Mythical founder and first king of Athens.
6. Mount Pentelikon.
7. The port of Athens.
8. The temple of Athena Nike.
9. Kislar Aga, the chief eunuch.
10. Similar sentiments, no doubt, motivated Lord Elgin some thirty-five years later.
11. The whereabouts of these fragments of the frieze removed by Chandler's group is not known; see Mary Beard, *The Parthenon* (London: Profile Books, 2002), p. 86.
12. Jacques Carrey, on whose drawings see T. Bowie and D. Thimme, *The Carrey Drawings of the Parthenon Sculptures* (Bloomington: Indiana University Press, 1971).
13. Here Chandler makes the common mistake of assuming that Vitruvius' account of Caryatids refers to the Porch of the Maidens of the Erechtheion. On this confusion see Alexandra L Lesk, "Caryatides probantur inter pauca operum: Pliny, Vitruvius, and the Semiotics of the Erechtheion Maidens at Rome" in *Arethusa,* Volume 40, Number 1, Winter 2007, pp. 25-42.
14. *Idem,* Vol. 1, Chapter 2.
15. From the Saronic island of Hydra in the Aegean sea.
16. Some decades later, Byron added to this mass of graffiti by infamously scratching his own name on one of the columns of this temple; Beard, *op. cit.,* p. 14.
17. *Idem,* Vol. 1, Chapters 9-10. The modern name for Alexandria Troas, which is situated on western coast of Turkey, is Eski Stambul.
18. A bath-gymnasium complex built by Herodes Atticus.
19. *Idem,* Vol 1, Chapter 42. William Pars here depicts Richard Chandler already on the ferry and dismounted, while Nicholas Revett and Pars himself are about to board.
20. *Idem,* Vol. 1, Chapters 43-4.
21. See *Ionian Antiquities,* Vol. I, 1769, Chapter III.
22. *Idem,* Vol. 1, Chapter 56. Modern-day Milas in South-western Turkey.
23. Probably Revett, to measure the entablature as can be seen in Pars' watercolor.
24. *Idem,* Vol. 2, Chapter 79.

Book Reviews

Mirror, Mirror…

CARL LAUBIN: PAINTINGS
*By John Russell Taylor and David Watkin. Designed by Norman Turpin.
London: Plus One Publishing, 2007.*

Reviewed by Richard W. Cameron

FOR STUDENTS OF CLASSICAL ARCHITECTURE the 1980s were exciting but fraught years—filled with the hope that postmodernism would evolve into a full-blown classical revival while we teetered on the edge of deconstruction and a resurrected mid-century modernism. Those of us who began our studies at that time all remember the "style" battles as they played out in the journals of the day— *Progressive Architecture, Architectural Record, Blueprint* et al. In the midst of this eclectic noise one journal often stood out—particularly because of its striking covers. They occasionally broke through the cloud of argument like a beautiful tune out of the fog, beckoning us to a different place: part an evocation of an idealized past and part a gently utopian future. The journal was AD (*Architectural Design*, published by Andreas Papadakis, who is sadly no longer with us), which was almost alone in publishing the work of the artists and architects working their way towards a classical revival. The most striking images AD published in those years (to my mind) were two paintings: one a limpid view along the Thames of a new housing project by Jeremy Dixon and Associates for the Isle of Dogs (*Dudgeon's Wharf*, 1986); and one a "Claudeian" view of Léon Krier's project for a new town on the island of Tenerife (*Atlantis at Sunrise*, 1987). Both of these paintings (for they are clearly that and not simply architectural renderings) have a kind of shimmering quality that simultaneously evoke painters like Claude and Corot while clearly being works of contemporary realism. I remember wondering at the time "who is Carl Laubin (the artist) and what is his background?" I found out eventually that he trained at Cornell as an architect and had worked for the London-based architect Jeremy Dixon for a number of years (in fact it was through Laubin's work for Dixon

Carl Laubin, *Dudgeon's Wharf,* 81cm x 110cm, Oil on Canvas.

that both became well-known in North America). The series of paintings that Laubin produced of Dixon's project for the Royal Opera House at Covent Garden conveyed a frolicking and lively reality, set against the background of Dixon's new buildings. They made the vision of a revived traditional architecture seem entirely believeable and of our time—if slightly theatrical and sanitized. Other striking images followed of projects by Léon Krier, John Simpson, and John Outram— each one more convincing than the last. And then the moment passed. Postmodernism ran its course and was quickly replaced by deconstuction and a return to conservative modernism. The new classicists went on and the movement grew but it has lacked the visibility and vitality that AD and Laubin's paintings gave it in the 1980s. And of course Carl Laubin kept on painting.

Now we have this marvelous new book *Carl Laubin: Paintings* by John Russell Taylor and David Watkin, which draws aside the veil on the artist and his practice—at least in part. We should all be grateful for this book for several reasons, but the first and most important is the publication of Laubin's work to date. Not only are the AD cover paintings included, but much else which is equally, if not more important. Laubin's early work was influenced by artists like Hopper and Hockney, and his own background as an architectural draughtsman trained at Cornell. Laubin's father was an instrument maker and an amateur painter, and Laubin received his early artistic training from him. Both essays by Prof. Watkin and Prof. Taylor (which run in parallel following Laubin's career and work and provide two independent assessments of it) give us a good feeling for his formation as an artist. So there are early paintings like *Holly Place,* which combine realistic painting with drawing in a finished work, playing with the conventions of both, or *Madame X,* which combines a quotation of the famous Sargent painting with fragments from architectural plans and profiles.

The other preoccupation in Laubin's early work is with photorealism, which while technically virtuoso is somehow less appealing. There are sweeping views of the English coast almost invariably including the figure of the artist's wife walking away from the viewer, paintings of boats, of the seashore, and the British countryside, all rendered in loving if sometimes hard-edged detail. These eschew any architectural preoccupation and focus exclusively on the landscape in the changing light. Prof. Watkin's essay does a thorough job of placing Laubin's work in its historical context tracing both the contemporary realist influences at work as well as the work of earlier painters like Claude, Canaletto, Guardi, and others. Prof. Watkin's focus on the capriccio is significant because as Laubin's career progressed he composed more and more elaborate variations on the capriccio, not so much in its seventeenth- and eighteenth-century imaginary topographical mode—though there are examples of this in his work—but the full-blown architectural fantasy model of Joseph Gandy's illustrations of the work of John Soane. Gandy's drawings, which influenced later architects like C. R. Cockerell and others, show Soane's work assembled as models and drawings in interiors of Soane's invention, often including the architect in the view. There is a febrility and obsessiveness to these drawings which adds to the virtuoso quality of the image and often leaves one with the feeling of a kind of architectural monomania—though highly pleasurable and stimulating. Laubin's paintings in this mode are almost too extraordinary to describe. From his *Almerico to Zeno* of 1992 to the extraordinary *Grotescha* of 1994—a commissioned painting for the National Trust—Laubin pushes this type of painting to technical and artistic levels that are genuinely novel. His eye for architectural detail, and for the material of building is unerring, and he exploits this in most of the paintings in one way or another. So we are presented with a series of images that almost overwhelm, first because of the high quality of the architecture being represented, and secondly for the compositional complexity. In one of these, *Rowe Interotta* of which there are several versions, the face of the influential architectural historian Colin Rowe, peers out, ghost-like, from behind the reconstructed and fragmented Tempietto of Bramante; a combination of Beaux-Arts analytique and postmodern fragment worship that is almost eerie.

Laubin has been commissioned by a number of modernist architects to paint views of their buildings, but in my opinion the results are less compelling, perhaps because Laubin's sympathies seem to lie so clearly with his beloved surface rendering of traditional materials and their presentation in light and shadow with the effects of weathering and time articulated in meticulous detail. The one exception is the moving series of paintings of the ruins of the World Trade Center entitled *Elegos.* The power of Laubin's technique renders this not only a compelling testament to the terrible attack on this country, but also a prescient view of what many of our cities will one day look like to future visitors.

If there is a regret about this book it is that there are too few of the drawings and studies Laubin makes in preparation for the final paintings. There are wonderful glimpses of them—like those for the Villa Rotunda paintings or *Si Monumentum Requiris*—which give us a sense of Laubin's method from pencil sketches and drawings studying the composition of the paintings, to loose oil studies that demonstrate his facility in a more impressionistic style (it seems he would be as facile in making paintings in the manner of Walcot as he is of Gandy). But it would be instructive and valuable to have more.

Laubin's voice, while it is absent in the written part of the book, speaks exquisitely and voluminously through his work, and the book's lavish color gives a glowing sense of the impact the paintings must have in a gallery or hanging on the wall of a private house. Many of the collectors of Laubin's paintings have commissioned multiple works, and one can imagine them, like the great Canaletto collections, their luminous views of great architecture shining out into majestic rooms and halls. The Hon. Simon Howard, whose family owns Castle Howard, is of particular note in this context. Envision Laubin's superb renditions of Vanbrugh's great house, along with his other buildings, and Hawksmoor's brooding, solemn Mausoleum adorning the walls of the very buildings they depict. There is a quality in all of this of a mirror world that is endlessly reflecting, refracting, recomposing, and representing the material world of architecture through Laubin's fertile imagination and his extraordinary facility as a painter. It comes very close, it seems to me, to fulfilling the best of the promise of postmodernism, while maintaining the rigorous standards of great painting and the architectural tradition. Of course if all of this becomes a bit overwhelming, one can return from the looking-glass world to the simple beauty of *Dudgeon's Wharf* and its depiction of a calm, rain-puddled world of Thames-side tranquility.

My final regret is that this book is not the catalogue to a gallery show in this country of Laubin's remarkable work. Even so, this book serves as a splendid introduction to the painter and his paintings—and we can always wait and hope.

Richard W. Cameron is a diretor of the Ariel Atelier. He also serves as vice-chairman of the ICA&CA's Board of Directors.

John Fowler Revisited

JOHN FOWLER: PRINCE OF DECORATORS
By Martin Wood. London: Frances Lincoln Ltd., 2007.

JOHN FOWLER: THE INVENTION OF THE COUNTRY-HOUSE STYLE
Edited by Helen Hughes. Shaftesbury: Donhead Publishing Ltd., 2005.

Reviewed by William Brockschmidt

THE NOTION OF THE ENGLISH COUNTRY HOUSE has, throughout its history, transcended a great variety of architectural expressions to represent an idealized lifestyle and elite status. Regardless of whether the aristocratic dwelling house is a Jacobean pile, a Palladian mansion, a "Gothick" folly or a Regency villa, it is the characteristically traditional decorating style of the mythic English country house that has captured the popular imagination. It may surprise many to learn that this attitude towards decorating, which emphasizes continuity, expressions of innate taste, unpretentious elegance, and unapologetic comfort, was created not so long ago in the vision of one of the twentieth century's most influential decorators, John Fowler.

Fowler is the subject of two recent books: *John Fowler: The Invention of the Country-House Style* was edited by Helen Hughes and released in 2005, and *John Fowler: Prince of Decorators* by Martin Wood was published in late 2007.

Nothing may delight the practicing classicist architect book-collector more than an architectural monograph or historical survey that features clear photographs accompanied with useful scale drawings. For the interior designer, however, nothing can compare with large, detailed photographs for reference and inspiration. Martin Wood, an English designer of textiles, interiors, and gardens, understands this well and has included in his book about the life and work of John Fowler over 400 color illustrations in large format and striking colors. In addition to the evocative photographs showing complete rooms, many of Fowler's instructional design sketches are shown juxtaposed with a photograph of the completed element. The sketches most often describe the elaborate curtain designs for which he was famously innovative. Fowler's interest in historic document textiles, wallpapers, and carpet patterns is presented with close-up details of the designs he created and of the historic patterns he copied and re-colored in his own interpretations. The splendid illustrations amply make this book invaluable to decorators who will use it as a visual catalog for inspiration without ever reading more than a few captions and chapter titles. In fact, the book has been designed so that one can effectively glean the evolution of Fowler's style merely by observing the photographs chronologically by chapter. Apparent is Fowler's sophisticated mastery of color, often in unusual hues or combinations, but so thoroughly integrated within the architectural elements, carpets, curtains, upholstery, furniture, and art that the effect is perfectly harmonized. Also evident is Fowler's genius in placing furniture for aesthetic effect and practical comfort. His respect for the details and proportions of fine period architecture, as well as inventive solutions for less-than-perfect conditions are perceptible within the photographs.

However, it is well worthwhile for the decorator to read Martin Wood's text, which thoughtfully integrates the life and work of John Fowler within the context of his era, from his early influences and development, to his celebrity as a sought-after style-maker, and finally to his authority as an historic figure in the history and evolution of the English Country House. The biography charts Fowler's early career as a decorative painter of "antique" wallpaper and furniture. After he established his own studio, John Beresford Fowler, he quickly gained renown and success as an enterprising and creative decorator. There are several illustrations of his well-published and influential flat on the King's Road in bohemian 1930s Chelsea in London, and several illustrations of other early published projects. By the time he joined the reputable society decorator, Sybil Colefax, eight years later, young Fowler was already recognized as one of England's top eight decorators. The partnership with Lady Colefax merged her established clientele with his younger set. However, the war diminished their business, and then her declining health and personal finances forced her to sell Sybil Colefax and John Fowler, Ltd., to the Virginian, Nancy Tree.

Nancy Tree, later Nancy Lancaster, was renowned for her highly personal and influential redecoration of two eighteenth-century James Gibbs-designed mansions, Kelmarsh Hall and Ditchley Park. Although she did not officially practice decorating within the firm, Nancy Lancaster worked as business-owner and client with John Fowler on her house in London, her latest country house, Haseley Court, and later her suite of rooms within the Colefax and Fowler shop. In this period, most of the Colefax and Fowler clients were Nancy Lancaster's English and American friends or connections, so for ten years she actively participated in the projects. Both Fowler and Lancaster were headstrong and opinionated, and although they were famously quoted as being "the most unhappy unmarried couple in England" for their constant bickering, they discovered much from each other. In particular, Fowler was inspired by her notions of American comfort and observed how she lived gracefully and stylishly within a great house.

The book essentially traces Fowler's life and career chronologically, but the author describes the full extent of the collaboration between John Fowler and Nancy Lancaster in an early chapter. Two other telling chapters also span Fowler's entire life and career: One describes his personal life and personality by focusing on his adored country house called "The Hunting Lodge," the design laboratory where he spent weekends and holidays with friends and invited guests, and where he also developed his beloved garden. Another chapter called "Elements of a Style; the Inspiration of the Eighteenth Century," describes the work practices of John Fowler. For those who do not wish to read the entire book, this chapter could be considered an independent essay, illustrating the prevailing tastes and trends throughout his career, the influences that he transformed into innovations, his preferences and

(opposite page): Staircase at the National Trust's Sudbury Hall, Derbyshire, as redecorated by Fowler.

sources for materials, and the way he worked with his clients, staff, artisans, and craftspeople. It discusses specifically how he used fabrics, passementerie, wallpapers, carpets, and furniture, and how he developed paint techniques to give vitality to historic houses. The chapter ends by describing how he achieved additional influence and authority by co-authoring with John Cornforth the reference book, *English Decoration in the Eighteenth Century (1974)*.

The other chapters sequentially chronicle the many projects of John Fowler. Within each project are portrayals of the clients and their houses, the decorating programs, and Fowler's decorative solutions in great detail. Earlier projects undertaken during wartime and immediate post-war rationing are characterized by chic austerity and creative uses of available or salvaged fabrics and recycled materials, such as dyed army blankets and table cloths. The more luxurious interiors that Fowler created when comfort and optimism returned to England in the 1950s lead to Fowler's preeminent position as a "haute couture decorator" in which he could select his clients. His renown continued throughout the 1960s when he was in his busiest and most prolific period. In these chapters there are many beautiful projects well-documented by color photographs and peppered with interesting anecdotes. However, when the individual details for the curtains, linings, trimmings, painted glazes, underglazes, and secondary and tertiary paint colors are all recounted for every project, these chapters of the biography can become a bit tedious. Conversely, as a decorating resource, one truly appreciates the extent of written detail and the quantity of photographs, some of which are obviously unstyled snapshots taken during site-visits. In fact, one wishes that the author had been able to supplement the photos by conjuring up a John Fowler paint-color chart to compare the photographic images with color chips illustrating the actual hues of tangerine-apricot, grey-white, lilac, or more elusively described colors such as "mouse back" and "the soul of blue."

Although John Fowler was urged by private clients to take on work into the early 1970s, the last twenty years of his life were also occupied by several projects for the National Trust, which had acquired many properties due to the burdens of post-war taxation. Beginning with Claydon in 1956, Fowler was asked to donate decorating services in order to restore and preserve stately houses in such a way as to attract visitors. Many of the houses, such as Sudbury Hall, were what Fowler called "dead houses" in that they no longer had any furniture or art, but were bare rooms. Throughout his decorating career, Fowler often took cues from existing conditions, in particular "paint scrapes" from which entire color schemes were inspired. In his work for the Trust, he would utilise his talents and creativity as a decorator to accentuate the architectural character and capture the spirit of the room. In *English Decoration in the Eighteenth Century* he describes his goals in his work for the Trust: "Of course all attempt to play up the character of the decoration could have been resisted, and the whole place could have been frozen, but particularly in a sparsely furnished house…whose sole use is to be shown to visitors, the impact on those visitors must be considered and they must be given an experience that is as rich and enjoyable as possible." Martin Wood admits that Fowler's approach received some criticism from historians and preservationists of the time, and that today's atti-

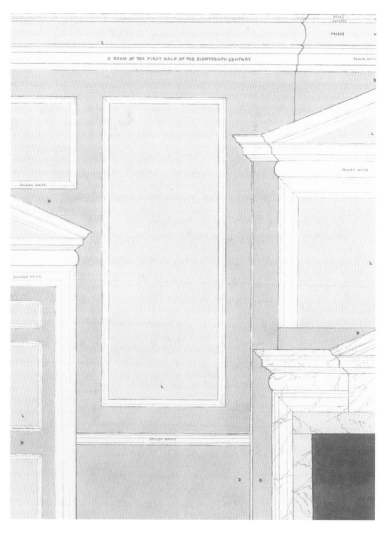

(above): Diagram from John Fowler's book on eighteenth-century English decoration, showing his scheme for painting panelling in three shades of white.

tudes towards restoration are such that a fashionable decorator would not likely be involved in period restoration work. However, Fowler's work on Trust properties is now worthy of preservation on its own terms as a twentieth-century interpretation by one of the period's most influential British decorators.

Martin Wood's *John Fowler: Prince of Decorators*, as the title implies, celebrates the man and the influential work of John Fowler. As such, it is an extraordinary visual assemblage and description of his work, and is an important reference for the decorators and an enjoyable biography for the enthusiast. On the other hand, *John Fowler: The Invention of the Country-House Style*, would best be a supplement to those interested in the work of John Fowler or a reference book to those interested in his influence on preservation and restoration or the evolution of the English country house in a more academic vein. The book is a collection of papers delivered at two conferences both co-organized by the Traditional Paint Forum, the Kelmarsh Preservation Trust, and English Heritage. The book was edited by Helen Hughes, the Head of Historic Interiors Research & Conservation for English Heritage and Events Organizer of the Traditional Paint Forum. The conferences sought to discuss John Fowler's work for the National Trust in terms of his legacy to the English country house tradition as both a fashionable decorator of the mid-twentieth century and an interpreter of historic house restoration. Because the events were organized by the Traditional Paint Forum, and also because the painting scheme was often the most effective way to enliven the decorative scheme of "dead" houses, the papers deal predominantly with Fowler's paint treatments in historic interiors. While admitting Fowler's contributions to the continuum of country house interiors, the papers typically admonish his interpretations, and caution against the role of the fashionable decorator within the realm of preservation.

It is helpful to have a general knowledge of Fowler's work when reading this collection of papers, as the illustrations included are limited to specifically serve points made in the arguments presented. Even the introduction by Helen Hughes presupposes an audience with substantial familiarity with John Fowler and his work with the Trust. The first paper, "Working with John Fowler" by Peter Inskip, an architect who worked with Fowler on some Trust properties, admirably describes John Fowler's working methods and character. Especially insightful are Inskip's recollections of the way Fowler reacted to evidence uncovered during the restoration process that would influence the final interpretation for a room. In light of current research, Inskip concludes that Fowler's "historical" treatment of picking out architectural details in three complementary shades was a romantic notion of how old paint appeared rather than any treatment used in the eighteenth century.

"John Fowler and the National Trust" by Tim Knox, the head curator of the National Trust, continues the theme of Fowler's interpretive painting schemes with examples, some of which were contentious at the time of the "restorations." While Knox admits that the National Trust, as a "guardian of historic-house museums, should not perhaps have permitted a decorator to impose his taste upon them in a way that a private proprietor might do" he also admits that Fowler's approach was grounded with historic sensitivity and provided neglected houses with a strong architectural character, which in the best cases are worth preserving as historic examples of his twentieth-century interpretations.

Christine Sitwell, Painting Conservation Advisor of the National Trust, points out in "Recent Investigations of Fowler Schemes" that recent scientific paint analysis confirms that Fowler actually misinterpreted paint evidence upon which his decorating schemes are based in two Trust houses. While crediting his regard for the problematic paint scrapes, she concludes that his interiors now require careful consideration because, as Cornforth's disclaimer explains, Fowler "strove for beauty within the limits of that evidence rather than a strict reproduction."

Private paint specialist, Patrick Baty, is more pointed in "Inspired by the Past" in which he points out inconsistancies, contradictions, and apparent misunderstandings written by Fowler and Cornforth in *English Decoration in the Eighteenth Century* regarding historic paint techniques and

materials. Ian Bristol, an architect and consultant, implies criticism of Fowler's interpretation of color in his paper "Color in Historic Houses in Public Ownership" in which he describes the development of more conservative and authentic restoration approaches for such historic house museums undertaken from the 1930s to 1980s. A paper by Marianne Suhl, a surveyor for the Society for the Preservation of Ancient Buildings and another paper by Ian Bristol focus on Nancy Lancaster's Kelmarsh Hall, in particular a thorough investigation of the evidence and quality of the famous pink walls.

Finally, Louise Ward, a design historian at the Royal College of Art, contributes "English Country-House Style: The English Country House as it might have been but never was," in which she describes how the "fiction" of the English country house can be traced to the taste and personality of Nancy Lancaster. She describes how the style was developed professionally with John Fowler to become the recognizable Colefax and Fowler aesthetic. However, as a style it was imitated and idealized, reinterpreted, and misinterpreted, becoming along the way a hoax and fantasy.

Although Ms. Ward's paper does not qualify as a conclusion since *John Fowler: The Invention of the Country-House Style* is not conceived as a book by one author, its tone does send a warning to the practitioner who seeks only to emulate without more than a mere appreciation or superficial understanding. However, one can be inspired not only by the visual beauty of John Fowler's country-house style, but by his modern attitudes towards the integration of past and present, beauty and comfort. In decorating and architecture, John Fowler admired and respected the artistic achievements of the past, yet he did not set out to recreate historically accurate period rooms, nor to create his own recognizable brand of style. He worked instinctively to emphasize the best qualities inherent in a room and his vast knowledge of historical details and materials provided him with a language to create rooms that were unique, personal, and beautiful—and so influential that the style would become part of the cultural imagination.

William Brockschmidt co-founded Brockschmidt & Coleman, LLC, in 2001. He is a Fellow of the ICA&CA.

Administration,
Members, and Sponsors

PROFESSIONAL MEMBERS

LATROBE SOCIETY
Professional
Dell Mitchell Architects, Inc.

BENEFACTOR CIRCLE
Professional
Larry E. Boerder Architects

PATRON
Professional
Allan Greenberg, Architects
Alvin Holm AIA Architects
Andrew V. Giambertone & Assoc.
    Architects, PC
Balmer Architectural Mouldings
Bulley & Andrews, LLC
Chadsworth's 1-800-COLUMNS
Dalgleish Construction Company
David Phoenix
Decorators Supply Corp.
Drake Design Associates
Duany Plater-Zyberk & Company, LLC
Eric J. Smith Architect, P.C.
Eric Stengel Architecture
Eric Watson Architect, P.A.
Ervin, Lovett, & Miller, Inc.
Exclusive Cultural Travel Programs
Fairfax & Sammons Architects, PC
Ferguson & Shamamian Architects, LLP
FZAD Architecture + Design, P.C.
G. P. Schafer Architect, PLLC
Giannetti Architecture & Interiors, Inc.
Hottenroth & Joseph Architects
Ike Kligerman Barkley Architects
Insidesign, Inc.
James Doyle Design Associates, LLC
Les Metalliers Champenois (USA)
London Boone, Inc./Mimi London, Inc.
The Marker Group
M. Deane Johnson, Inc.
Mayfair Construction Group, LLC
Merritt Woodwork
Katherine Pasternack
Peter Pennoyer Architects
Project Solutions, LLC
R. D. Rice Construction, Inc.
Robert A. M. Stern Architects, LLP
Robinson Iron Corporation
SBD Kitchens, LLC
Seaside Community Development Corp.
Sebastian Construction Group
Symm Group Limited
TJS Partners, Inc.
White River Hardwoods
William Hefner Architecture, Inc.
Zeluck Inc./Fenestra America
Zepsa Industries

DONOR
Professional
Appleton & Associates, Inc.
Authentic Provence, Inc.
BAMO, Inc.
Barbara Tattersfield Designs, Inc.
Biglin Architectural Group
Lisa Singleton Boudiette
Brian O'Keefe Architect, P.C.
Caccoma Interiors
Campbell Design Associates, Inc.
Charles Warren, Architect
Charlotte Moss Interior Design
Connor Homes
Cowtan and Tout
DSI Entertainment Systems
Fokine Construction Services
Fondation de Coubertin
The Green-Wood Cemetery
Hilton-VanderHorn Architects
Historical Arts & Casting
J. P. Hall Architect, PC
James F. Carter Architect
Jeff Allen Landscape Architecture
JMS Design Associates
John B. Murray Architect, LLC
KAA Design Group, Inc.
Ken Tate Architect, P.A.
LaPolla Painting and Designs Studio, Inc.
Laura Blanco Interiors
Laura Casale Architect
Leonard Porter Studio, LLC
Margolis, Incorporated
Mark P. Finlay Architects, AIA
McCoy Construction
Merrill, Pastor and Colgan Architects
Michael G. Imber, Architects
Michael Middleton Dwyer, Architect
Neil Hauck Architects, LLC
Page Duke Landscape Architects
Reclamation Lumber
Restore Media, LLC
Richard Skinner & Associates, PL
Saint Jacques Artisans Workshops
Scofield Historic Lighting
Soho Construction Group, Inc.
Thomas M. Kirchhoff Architect, AIA, PA
Tucker & Marks
University of Notre Dame
Urban Design Associates
Vintage Millworks, Inc.
William R. Eubanks Interior Design, Inc.
Womack Interiors

SUSTAINER
Professional
A Classical Studio, Inc.
Aedicule Fine Framemaking
Agrell Architectural Carving, Ltd.
AJ.T Architect PC
Alexandros C. Samaras & Associates, SA
Alisberg Parker Architects, LLC
Andre Junget Illustration
Angela Free Design, Inc.
Antonia Hutt & Associates, Inc.
Archer & Buchanan Architecture, Ltd.
Athalie Derse, Inc.
Austin Patterson Disston Architects, LLC
The Beehive Foundation
Berndsen Company, Inc.
Bisazza USA, North America
Minor L. Bishop
BKSK Architects, LLP
Brockschmidt & Coleman, LLC
Brothers' Custom Windows & Doors
BSF Properties, Inc.
Budd Woodwork, Inc.
C2 Limited Design Associates
Cannon Design
Carolina Design Group
Carolina Residential Design
Carpenter & MacNeille,
    Architects & Builders, Inc.
Catalano Architects
Chesney's
The Classical Arts Studio
Clawson Architects, LLC
Commercial Design Group -
    California Office
Cooper, Robertson & Partners
Core Home, Inc.
Cove Construction
Cronk Duch Architecture
H. Beck Crothers
Cullman & Kravis, Inc.
Cumberland Architectural Millwork, Inc.
Curtis and Windham Architects Inc.
D. Stanley Dixon Architect, Inc.
The D. H. Ellison Co.
Daron Builta, Inc.
David Desmond, Inc.
David Jones Architects
Design Built Consulting, Inc.
DiBiase Filkoff Architects
Don B. McDonald Architect AIA, Ltd.
Donald W. Powers Architects, Inc.
Donald Whittaker—The Design Guy Team
Dorosinski Campbell Design Associates, Inc.
Douglas Durkin Design, Inc.
Duncan McRoberts Associates
E. Frank Smith Residential Design, Inc.
E. M. Rose Builders, Inc.
Eberlein Design Consultants, Ltd.
Ecocentrix, Inc.
Ekman Design Studio, Inc.
Elleco Construction

EverGreene Architectural Arts, Inc.
F. H. Perry Builder, Inc.
F. L. Bissinger, Inc.
Fire Rock Products, LLC
The Florentine Craftsmen
Flower Construction
Foutz Construction
Fusch Architects, Inc.
G. Morris Steinbraker & Son, Inc.
Geoffrey Mouen Architects
Georgina Rice & Co., Inc.
Gillian C. Rose Interior Design, LLC
Gleysteen Design, LLC
Gold Coast Metal Works, Inc.
Golenberg & Company Construction
Graham Landscape Architecture, Inc.
The Grand Prospect Hall
Graphic Builders, Inc.
Gregory Lombardi Design, Inc.
Gregg Wiess & Gardner Architects
Griffiths Constructions, Inc.
Group 3 Architecture-Interiors-Planning
Haifa General
Hammersmith Studios
Hammond Beeby Rupert Ainge, Inc.
Harrison Design Associates
Hartman-Cox Architects
Heaven N Earth
Henry H. Lewis Contractors, LLC
Historical Concepts
Horizon Builders, Inc.
Horizon Houseworks
Housing Trends, Inc.
Hubert Whitlock Builders, Inc.
Hull Historical, Inc.
International Fine Art
    Conservation Studios, Inc.
Jack Arnold
Jacquelynne P. Lanham Designs, Inc.
Jamb
James Leslie Design Associates Corp
Jane Antonacci Interior Design
JD Group, Inc.
Jean Larette Interior Design
Jeffrey Preuss
Johanna's Design Studio
John Blatteau Associates
Jonathan Browning Studios, Inc.
Jonathan Lee Architects
Joseph Minton, Inc.
Kaplan Gehring McCarroll
    Architectural Lighting
Kass & Associates
Kate Johns, AIA
Kensington & Associates
Kirk Stathes Architect, Inc.
KL Megla, LLC
KM Designs, Inc.
KMNelson Design
Knight Architecture, LLC
L. M. Silkworth Architect, P.A.
Lambert Landscape Company

Land Plus Associates, Ltd.
The Lane Group, Inc.
Lane-McCook & Associates, Inc.
Lantern Masters
Leeds Custom Design
Leonard Metal Art Works, Inc.
Leta Austin Foster & Associates, Inc.
Loop Worx
The Lotus Collection
Ludowici Roof Tile
Lundy Flitter Beldecos & Berger, P.C.
Lynn Beavers & Associates
Madison Cox Design, Inc.
Madison Spencer Architects
Robert C. Magrish
Mary Follin Design
McCrery Architects, LLC
Melinda Ritz Interiors
Merrimack Design Associates
Meyer Architecture
MG Partners
Michael Goldman Architect, P.C.
Michael Matrka, Inc.
Michael Whaley Interiors, Inc.
Millworks by Design
Millworks, Etc.
Mitchell Studio, LLC
Moberg Fireplaces, Inc.
Molly Isaksen Interiors, Inc.
Morales-Kessee Design Associates
Nancy Boszhardt, Inc.
Nanz Custom Hardware
NCG Architects
John R. Neal
Ned Forrest Architects
Neumann Lewis Buchanan Architects
New World Home, LLC
NHM Interiors
North Pacific
Oak Grove Restoration Company
Offenhauser Associates, Inc.
Old World Stone, Ltd.
Orleans Realty, LLC
P. S. Kennedy-Grant Architect
Pak Heydt & Associates
Parc Monceau Fine Antiques & Accessories
Paskevich & Associates Architects
Patricia Benner Landscape Design, Inc.
Pavé Tile & Stone, Inc.
Penelope Francis & Co.
Peninsula Custom Homes
Perry Guillot, Inc.
Peter Block & Associates Architects, Inc.
Peter Zimmerman Architects, Inc.
Pineapple House Interior Design
Plath & Company, Inc.
Portera Antique Spanish Doors
Preservation Foundation of Palm Beach
Pyramid Builders
R G Architects, LLC
R. S. Granoff Architects, P.C.
Randall A. Ridless, LLC

Randall Architects, Inc.
Real Illusions, Inc.
Rebecca Bradley Interior Design
Remains Lighting
Restoration Timber, LLC
Revival Construction, Inc.
Richard Holz, Inc.
Robert Dean Architects
Robert Frear Architects, Inc.
Robert S. Bennett Architect
Robin Bell Design, Inc.
Ruby Architects, Inc
Ryall Porter Architects
Ryan Associates - New York Office
Ryan Associates - San Francisco Office
Sater Group, Inc.
Shannon Hall Designs
Shears & Window
Sheldon Richard Kostelecky Architect
Shelley Morris Interior Design, Ltd.
Shostak Style, Inc.
Sloan Architects, PC
SM Architects, Inc.
Smith Ekblad & Associates
Spitzmiller & Norris, Inc.
Sroka Design, Inc.
Stancil Studios
Studio for Civil Architecture, PLLC
Studio H Home Couture
Susan Lustik, Inc.
Suzanne B. Allen & Company Design, LLC
Tanglewood Conservatories
The Taylor & Taylor Partnership
Taylor Development
Thomas Gordon Smith Architects
Thomas Jayne Studio
Thomas Norman Rajkovich Architect, Ltd.
Thomas Riley Artisans' Guild
Timothy Bryant Architect
Todd Alexander Romano
Tony Quinn Masonry
Town & Country Conservatories
TR Building and Remodeling, Inc
Traditional Architecture, Inc.
Traditional Cut Stone, Ltd.
Vigini Paint and Decorating, Inc.
Vigneau & Associates Interior Design
Villa Savoia, Inc.
Village Homes
Vitoch Interiors, Ltd.
Von Morris Corporation
Walter B. Melvin Architects, LLC
Weaver Design Group
Webster & Company, Ltd.
Wendy Posard & Associates
Westye Group Southeast
William B. Litchfield Residential Design, Inc.
William H. Childs, Jr. & Associates
Wilson Kelsey Design, Inc.
Zivkovic Connolly Architects, P.C.

INDIVIDUAL
Professional
David Ager
Frederick L. Ames
Brad Anderson
Christine Anderson
Richard Anderson
Walter S. Arnold
George Athans
Lorna Auerbach
Michael Avery
Janice Barker
Charlie Barnett
Richard F. Barrett
Bob Becker
Deborah Belcher
Jill Biskin
David J. Black
Carol Boerder-Snyder
Tom Boland
Joan Boone
Margaret C. Bosbyshell
James Boyd
Brian P. Brady
Ronald Bricke
William Briggs
Jean-Luc Briguet
Brad Brotje
Robert T. Brown
Ernesto Buch
Ken Burney
Daniel Busbin
Gerald Buxbaum
Brian P. Calandro
Frank J. Capone
Donald Carey
Denis Cassidy
Greta Cassudakis
Rodolfo Castro
Rachele Chafir
Tommy Chambers
Richard Charbonneau
John H. Cluver
Mark Cole
Cate Comerford
Morgan Conolly
James Cooper
Jack Crane
Philip L. Crotwell
Troy W. Curry
Nick Cusano
Charles Davey
Anne Decker
Allan Cooper Dell
Charles Denning
Laura DePree
Fernando Diaz
Curt DiCamillo
Jeff DiCicco
Elizabeth Dinkel
James W. Dixon
Gregory Dixon

John F. Dorr
Ralph Duesing
James Dupree
Lenore Eisner
Ralph E. Eissmann
Anya Ellia
David Escobedo
Krista Everage
David A. Ewald
Ralph W. Fallon
Marlene Farrell
Eugenia W. Farrow
Rebecca B. Flannery
Rosemary Battles Foy
Suzanne Furst
Monty Gaither
Kathleen M. Galvin
Kaja Gam
Francis M. Garretson
Thomas W. Gibb
Donald Glockner
Charles Paul Goebel
Wayne L. Good
Steven Goodwin
Dan K. Gordon
Jack L. Gordon
Cindy Grant
Donald J. Grubb
Angelo Gueli
David D. Harlan
Charles B. Harrison
Constance Haydock
Norine Haynes
Laura Heery Prozes
Judith F. Hernstadt
William Heyer
Joseph Hill
Jeffrey Hitchcock
Michael Holz
Kimberly Hopper
Chery S. Horacek
Harry G. Howle
Steve Humbert
Mark A. Hutker
William Rush Jenkins
Jeff Jenkins
Kenneth L. Jennings
Peter L. Jensen
Timothy Joslin
Gary W. Justiss
Robert Kaler
Justin Kapela
Buzz Kaplan
Gary Katz
Virginia Kelsey
Douglas A. Kertesz
Firoozeh Khorrami
Dimitrios Klitsas
John F. Koncar
Regina Konet
Sergey Konstantinov
Brent A. Kovalchik

Robert B. Kramer
Judy Kushner
Joel Laseter
Jeffrey Levinson
Isaac Lewin
Frank Lewis
Salvatore A. Liberti
Dietrich Logan
Jan Lorenc
J. Steven Lovci
Thomas E. Low
Joseph Lucier
Linda D'Oranzio MacArthur
Andrew Malone
David Mango
James Margulies
Jeffrey A. Marks
John P. Marrs
Robert Martignoni
James Marzo
Thomas P. Matthews
W. Travis Mattingly
Roy Mattson
Kirsten McCoy
Patrick O. McGinty
Charles F. McLarty
Margaret McMahon
Nancy A. McNeilly
David B. Meleca
Judith Melinger
Gary Mertz
Michael Mesko
Andrea Michaelson
Deborah Mills
Peter D. Moor
Craig Morrison
Stephen Mouzon
Steven Murphy
Bradley S. Neal
Adrienne Neff
Mario Nievera
Kirk Nix
James Noble
Sean P. Nohelty
David M. Novak
Joseph Odoerfer
William D. B. Olafsen
Gerald Olesker
Ruthann Olsson
Brendan T. O'Neill
Rita Orland
Euclides Pagan
Arturo Palombo
Melinda Papp
E. C. Parker
J. Randall Parker
Daniel Parolek
Chris Pellettieri
Justin C. Petrecca
Frank Ponterio
Anthony M. Pucillo
Willem Racke

Jennifer Ratchford
David W. Rau
John Reagan
Adrienne Retief
Dan Ritosa
Christian Rogers
Don Ruth
Devin Rutkowski
Scot Samuelson
Raymond J. Santa
Darrell Schmitt
Sean W. Sculley
Cary Shafer
Melissa Shanks
George Shaw
Les Shepherd
Marla Sher
Charles Shipp
Azadeh Shladovsky
Robert Sinclair
Kaveri Singh
Samuel Sinnott
William Sloan
Jeffrey Small
Victor P. Smith
Patricia Smith
Landon Smith
R. D. Sondles
Lee Staton
Laurie J. Steichen
David Stocker
Leland Stone
Debbie C. Stuart
Richard Dana Swann
Hal Swanson
Lori Swanson
Anna Sweeney Crockett
Andre Tchelistcheff
Erich Theophile
Dan Thompson
Tryggvi Thorsteinsson
John B. Tittmann
Craig P. Vaughn
Dirk L. Veteto
Shepard E. Vineburg
Philip C. Volkmann
M. L. Waller
Doug Walter
Kirk Watson
Sherri L. Weaver
Marilyln Weiss
David White
Dan Wigodsky
Charles M. Wilkes
Edward Williams
B. Stephen Wiseman
Norm Wogan
Kevin Wolfe
Robert Yorburg
Linda Yowell

GENERAL MEMBERS

LATROBE SOCIETY
Marshall G. Allan and Karen LaGatta
Marc Appleton and Joanna Kerns
Naja Armstrong
Norman D. Askins
F. Ronald Balmer
Joe Boehm
Jon Berdsen
Gary L. Brewer
Christopher H. Browne
Rhett Butler
Richard W. Cameron
Richard A. Clegg
Jacob Collins
Jeffrey L. Davis
Antoinette Denisof
Richard H. Driehaus
Anne Fairfax and Richard Sammons
Mark Ferguson
Maureen W. Footer
Mr. and Mrs. George J. Gillespie III
Ray Gindroz
Jim Hanley
William H. Harrison
Amanda Haynes-Dale
Kathryn M. Herman
Charles Heydt
Michael G. Imber
Deirdre E. Lawrence and
    Clem Labine
Tom Maciag
Peter H. Miller
Dell Mitchell
John Murray
Yong Pak
Greg Palmer
Katie Ridder and Peter Pennoyer
Elizabeth Plater-Zyberk
Foster Reeve
R. Douglass Rice
Jaquelin Robertson
Janet Ross
Alfred Ross
Barbara Sallick
Suzanne and David Santry
Gilbert P. Schafer III
Oscar Shamamian
Michael Simon
Andrew Skurman
Eric Smith
Nick Stern
Todd Strickland
James Sykes
Aso Tavitian
Suzanne Tucker and
    Timothy Marks
D. Clay Ulmer
Jean Wiart

Bunny Williams and
    John Rosselli
Russell Windham
Roy Zeluck
Lloyd P. Zuckerberg and
    Charlotte Triefus

BENEFACTOR CIRCLE
Suzanne and Ric Kayne
Jane Cheever Powell
Seth Joseph Weine

PATRON
Martha and James Alexander
Tim Barber
Kevin P. A. Broderick
Suzanne Clary
M. Lily Datta
Sharon Saul and Christopher Davis
David H. Ellison
Jorge Lóyzaga
Anne Girard Mann
Nancy Brown Negley
Paige Rense
James R. Utaski

DONOR
Betsy Allen
Mary M. Ballard
Constance Goodyear Baron
Paul Beirne
Marifé Hernández and Joel Bell
Shelley G. Belling
Michael C. Booth
Frances and John Cameron
Edward Lee Cave
James F. Cooper
David Dowler
Ronald Lee Fleming
Christopher Forbes
Emily T. Frick
Todd Furgason
Edmund Hollander
Richard L. Kramer
Michael Lykoudis
Paula Nataf
David Orentreich
Randy Ratcliff
Alan J. Rogers
Stephen Salny
Anita Sweeney
Linda Stabler-Talty and
    Peter J. Talty
Richard Trimble
Stephanie Walden

SUSTAINER
Emerson Adams
Eleanor Alger
Debra Antolino
Catherine Cahill and
    William Bernhard
Morrison Brown
Robin Browne
Valerie Carney
Chris Carson
John Clark
Gary L. Cole
Sherwood Cox
Andrew Cullinan
Scott Reed Dakin
Eric Inman Daum
Diana Davenport
Angelo Davila
Ron de Salvo
Timothy Deal
Nancy M. Dedman
Seth Faler
Mary Campbell Gallagher JD, PhD
Mark J. Gasper
David H. Gleason
Gwynne Gloege
Peter Louis Guidetti
Jas Gundry
Kahlil Hamady
Stephen Harby
Thomas S. Hayes
Frederick H. Herpel
Helga Horner
John Jamail
Evelyn and Michael Jefcoat
David Karabell
Jeff Kaufman
Richard Kossmann
Scott R. Layne
Catesby Leigh
Alan P. Levenstein
David Lewandowski
J. Carson Looney
Calder Loth
Sandra Mabritto
Robert MacLeod
Steven Markey
Helen Marx
Victoria McCluggage
Mark W. McClure
John P. McGrath
Richard D. Miller
Chas A. Miller
William L. Mincey
Susan C. Morse
Paula Moss
Stephanie Murray
Nancy Newcomb
Suzanne Rabil
Lawrence H. Randolph
Paul Stuart Rankin
Elizabeth and Stanley D. Scott

Harold R. Simmons
P. Allen Smith
L. Caesar Stair
Jack Taylor
Richard John Torres
Robert N. Wakefield
Gail Whelan
John H. Whitworth
Nalla Wollen
David Michael Wood
Douglas C. Wright
Molly Wythes
John Yunis
Fred S. Zrinscak

CONTRIBUTOR
Michael Allen
Lawrence Angyal
Peter Batchlor
Johanna Bauman
Marguerite Bierman
Deborah Black
Michael Black-Schaffer
Louis H. Blumengarten
Mosette Broderick
David Brussat
Thomas Anthony Buckley
Caitlin Burck
Robert E. Caines
Monica Cheslak
Kenneth Clark
Andrew B. Cogar
Monty Cornell
Edward T. Davis
Robert M. Del Gatto
Alden Lowell Doud
Elizabeth M. Dowling PhD
Carter Ellison
Rachel Epstein
David Esterly
Irwin Federman
Suzanne Fitzgerald-Knowlton
Richard Ford
Josh Friedman
Mac Griswold
Philippe Hans
James Hellyer
Nicholas Biddle Hill
Christopher Hough
Leslye Howerton
Cheryl Hurley
Rhonda and Roger P. Jackson
Richard John
Joseph F. Johnston
Corinne Jones
Bruce C. King
Suzanne Klein
George Lanier
William Malmstedt
Michael Maloof
Haskell R. Matheny
Louis Newman

Noble Gregory Pettit
Paul R. Provost
William Dean Randle
John Reagan
Stephen Renton
Donald H. Roberts
Kibby Schaefer
Helen Rockwell
Maryel Schneider
Douglas Segars
Steven W. Semes
Ann G. Seidler
In Shields
Salli Snyder
Stephen R. Sonnenberg
Charles Stick
David E. Stutzman
Debbie Swann
Kendra Taylor
William Trautman
Kristen and Paul D. Trautman
Paul R. Tritch
Nancy R. Turner
Riccardo S. Vicenzino
Andrew von Maur
William B. Warren
Leonard Woods
William R. Yamanoha

DUAL
Malouf Abraham
Dawn Abrecht
Sukie Amory
John H. Anderson
Richard Anderson
Martha Angus
Brent Baldwin
Elizabeth Ballard
Edward S Barnard
Tim Barrett
William H. Bates III
D. Troy Beasley
Karen Bechtel
Myron Beldock
Raffi R. Berberian
Gregory Bettenhausen
Mark Billy
Brian Bishop
Mary and Robert Black
Elizabeth Bramwell
Sandra Breakstone
Pascal Brocard
Horace Wood Brock
Kate and Alexander Brodsky
Harry P. Broom
William Bruning
Bruce Budd
George M. Bulow
John Burgee
Richard T. Button
Thomas Callaway
James C. Cammarata

Thomas Rex Campbell
Torrey Stanley Carleton
John Casarino and
    William McBain
Thomas A. Cassilly
Margaret Chambers
Cathy and Paul Chapman
Blanche Cirker
Daniel Clancy
Steven R. Cohen
J. Christine Cooper
John Dale
Leslie Barry Davidson
Nat Day
Stewart Desmond
Kim Doggett
Marc Donnelly
Elana Donovan
Franciska K. and Robert G. Dyck
Laura I. and William Egelhoff
Paul Wentworth Engel
Arthur and Janet Eschenlauer
James N. Evans
Coburn Darling Everdell
Estelle Fabre
Diane Elaine Farrar
David Flaharty
Laura W. Fleder
Edwin H. Frank
Charles J. Frederick
Ryan Gagnard
Malin Giddings
Max Golestan-Parast
Kay Golitz
Marianne and Jay Graham
Nancy Greenberg
Max M. Guenther
Nancy and Kenneth Gunther
G. William Haas
James Haas
Carmen Dubroc and
    Lewis I. Haber
Donald Hadsell
Helen Haje
Jane Havemeyer
Charles Haworth
Franklin Headley
W. A. Heath
Douglas Heckrotte
Kirk Henckels
Howard and Consuelo Hertz
Albert P. Hildebrandt
Peter Hodson
Richard Holt
Mark Howard
Brandon Ingram
Diane O. Jacoby
John M. Jascob
Henry Pinckney Johnson
Dorothy and David Kamenshine
Meg and Lawrence Kasdan
Raymond Kaskey

Michael Kathrens
Barbara Kraebel
Richard Landry
Gary Lencioni
Alan LeQuire
George Lewis
Judith and Felix Lief
Charles Lockwood
Kelley Tucker and
    Stephen Longmire
Jennifer Maples
David B. Markey
James C. Marlas
Christopher Mason
Patricia J. Matson
Charles Mazzola
David Mark McAlpin
Mary Ryan McCarthy
Steven L. McClain
Barbara Wilson and
    James R. McKeown
Denis McNamara
Newton Merrill
Albert S. Messina
Christopher C. Miller
Orloff Miller
Susan Miniman
James T. Mitchell
William R. Mitchell
Charles Mohaupt
Jason Moser
Ryan Moss
Robert Mueller
Grace Mynatt
Alfred Nazari
Douglas Newby
James Scott O'Barr
Sean O'Kane
Diane Oxley
Alex B. Pagel
Daniel J. Pardy
Bret Parsons
Rose T. Patrick
H. Drexel Patterson
Frank K. Pennino
Jack Peterson
Martha Picciotti
Edward Pollak
Annabelle F. Prager
Lynette Proler
Jonathan D. Rabinowitz
Catha and Viggo Rambusch
Rosalie W. Reynolds
Donna B. Rich
Gregory M. Richard
Frank Rogers
Colleen M. Rogers
Glenda Ruby
Richard D'Attile and Vern Ruiz
Mortimer Sackler
Alireza Sagharchi
Elisabeth A. Saint-Amand

Marvin Schwartz
Lise Scott
Justine Sears
Les Sechler
Elliot Shalom
Bailey Sharp
Louise Shaw
Kristen and Gregory Shue
Teresa Power Silverman
John Sinopoli
Yasuko Noguchi and George Sheldon
Susan Sloan
James Smiros
Martin Avery Snyder
Walter South
Michael Sovern
F. T. Spain
Joseph Peter Spang
Siew Thye and Bryon Stinson
Nina Strachimirova
Eric P. Svahn
Sally Swing
Mia Taradash
Jay Tartell
Michelle P. Tate
Raun Thorp
Karen Topjian
P. Coleman Townsend
Peter B. Trippi
Andrew Tullis
Wendy Watson and John Varriano
Susan B. Wallace
Marigil M. Walsh
Franklin Walton
Carroll William Westfall
Roby and Robert C Whitlock
Hutton Wilkinson
Roderick Wilson
Nancy Allerston and Erich Winkler
Christopher Wiss
Nancy Sweers and Guy Woelk
Robert L. Woodbury
Adam Wright
Michael J Young
Carol and John Young

INDIVIDUAL
Peter Aaron
Jacob Albert
Drury B. Alexander
Beverly Allen
Hugh Anderson
Edward D. Andrews
Mason Andrews
Marie-Rose Andriadi
Joshua Arcurio
Charlotte P. Armstrong
Regina Armstrong
Jean Arrington
Ann Ascher
Frederick W. Atherton
Beth Ayer

Frances Bailey
Terry Bailey
Christine Baker
William W. Ball
Steven Ballenger
Leonora M. Ballinger
Betsy Barbanell
Frank Barham
Ann Barton
Yvonne Bartos
Steve Bass
Karen Beam
David A. Beckwith
Thomas Beeby
Paul Belotti
Devereaux Bemis
Kristy Benner
Ronald Bentley
Ivan Bereznicki
John L. Beringer
Ian Berke
Seth P. Bernstein
Inez Bershad
John Bews
Nora M. Black
James Bleecker
Russell Bloodworth
Thomas A. Blount
Richard Blumenberg
R. Louis Bofferding
Glen B. Boggs
Charles P. Bolton
Dori Bonn
Valerie J. Boom
Ellen Borker
Clary Bosbyshell
Richard Bouchard
Linda Boyce
Brian P. Brady
Holland Brady
Diane Brandt
Martin Brandwein
Donald Brinsky
Lisa Brown
Joan Brown
Dan Brown
Frank Brown
Aimee Buccellato
Barbara Buff
Robert Bump
Andrew Burke
Jonathan P. Butler
Ralph Cadenhead
Tim Campbell
James A. Campbell
Dee Carawan
Monica T. Carney
Robert M. Caro
Christopher M. Carrigan
Kathleen Casanta
Celeste Caskey
Heather Cass

Peter Cella
Arnold B. Chace
Karla Champion
Carl Chapman
Winston B. Chappell
John Chase
Sarah Mueller Chernoff
Jason Childers
Pinares Childers
Lucylee Chiles
Antoinette Cindrich
Bruce Clymer
Melanie Coddington
Etienne Coffinier
Anna B. Coiner
Melody Cokeley
Todd Cole
Mary Howland Cole
Suzie Coleman
Barbara Colvin-Hoopes
Faye Cone
David Cornelius
John Cotugno
John Craig
Anthony Crisafi
Tim Cronin
David Crouse
Richard Crum
Kevin G. Crump
John Danzer
John DaSilva
Nicholas Daveline
Sheryl Davis
John E. Day
Daniel P. DeGreve
Amy Delin
Joseph Dennan
Jocelyne Denunzio
Perry Des Jardins
Samuel J. DeSanto
Peter F. Dessauer
Lori DeWaal
Dale Dibello
Robert Dickensheets
Rochelle Marie Didier
Michael Dillon
Cheree Dillon
Mason H. Disosway
Gerald E. Dolezar
Michael Doumani
Stuart A. Drake
Andrew Dulcie
Molly M. Dunlap
Saranne Durkacs
Julia Dworschack
Gary I. Dycus
Don Edson
Mohamed Elkordy
Whitney Rietz Eller
Chris Eller
Carol Ann Ellett
Janette Emery

Mark Enos
Jessica Esquivel
Mary Anne Eves
Mark Dillen Failor
Sara C. Fair
Laura Falb
Patricia Fast
Richard N. Faust
Marcia Feinstein
John Feldman
Laurie Gunther Fellows
April Fey
David Finlay
Neil Flax
Sheryl Fleischer
Peter D. Fleming
Andre Fleuriel
Bronwyn Ford
David W. Fox
Bruce Fox
Ruth Frangopoulos
Philip J. Franz
Susan Hume Frazer
M. Jane Gaillard
Jim Galloway
Larry W. Garnett
James Garrison
Patrick Gaughan
Celeste P. Gebhardt
Beth Gensemer
Joanne Georgiou
Heidi K. Gerpheide
Grant Gibson
Richard Giesbret
Tracy Gilmore
Raymond Givargis
Carole Glaser
Jan Gleysteen
Juan Felipe Goldstein
Danny Gonzales
Jessica Goodyear
Neil Gordon
Justin Gordon
Kristine Gould
Alexandra W. Grannis
Bonnie Grant
Michael T. Gray
John L. Gray
Leonard Greco
Nancy Green
Gail Green
Bryan Green
William Greene
Connie Greenspan
Gregory Greenwood
Julia W. Greer
Robert Griffin
Jeff Groff
Catherine Gulevich
Jim Hackett
Susan Hager
Erik Haig

Thomas Hall
Edward Hall
Kristen J. Haller
Burks Hamner
Tom Hanahan
Alice Hancock
R. Gary Hancock
Edwin Hardy
Kevin L. Harris
James Hayes
Suzanne L. Haynes
Adriana Hayward
George T. Heery
Christopher Heiler
Edwin Heinle
Huyler C. Held
Aaron Helfand
Ronald G. Herczeg
Richard Hershner
Deborah Hershowitz
Patrick Hickox
Casey Hill
Jennifer Hollingsworth
H. Randolph Holmes
Stephen Roberts Holt
James A. Hoobler
E. Randolph Hooks
Thayer Hopkins
Carter Hord
Natalie Howard
Susan Howell
Yong Huang
Amily S. Huang
James Hyatt
John Iglar
Alfred Izzo
Mark Jackson
A. Woolsey James
Richard H. Jenrette
Charles A. John
Marion Johnson
Robert S. Johnson
George R. Johnston
Andrew Berrien Jones
Marianne Jones
Diana Justice
Eve M. Kahn
Susan Kahn
Michael Kaiser
John Kasten
Arthur Keller
John Woodrow Kelley
James Kelly
Christa M. Kelly
Margaret Kendrick
Philip Kessler
Margaret Derwent Ketcham
Michelle Kinasiewicz
Theodora Kinder
Lauren S. King
Max King
Catherine Lee Kirchhoff

Grant Kirkpatrick
Stephen Klimczuk
Dimitrios Klitsas
Corinna Knight
Trian Koutoufaris
Joseph Kowalski
Brian Kramer
Laura Krey
Brian N. LaBau AIA
Jonathan LaCrosse
Elizabeth LaDuke
D. E. Lafave
Rocky LaFleur
Christopher Lagos
Salem Richard LaHood
James Lamantia
Nicholas Lamb
Gene Lambert
Suzanne Lammers
Janice Langrall
Dana Laudani
Andrew Laux
Anne C. Lawrence
W. Jude LeBlanc
Kathleen O. Leeger
Annette Lester
Margaret Monsor Leung
Jennifer Levin
Timothy L. Lindsay
Kent Lineberger
Wayne A. Linker
Jennifer Littke
Donna Livingston
Janet Lohman
Thomas W. Lollar
David Long
Maria C. Longo
David Garrard Lowe
John Lunday
Valera W. Lyles
Alice Ann Lynch
Melissa Mabe-Sabanosh
Donald MacDonald
James MacNutt
Robert Magoon
Christine Mainwaring-Samwell
Robert Maisano
Suzan Gay Makaus
Alan Malouf
Rosario Mannino
Laurence E. Mansfield III
Tripp March
Michael J. Margulies
James Marino
Hannah Marks
John Martin
Brenda Martin
Toni Martucci
Randolph Martz
Doris L. Master
Marcy V. Masterson
Nicholas Matranga

Christopher Mattioli
David Mauzé
Art May
John Mayfield
Diane Maze
Virginia S. McAlester
Jennie McCahey
Daniel McCarthy
Anthony McConnell
Thomas A. McCrary
Katy McCullough
Justin McEntee
Mary McGrath
Donna McKee
Daniel McMillan
George McNeely
Elizabeth A. McNicholas
Erica McNicholas
William McWhorter
Susan C. Meals
Robert Meiklejohn
Marcelo C. Mendez
Vera Mendoza
Jean Mercier
Manuel Mergal
Ruben Mijares
John F. Millar
Jonathan Miller
Lisa Miller
Briana Miller
Marian Miller
Jeffrey L. Miller
Walter Miller
Adrian Milton
Maureen Monck
Eliza Montgomery
Michelle Moody
Wendy Moonan
Denise Moore
Anne Sophie Moore Jones
Josephine Morales
Jeremy Morrelli
David Morton
Matthew J. Mosca
Geoffrey Mouen
Mark A. Murphy
Andrew Muscato
John R. Muse
David J. G. Nastasi
Andrew G. Nehlig
J. Mark Nelson
Merise Nelson
Mark W. Nester
Alan Neumann
Deborah Nevins
Thomas Newman
George Nichols
Sudie Nostrand
John James Oddy
Kevin K. Ohlinger
Luis Ortega
Patricia Ostrander

Kate Ottavino
Cory Padesky
Michael Paietta
Jennifer Paloski
Jonathan Parisen
David Park
Walter Parrish
Phillip Parton
Luke Paskevich
Lenore Passavanti
Guy Pearlman
Katherine Pearson
Kathryn L. Perkins
Betty Perlish
Finley Perry
BJ Peterson
Niles Peterson
Hugh D. M. Petter
M. DeWitt Petty
H. Lee Pharr
Marc Phillips
David Picotte
Destiny Brooke Pierce
Patrick Pigott
Daniel Pisaniello
Christopher M Pizzi
Cody Pless
Anatole Plotkin
Stephen Poe
Carol Poet
Patricia Poundstone
Nancy Goslee Power
Shirley Price
Brij Punj
John J. Quinn
George A. Radwan
John W. Rae, Jr.
Natasha Rahban
Jan S. Ramirez
Mark Ramsey
Paul Andrija Ranogajec
Andrea Raynal
Miles Redd
Ben Reeves
Peter J. Rehme
Stephen Reinel
Carol Reznikoff
Nancy Richardson
Wade Rick
David Rinehart
Kyle Roberts
Kathleen A. Robison
Lee Rogers
Tom Romich
William C. Rorick
Melvin Rose
Jane Ellen Rosen
D. Crosby Ross
Frank A. Ross
Kevin Rosser
Barbara Rossi
David Rowland

Karen E. Rubin
Donald Rubin
Joseph Ruggiero
Donald H. Ruggles
Nelson L. Ruiz
Robert C. Russek
William Rutledge
Lynne Rutter
Michael Ryan
William Sacrey
Samantha Salden
Nikos Salingaros
Siamak Samii
Anne Samuel
Alina Sanchez de Myklebust
Ken Sanden
Charles A. Scarallo
Barbara Scavullo
Molly Schaefer
Marcia Meehan Schaeffer
Barbara Kolonay Schaffel
Lee Schettino
James Lucian Schettino
James Schettino
Victoria Ann Schlegel
Erin E. Schneider
Beverly McGuire Schnur
Jack Schreiber
Jennifer K. Schreiber
David P. Schuyler
Joel A. Schwartz
Janet Schwartz
Robert F Shainheit
June Shapiro
Steve Shard
Lisa Shire
Scott L. Shonk
Jeffrey Shopoff
Kristen Shue
Nathan Royce Silverstein
Daniel Sinclair
Howe K. Sipes
Diane Sipos
Vicki Slockbower
Susanne Smith
Lee Smith
Dean Smith
Michael Smith
Gregory T. Smith
Douglas A. Smith
Clinton Ross Smith
Demetra Canna Smith
Joel Snodgrass
Sandra Sobel
Jeremy Sommer
Jeffrey P. Soons
Randy J. Soprano
Patrick Soran
Marta Sovilj
Joann S. Speas
Brian Speas
Clayton E Spence

Barrie Curtis Spies
D. Scott Springer
Steve James Stannard
Frank Starkey
Carl Steele
Catherine B. Stein
Ailene Steinberg
Ania Stempi
Alan H. Stenzler
Martha Roby Stephens
Vivienne H. Stevens
Patricia Galt Steves
Edward Stick
David W. Stirling
Elise Stirzel
R. Adam Storch
Christoph Streubert
Ashley Strickland
John Blaine Summitt
Jerl Surratt
Leonard Sussman
Stephen Sutro
Stephanie Swann
Bart Swindall
Vince Tarango
Mark Taylor
Henrika Dyck Taylor
Stephanie Tegnazian
E. Clothier Tepper
John Thompson
Shannon Thompson
Margaret Anne Tockarshewsky
Celia Tompkins-Hegyi
Sabina Toriello
Edward Trafidlo
Violette Travers
John S. Troy
Karen Tubridy
Matthew Turner
John K. Turpin
Michael J. Tyrrell
Christine Ussler
Julie Valadez
Gregory Van Boven
Josh Van Donge
Patrick Van Pelt
Walton Van Winkle
Jeanne Vanecko
David Vasquez
Leslie-jon Vickory
Raymond Vinciguerra
Sandra Vitzthum
Adelene Vogel
Amanda Wachsmuth
William Waibel
Benjamin L. Walbert
Stephen Wang
Dancie Perugini Ware
Margo Warnecke Merck
Sandra Warshawsky
Michael Watkins
Joan Watkins

Joe Wayner
Jim Webb
Sandra Weber
Irwin Weiner
Margot Wellington
Frank Wen
Karen Wesson
Paul Whalen
Timothy Whealon
Walter Wheatley
Bruce W. Whipple
Brooks S. White
David N. White
Rudolph Widmann
Jerry Williams
Jann Williams
Scott Wilson
Bertram Winchester
Christine Wolfe Nichols
John M. Woolsey
Greg L Wyatt
Howard Yaruss
Fariba Yazdani
Margot Zengotia
Richard Zini
Nancy Zito
Bob Zoni

Current membership roster as of September 1, 2009

SPONSORS

The publication of *The Classicist No. 8* has been made possible
thanks to the generous contributions of the following:

The Beehive Foundation
E. R. Butler & Co.

Marshall G. Allan and Karen LaGatta
Balmer Architectural Mouldings
Timothy Bryant Architect
Chadsworth's 1-800-COLUMNS
Rodney M. Cook Interests
D. H. Ruggles & Associates, P.C.
Dyad Communications, *design office*
Fairfax & Sammons Architects PC
Ferguson & Shamamian Architects
G. P. Schafer Architect, PLLC
Gold Coast Metal Works, Inc.
Jamb
James Doyle Design Associates, LLC
John B. Murray Architect, LLC
Ken Tate Architect, P.A.
Les Metailliers Champenois (USA)
Mark P. Finlay Architects, AIA
Mona Hajj Interiors
Oliver Cope Architect
Peter Pennoyer Architects
Robert A. M. Stern Architects, LLP
Wadia Associates, LLC
Zeluck Inc. / Fenestra America

Andre Tchelistcheff Architect
Appleton & Associates, Inc.
David D. Harlan Architects, LLC
Flower Construction
Hammersmith Studios
Historic Doors
Michael G. Imber, Architects
White River Hardwoods

Campbell & Strasser
Kais Custom Builders
Traditional Cut Stone
Zepsa Industries

Antonia Hutt & Associates, Inc.
George Knight

Balmer Architectural Mouldings Inc.

271 Yorkland Blvd. Toronto, ON, M2J 1S5 Canada

Tel: 416 491 6425 Fax: 416 491 7023

www.balmer.com

Timothy Bryant Architect

66 West Broadway · New York, New York 10007 · timothybryant.com

DHR
ARCHITECTURE

DENVER ⚜ PARK CITY
303-355-2460
DHRARCHITECTURE.COM

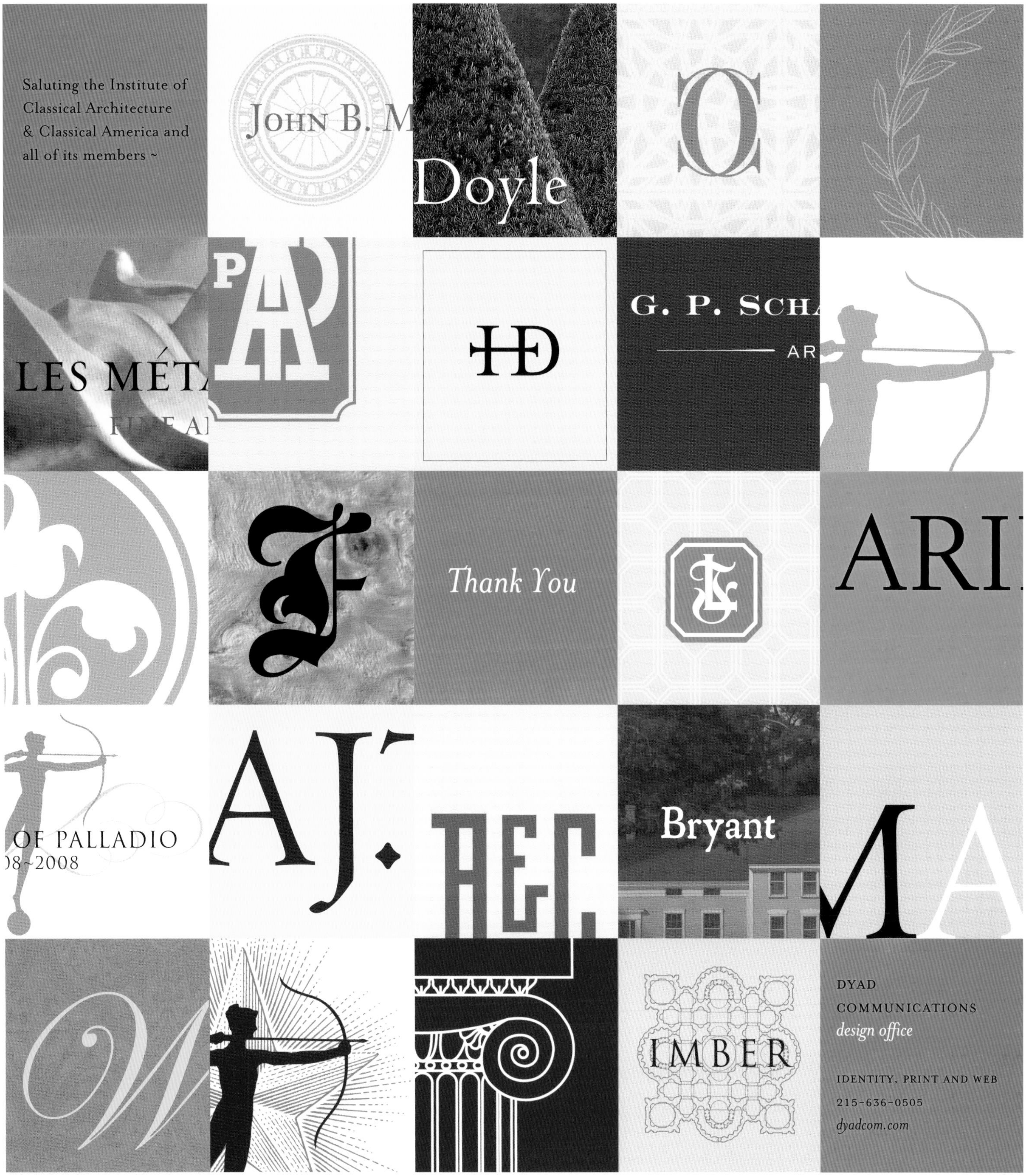

Saluting the Institute of
Classical Architecture
& Classical America and
all of its members ~

JOHN B. M

Doyle

LES MÉT
~ FINE A

G. P. SCH
AR

Thank You

ARI

OF PALLADIO
08~2008

AJ.

Bryant

MA

IMBER

DYAD
COMMUNICATIONS
design office

IDENTITY, PRINT AND WEB
215-636-0505
dyadcom.com

PHOTOGRAPHY BY DURSTON SAYLOR

Photo: Scott Frances

FERGUSON &
SHAMAMIAN
ARCHITECTS, LLP

270 LAFAYETTE STREET, NEW YORK, NEW YORK 10012
TELEPHONE: 212-941-8088   TELEFAX: 212-941-8089   www.fergusonshamamian.com

PHOTO BY JONATHAN WALLEN

G. P. Schafer Architect, pllc

—— ARCHITECTURE & DESIGN ——

WWW.GPSCHAFER.COM

Gold Coast Metal Works, Inc.
Fine Architectural Ironwork, New York - Olomouc

118 Bay Avenue, Huntington Bay, N.Y. 11743
Phone: 631-424-0905, Fax: 631-424-4867
e-mail: info@gcmw.com   www.gcmw.com

3 Dove Walk, Pimlico, London SW1W 8PS, England
T +44 20 7730 2122
www.jamb.co.uk

Traditionally hand-crafted stone and marble mantles, grates and accessories.

Jamb.

3 Dove Walk, Pimlico, London SW1W 8PS, England
T +44 20 7730 2122
www.jamb.co.uk

Traditionally hand-crafted lighting.

James Doyle Design Associates
LANDSCAPE DESIGN

B̈

E . R . B U T L E R & C O .

E. & G.W. Robinson Crystal Collection

E . R . B U T L E R & C O . is pleased to offer the E. & G.W. Robinson collection of Early American pressed and hand-ground crystal door and cabinet knobs. In the eighteenth and nineteenth centuries crystal knobs adorned doors, cabinets and drawers; their clarity and brilliance continue to suggest the "cleanliness, purity, refinement and good taste" for which they were valued.

E.R. Butler & Co., as the successor to E. & G.W. Robinson, continues to produce crystal knobs of superior design and workmanship. Our crystal knobs attach to their solid brass turned shanks with a technique patented by Enoch Robinson in 1837. With his "Method of Attaching Glass Knobs to Metallic Sockets" a denticulated knob is held in place by a keystoned socket. Our collection includes an historic variety of shapes, colors and sizes. Round, oval, octagonal or faceted knobs may have full, concave or flat surfaces. Crystal knobs may be clear, milk, opalescent, amber, ruby, ox-blood, amethyst, cobalt, emerald or black, as well as silvered or etched.

The knobs are available in three sizes: 2 ¼ and 1 ¾ inch diameter and projection for doors and 1 ¼ inch for cabinets and fine furniture. Three historical shank types (Robinson, Nashua and Hall), representing the evolution of Robinson's invention, are available in many standard, custom plated and patinated finishes. All knobs are fully complemented by a range of architectural trim including hinges, handles, locks, cane bolts, cylinder rings and covers, key escutcheons and covers, thumb turns, doorstops, etc.

TYPE I
(Robinson)

TYPE II
(Nashua)

TYPE III
(Hall)

SHELL SHANK OPTIONS

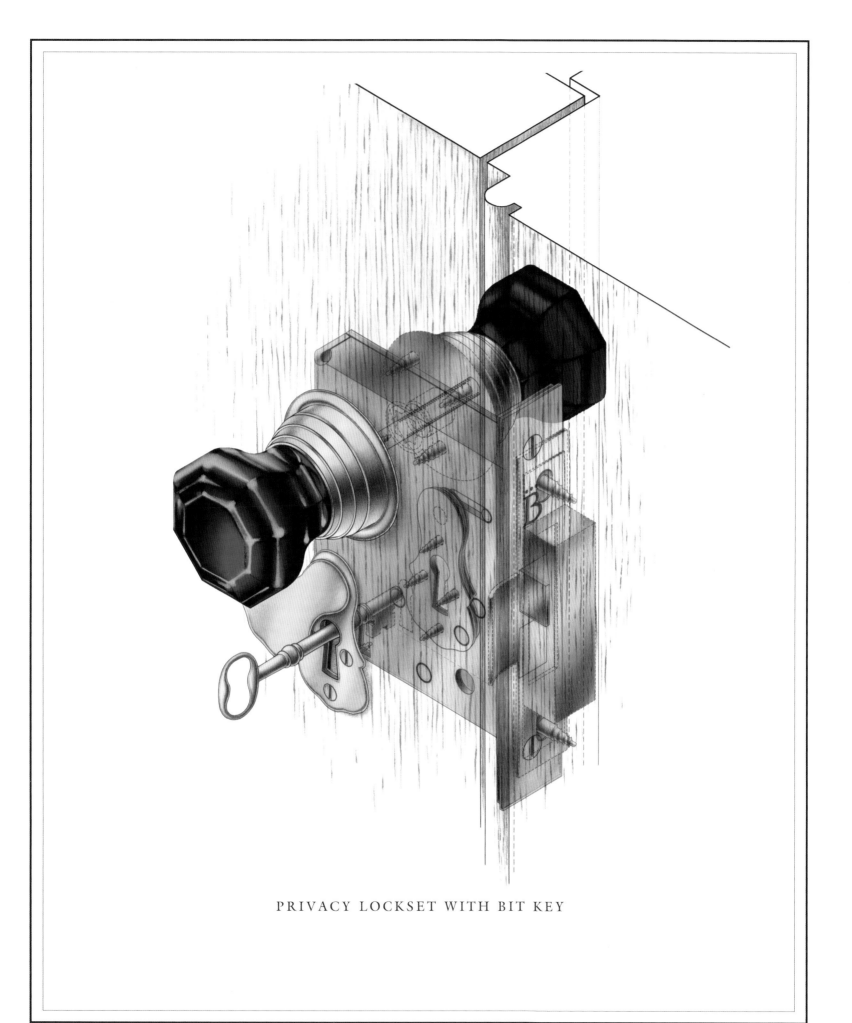

PRIVACY LOCKSET WITH BIT KEY

B̈

E.R. Butler & Co.

WWW.ERBUTLER.COM

CATALOGUES AVAILABLE TO THE TRADE

SHOWROOMS BY APPOINTMENT ONLY

Technical Drawing: John Sykes Fetterman   Rendering: Margitta Zachert   Typography: John Packer

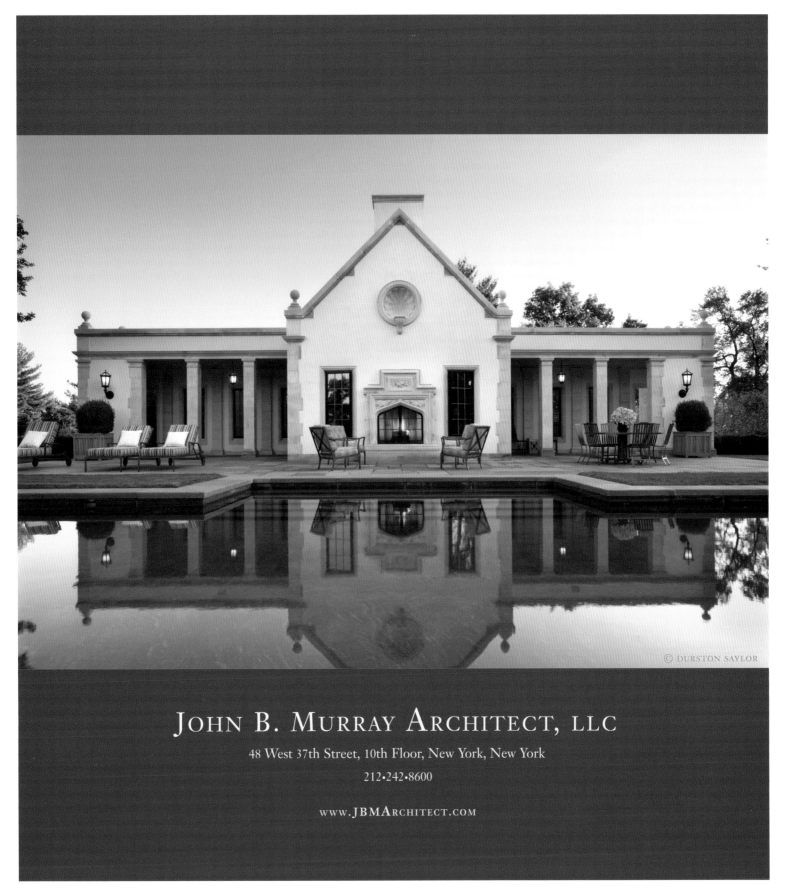

© DURSTON SAYLOR

JOHN B. MURRAY ARCHITECT, LLC

48 West 37th Street, 10th Floor, New York, New York

212·242·8600

WWW.JBMARCHITECT.COM

Ken Tate Architect

206 Covington Street Madisonville, LA 70447   985 845 8181   *kentatearchitect.com*

LES MÉTALLIERS CHAMPENOIS

➤ FINE ARCHITECTURAL METALWORK ➤

77 2nd Avenue Paterson, NJ 07514
WWW.L-M-C.COM

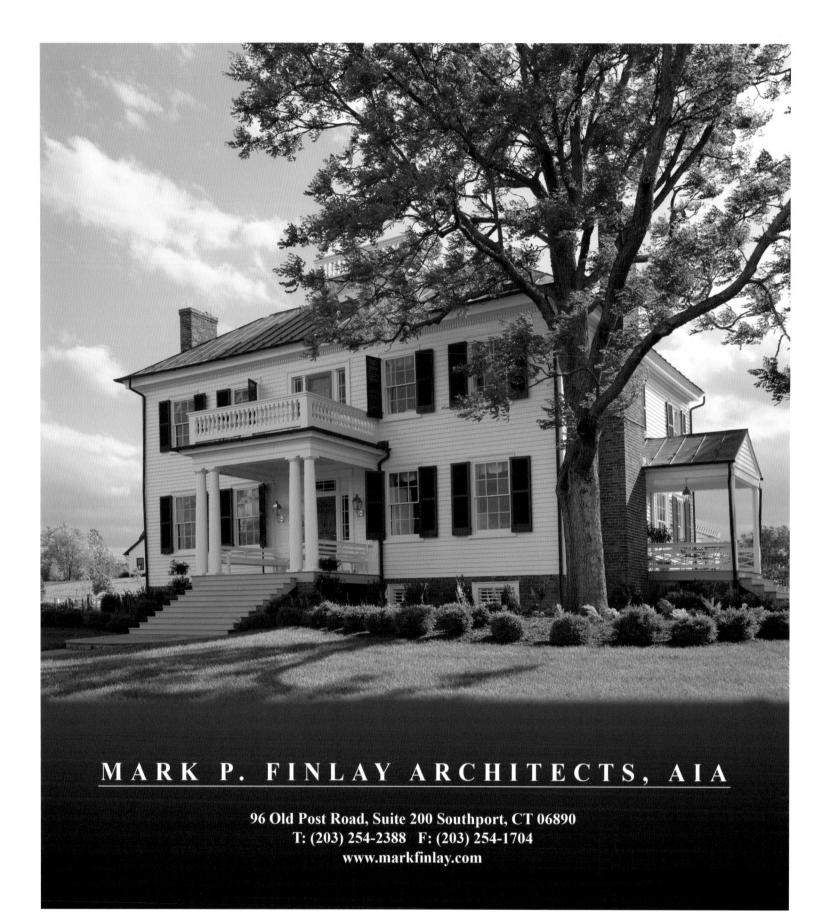

MARK P. FINLAY ARCHITECTS, AIA

96 Old Post Road, Suite 200 Southport, CT 06890
T: (203) 254-2388 F: (203) 254-1704
www.markfinlay.com

A JOHN RUSSELL POPE HOUSE RENOVATION IN BALTIMORE, MARYLAND

MONA HAJJ INTERIORS

13 East Eager Street, Baltimore, Maryland 21202 USA
T 410.234.0091 F 410.234.0198 mh@monahajj.com
www.monahajj.com

OLIVER COPE · ARCHITECT

151 WEST TWENTY-SIXTH STREET, NEW YORK, NEW YORK 10001
www.olivercope.com   *(212) 727-1225*

PETER PENNOYER ARCHITECTS
New York City

PPAPC.COM

Robert A.M. Stern Architects

460 West 34th Street, New York, New York, 10001
Tel 212 967 5100 fax 212 967 5588
WWW.RAMSA.COM

WADIA ASSOCIATES
RESIDENTIAL ARCHITECTURE OF DISTINCTION

~ WADIAASSOCIATES.COM ~

THE ART OF WINDOW MAKING

....

800-233-0101 OR VISIT WWW.ZELUCK.COM
Zeluck Windows & Doors meet Dade County, Hurricane Impact and IBC Specifications

Architect/Builder Kean Williams Giambertone

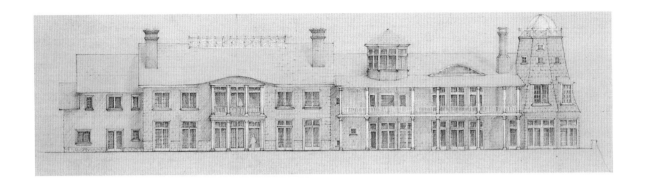

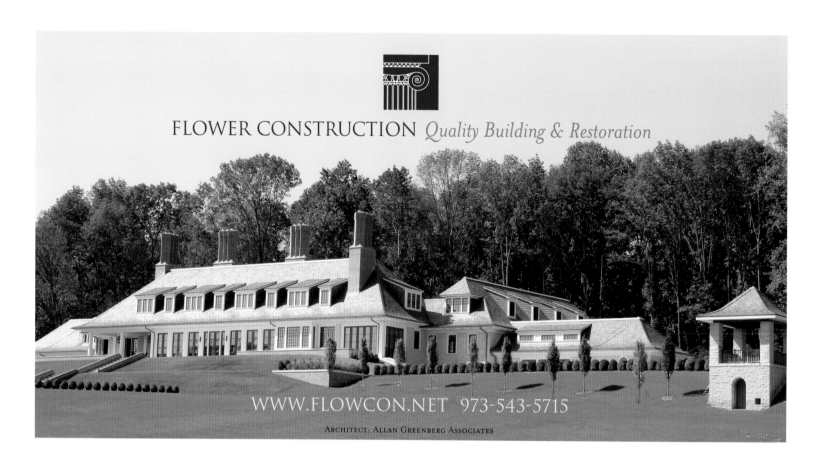

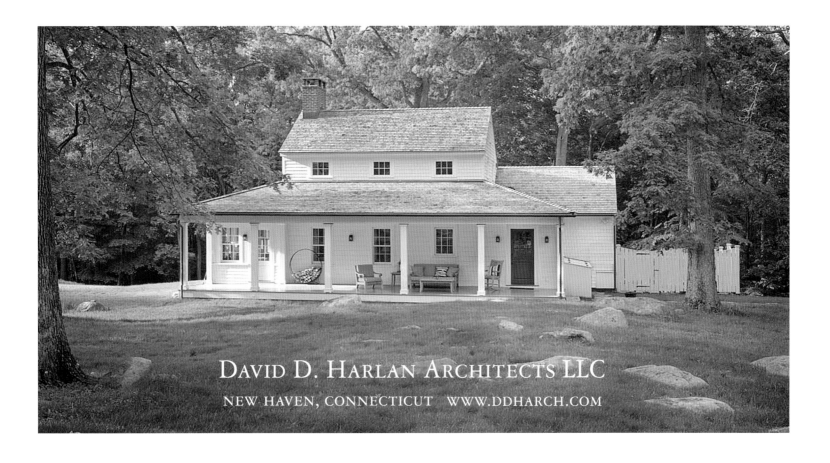
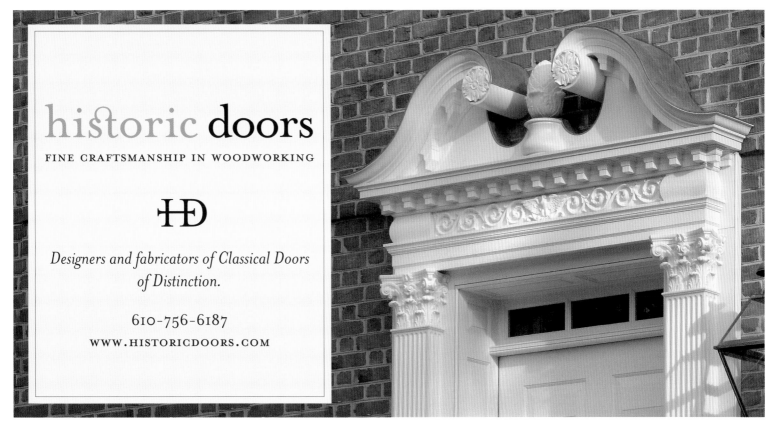

✤

Production:
Composed with Quark XPress 8.1 and Mac OS X

Text: Japanese Matte Art 140gsm
Cover: Japanese Matte Art 230gsm
Separations: 300 Line Screen
Printing: Offset Lithography
Binding: Perfect Bound
Edition: 3,500

Typefaces:
Centaur, designed by Bruce Rogers
for the Metropolitan Museum in 1912–14,
based on the Roman type cut in Venice by Nicolas Jensen in 1469.

Trajan, designed by Carol Twombly in 1988,
based on the inscription carved on the pedestal of
Trajan's column Rome, 113 A.D.

✤